Rural Transformations and Agro-Food Systems

T0362194

The economic and political rise of the BRICS (Brazil, Russia, India, China and South Africa) and Middle-Income Countries (MICs) have important implications for global agrarian transformation. These emerging economies are undergoing profound changes as key sites of the production, circulation and consumption of agricultural commodities; hosts to abundant cheap labour and natural resources; and home to growing numbers of both poor but also, increasingly, affluent consumers. Separately and together these countries are shaping international development agendas both as partners in and potential alternatives to the development paradigms promoted by the established hubs of global capital in the North Atlantic and by dominant international financial institutions. Collectively, the chapters in this book show the significance of BRICS countries in reshaping agro-food systems at the national and regional level as well as their global significance. As they export their own farming and production systems across different contexts, though, the outcomes are contingent and success is not assured. At the same time, BRICS may represent a continuation rather than an alternative to the development paradigms of the Global North.

The chapters were originally published in a special issue of *Third World Thematics: A TWQ Journal*.

Ben M. McKay is an assistant professor of Development and Sustainability in the Department of Anthropology and Archaeology and fellow of the Latin American Research Centre at the University of Calgary in Canada.

Ruth Hall is a professor at the Institute for Poverty, Land and Agrarian Studies (PLAAS) at the University of the Western Cape, South Africa. She is a co-founder of the Land Deal Politics Initiative and the BRICS Initiative in Critical Agrarian Studies, and coordinates the work of the Future Agricultures Consortium in Southern Africa.

Juan Liu is an assistant professor at the College of Humanities and Social Development, Northwest A&F University, China, and a postdoctoral researcher at ICTA, Universitat Autónoma de Barcelona, Spain. She is in the global secretariat of the BRICS Initiatives for Critical Agrarian Studies (BICAS) and is co-editor of the BICAS Working Paper Series.

ThirdWorlds

Edited by Shahid Qadir, *University of London, UK*

ThirdWorlds will focus on the political economy, development and cultures of those parts of the world that have experienced the most political, social, and economic upheaval, and which have faced the greatest challenges of the postcolonial world under globalisation: poverty, displacement and diaspora, environmental degradation, human and civil rights abuses, war, hunger, and disease.

ThirdWorlds serves as a signifier of oppositional emerging economies and cultures ranging from Africa, Asia, Latin America, Middle East, and even those 'Souths' within a larger perceived North, such as the U.S. South and Mediterranean Europe. The study of these otherwise disparate and discontinuous areas, known collectively as the Global South, demonstrates that as globalisation pervades the planet, the south, as a synonym for subalterity, also transcends geographical and ideological frontier.

Recent titles in the series include:

Rural Transformations and Agro-Food Systems

The BRICS and Agrarian Change in the Global South

Edited by
Ben M. McKay, Ruth Hall and Juan Liu

LONDON AND NEW YORK

First published 2018
by Routledge
2 Park Square, Milton Park, Abingdon, Oxon, OX14 4RN, UK

and by Routledge
52 Vanderbilt Avenue, New York, NY 10017

First issued in paperback 2020

Routledge is an imprint of the Taylor & Francis Group, an informa business

British Library Cataloguing in Publication Data
A catalogue record for this book is available from the British Library

ISBN 13: 978-0-367-58870-0 (pbk)
ISBN 13: 978-1-138-54243-3 (hbk)

Typeset in Myriad Pro
by RefineCatch Limited, Bungay, Suffolk

Publisher's Note
The publisher accepts responsibility for any inconsistencies that may have
arisen during the conversion of this book from journal articles to book chapters,
namely the possible inclusion of journal terminology.

Disclaimer
Every effort has been made to contact copyright holders for their permission to
reprint material in this book. The publishers would be grateful to hear from any
copyright holder who is not here acknowledged and will undertake to rectify
any errors or omissions in future editions of this book.

Contents

Citation Information

The chapters in this book were originally published in *Third World Thematics: A TWQ Journal*, volume 1, issue 5 (2017). When citing this material, please use the original page numbering for each article, as follows:

For any permission-related enquiries please visit:
http://www.tandfonline.com/page/help/permissions

Notes on Contributors

Alberto Alonso-Fradejas is a PhD candidate at the International Institute of Social Studies (ISS) in The Hague, The Netherlands, a research associate of the Transnational Institute (TNI), and a fellow of the Guatemalan Institute of Agrarian and Rural Studies (IDEAR).

Daniela Andrade is a PhD researcher at the International Institute of Social Studies (ISS) in The Hague, The Netherlands. Her research interests include political economy of development, agrarian change and agriculture (especially in Brazil and Mozambique).

Zoe W. Brent is a PhD candidate at the International Institute of Social Studies (ISS) in The Hague, The Netherlands, and a researcher with the Agrarian Justice team at the Transnational Institute (TNI).

Melodie Campbell is a town and regional planner and as such is inclined to seek out and gain understanding into the patterns and trends which manifest spatially. Her master's dissertation piqued an interest in food systems and the influential role of supermarkets in shaping food retail environments. A short stint at the Institute of Poverty, Land and Agrarian Studies (PLAAS) during 2014 allowed her to grapple still further with the embeddedness of food systems within regional and global systems.

Ruth Hall is a professor at the Institute for Poverty, Land and Agrarian Studies (PLAAS) at the University of the Western Cape, South Africa. She has published several books on land reform and agrarian change in South Africa and broader trends of land grabbing in Africa. She is a co-founder of the Land Deal Politics Initiative and the BRICS Initiative in Critical Agrarian Studies, and coordinates the work of the Future Agricultures Consortium in Southern Africa.

Juan Liu is an assistant professor at the College of Humanities and Social Development, Northwest A&F University, China, and a postdoctoral researcher at ICTA, Universitat Autónoma de Barcelona, Spain. She is in the global secretariat of the BRICS Initiatives for Critical Agrarian Studies (BICAS) and is co-editor of the BICAS Working Paper Series. Her research interests include: internal migration and left-behind population, social policies, rural politics, land politics, and political economy/ecology of agriculture, food and environment.

Anna Rosa Maria Lopane is a PhD candidate in the Graduate Program in Development Social Sciences, Agriculture and Society of the Rural Federal University of Rio de Janeiro (CPDA/UFRRJ) with a scholarship from CNPQ (Brazil). She holds a master's degree in International Development and Cooperation (UNIBO/Italy) and a master in Development, Agriculture and Society (CPDA/UFRRJ). She is a research assistant of Markets, Networks and Value Nucleus (MRV/CPDA).

Giuliano Martiniello joined the Faculty of Agriculture and Food Sciences as an assistant professor of Rural Community Development in Fall 2015. He is broadly interested in the political economy, political sociology and political ecology of agrarian change and rural development with particular reference to large-scale land acquisitions, labour and land tenure regimes, land reforms, urban–rural articulations, agricultural modernisation, agribusiness, smallholders' commercialisation and integration in global value chains, food security/sovereignty and rural social movements.

Ben M. McKay is an assistant professor of Development and Sustainability in the Department of Anthropology and Archaeology and fellow of the Latin American Research Centre at the University of Calgary in Canada. He has carried out research and maintains research interests on the politics of agrarian transformation in Latin America. He is also part of the BICAS secretariat and co-editor of the BICAS Working Paper Series.

Carolina Milhorance is a research fellow at the French Agricultural Centre for International Development (CIRAD). She received her PhD in political science from the University of Brasília (UnB) and the University of Paris Saclay in 2016, and she holds a MA in International Affairs and Sustainable Development from Sciences Po Paris. Her research focuses on Brazil-Africa and triangular co-operation in the rural sector, on the adoption of international norms and on the role of International Organisations in processes of policy transfer.

Alexander Mikhailovich Nikulin is an established Russian scientist who started his scientific career in the field of peasant studies under the guidance of Teodor Shanin in the 1990s. He is an author of many historical, theoretical and empirical works on the social and economic development of Russian agriculture and rural areas in general, especially from a comparative perspective. In 2016, he established as an Editor-in-Chief the journal *Russian Peasant Studies*, which will become a quarterly publication on economic and social questions of rural and agricultural development in Russia and worldwide, and questions of agrarian history and the methodology of rural sociology and peasant studies in the past and present.

Sérgio Sauer is a professor at the University of Brasília at the Planaltina campus (FUP/UnB) in the Post- Graduation Program on Environment and Rural Development (Mader).

Irina Vladimirovna Trotsuk started her career as a sociologist conducting quantitative and qualitative studies on the value orientations of different Russian generations and comparing such empirical data with other post-socialist societies. Since 2005 she has been part of a scientific group which publishes an annual collective monograph on the theory, history and present state of peasant studies, under the guidance of Teodor Shanin and Alexander Nikulin. She is a member of the editorial boards of *Russian Peasant Studies* and the Bulletin of RUDN University, Sociology Series.

Valdemar João Wesz Junior is a professor at the Federal University of Latin American Integration (UNILA) and a researcher at the Observatory on Public Policies for Agriculture (OPPA/CPDA/UFRRJ). He has master's and PhD degrees in Social Science in Development, Agriculture and Society from the Federal Rural University of Rio de Janeiro (CPDA/ UFRRJ), with undergraduate studies in Rural Development and Agribusiness Management at the State University of Rio Grande do Sul (UERGS).

John Wilkinson is an associate professor at the Graduate Center: Development, Agriculture and Society (CPDA), Rural Federal University, Rio de Janeiro, Brazil (UFRRJ), where he researches and lectures on the world of agrifood systems and economic sociology, about both of which he has published widely in Latin America, Europe and the US.

Yunan Xu is a PhD candidate at the International Institute of Social Studies (ISS) in The Hague, The Netherlands, and is funded by the China Scholarship Council (CSC).

Jiayi Zhou is a researcher at the Stockholm International Peace Research Institute (SIPRI), with a focus on international development and non-traditional security. She has recently co-authored a monograph *on China's Silk Road Economic Belt*: *Considering security implications and EU-China cooperation prospects*, and has published articles in *The Journal of Slavic Military Studies*, *European Centre for Minority Issues*, *Small Wars Journal*, and other outlets. She received her education from the Erasmus University Rotterdam, and the Maxwell School of Syracuse University. Her research interests are in the post-Soviet space, food security and agrarian change, and geopolitics.

researches and lectures on the world of unified systems and economic sociology, about both of which he has published widely in Latin America, Europe and the US.

Yunan Xu is a PhD candidate at the International Institute of Social Studies (ISS) in The Hague, The Netherlands and is funded by the China Scholarship Council (CSC).

Jiayi Zhou is a researcher at the Stockholm International Peace Research Institute (SIPRI), with a focus on international development and non-traditional security. She has recently co-authored a monograph on China's Silk Road economic belt. Currently, her research interests are in the post-Soviet space, food security and agrarian change and geopolitics.

The rise of BRICS: implications for global agrarian transformation

Ben M. McKay ⓘ , Ruth Hall and Juan Liu

ABSTRACT

This article introduces this collection, which focuses on the economic and political rise of the BRICS countries (Brazil, Russia, India, China, and South Africa) and its implications for global agrarian transformation. These emerging economies are undergoing profound changes as key sites of the production, circulation, and consumption of agricultural commodities; hosts to abundant cheap labour and natural resources; and home to growing numbers of both poor but also, increasingly, affluent consumers. Separately and together these countries are shaping international development agendas both as partners in, and potential alternatives to, the development paradigms promoted by the established hubs of global capital in the North Atlantic and by dominant international financial institutions. Collectively, the findings show the significance of BRICS countries in reshaping agro-food systems at the national and regional level, and their global significance. As they export their own farming and production systems across different contexts, though, the outcomes are contingent and success is not assured. At the same time, BRICS may represent a continuation rather than an alternative to the development paradigms of the Global North.

Introduction

Profound agrarian changes are underway in emerging economies such as Brazil, Russia, India, China, and South Africa (BRICS). These vary from land concentration, changing rural–urban linkages, migration, the rise of corporate agribusiness, contract farming schemes for smallholders, class differentiation between smallholders, family farmers, and labourers, new forms of agri-businesses upstream and downstream of farming, vertical (and horizontal) integration in value chains, and supermarketisation. Such agrarian transformations in turn interact with changes in the rural societies and agrarian economies in neighbouring countries as BRICS countries expand their presence in their respective regions through both state and private sector-led partnerships and investment deals. These transformations do not represent simply the extension of BRICS countries into their respective regions, where they are playing important roles as regional powers. Rather, their roles interact with dynamic changes already underway within these regions, marked partly by the rise of another set of powerful actors: Middle Income Countries (MICs) like Argentina, Chile, and Peru in South America; Indonesia, Malaysia, Thailand, and Vietnam in Southeast Asia; and Kenya and Nigeria in Africa.

The rise of BRICS countries alongside some powerful MICs, and the emerging alliances within and between them, has sparked debate about whether they herald a new era in the global political economy as an alternative to the conventional North Atlantic-anchored neo-liberal prescriptions for development – or whether their models of development are problematic, in similar or perhaps new ways.[1] More profoundly, the BRICS countries challenge existing conceptions of a North–South divide as the most significant dimension of global inequality in power and wealth, but without challenging capitalism as a system, or seeking to fundamentally transform the underlying social relations of capitalist agricultural production. This presents new challenges and opportunities for scholars, activists, policy-makers, development practitioners, and others. Agro-food system change and agrarian dynamics need to be understood in what seems to be an evolving polycentric world order – and new and innovative initiatives in knowledge production are required in response.

In addressing this research challenge, it is important to build on and extend the focus of existing knowledge about BRICS and MICs. The rise of BRICS countries and MICs has been accompanied by the emergence of new spheres of research, academic dialogue, and exchange in recent years. Most of these initiatives are BRICS-oriented and Africa-centred, tracking the impact of, mainly, China and Brazil on Africa.[2] Many of these studies are from international relations and international political economy traditions, with much less engagement by researchers from agrarian political economy. This body of emerging literature has provided us with important perspectives, but there remain key themes which are underexplored, including their influence in their respective regions. This present collection contributes to building a new literature with a particular focus on the emerging dynamics and implications for agrarian change.

This collection of essays emerges from the BRICS Initiatives in Critical Agrarian Studies (BICAS), which is a collective of academic researchers largely based within BRICS countries themselves. Scholars in the network are concerned with understanding the implications of the rise of emerging economies for national, regional, and global agrarian transformations. This collection contributes to the BICAS agenda, with the aim not only of contributing to understanding new dynamics of agrarian change but also to promoting further research and dialogue. It addresses, to various extents, four thematic research clusters with reference to Brazil, Russia, China, and South Africa. Unfortunately, this collection does not feature an analysis into the agrarian dynamics within India nor the influence of Indian capital elsewhere – an omission to hopefully be addressed as the network expands.

The four themes addressed are: (i) national agrarian dynamics within BRICS countries; (ii) BRICS countries and intra-regional agrarian transformations; (iii) new dynamics and multiple centres of power in the agro-food system; and (iv) BRICS and MICs in relation to the old hubs of global capital. The remainder of this introductory article introduces these four research clusters as well as outlining the contributions of the individual papers within this collection. However, many articles address issues related to multiple research clusters in complementary and overlapping ways. The rise of BRICS countries and its implications for global agrarian transformation represents a huge topic of research. This collection in no way provides a complete nor comprehensive analysis into all of these new and changing dynamics. Rather, it hopes to make a contribution to the much larger and ongoing research global initiative of BICAS[3], with the intention of encouraging other researchers to deepen enquiry and theorisation in this field.

National agrarian dynamics

Rather than engaging with BRICS as a political–economic bloc or organisation,[4] this collection addresses the BRICS countries themselves and the changes underway within their national territories, in their respective regions, and their emerging political and economic relations and activities in other regions. Several essays in this collection provide in-depth analyses into the agrarian dynamics and transformations *within* BRICS countries themselves. It is crucial to understand the agrarian, food and environmental changes taking place within these emerging economies in order to further understand the broader implications for global agrarian transformation.

In this collection, Andrade analyzes the rise of Brazil as a global agribusiness power and the overall transformations of production, trade, and capital flows which have emerged since the neoliberal reforms in the 1990s.[5] She argues that the macroeconomic policies which deregulated the national economy and opened it up to financial speculation have undermined the industrial sector, leading to a reprimarization of the economy and particularly the country's exports. This was not only due to the global commodities boom nor the increased demand for primary commodities from China, but also 'the outcome of policy-induced constraints on production'.[6] Andrade provides an explanation as to the core of the crisis that erupted in Brazil in 2014, linking it to Brazil's rise as a global agribusiness power and the country's insertion into global circuits of financial capital accumulation resulting in, and even concealing, an overall loss of economic power and political autonomy. The Brazilian agricultural development model has been promoted, for instance, by development agencies and international financial institutions, as one to replicate, not only in Latin America but also in Africa.[7] However, Andrade's analysis should caution those governments looking to reproduce such a model, by drawing attention to the vulnerabilities that arise from financial speculation in the agricultural sector.

In their analysis of national agrarian dynamics within Russia, Nikulin and Trotsuk revive the utopian visions of rural–urban reciprocity that were articulated in the work of the key Russian agrarian thinker, A.V. Chayanov, in the early twentieth century.[8] They argue that Chayanov's work offers important insights into understanding contemporary agrarian transformations in Russia and the world. Nikulin and Trotsuk reveal the diversity of Russia's agrarian pathways and the various agricultural 'worlds' which coexist. Moscow and Saint Petersburg continue to expand, absorbing rural territory and skilled labour and, perhaps paradoxically, have become the centre of agricultural production through giant agro-holdings. While it appears that mega-cities are pulling in capital, labour, and land, the authors point to the Belgorod region as a counterexample of what can transpire when Chayanov's neopopulist ideas are put into practice. Belgorod's development model is one based on a symbiotic relationship between the rural and urban, agricultural and industry, tradition and modernity. It is highlighted as a successful mixed economy with high rates of economic growth and quality of life. Despite the overall urban and agro-industrial bias throughout the country, the authors argue that elements of Chayanov's utopian insights can – and should – be applied, not only to understand but also to influence new trajectories of agrarian change.

Across the literature, there are contested interpretations of agricultural commercialisation and what constitute 'success stories' – whether in the Brazilian Cerrado, Russian massive agro-holdings or India's Special Economic Zones (SEZs).[9] These contestations centre on what constitutes positive agrarian outcomes but also on how the real economy and speculation interact. While dominant development institutions continue to promote large-scale industrial agriculture, critical studies have pointed to its accelerating biophysical contradictions[10], while others reveal the very extractive character – socially, economically, and environmentally – of this agricultural development model.[11] The papers in this collection also show the social, cultural, and economic implications of the dominant model of agricultural development and that alternatives to large-scale and corporatist production and value-chain concentration can and do exist, and that can be learnt from these experiences.

Intra-regional agrarian transformation

As political and economic powers in their respective regions, the rise of BRICS countries has significant implications for agrarian transformation intra-regionally. This includes both capital and labour flows in and around these new hubs of global capital accumulation, and land concentration or 'land grabbing' across national boundaries.[12] Brazil, for example, has led the way in agro-industrial development in the Latin American region, spreading not only its technologies and expertise but also capital investment, with Brazilian farmers moving to and investing in land, most prominently in Paraguay and Bolivia.[13] In Africa, South African capital and farmers are extending their reach throughout the continent – going beyond agriculture to construction and infrastructure and leading to a concentration of control over land, labour, and capital.[14]

In this collection, Martiniello uses a case study of South African sugar giant Illovo's acquisition of Kilombero Sugar Company Limited in Tanzania to explore the socio-ecological implications of such large-scale agricultural investments.[15] While contract farming and outgrower schemes have been promoted by influential development institutions such as the World Bank, Martiniello reveals how small-scale farmers became adversely incorporated into the agro-industrial value-chain by means of this outgrower scheme. Rather than protecting outgrowers against market risk, he shows how the scheme exposed small farmers to the risks and oscillations of volatile market prices and low harvests and 'have been used as an instrument to optimise the capacity utilisation of mills, and as a buffer against risks of under-production'.[16] Martiniello's case study illuminates the more generalisable trends of what Hall calls the 'South Africanisation' of the region which, as she explains, is 'not in the literal sense of South Africa becoming the coloniser of the region (though elements of that view may indeed be true!) but rather in the sense that the changes underway – concentration of control over land, labour and value chains (capital) – are rendering the agrarian structure of several countries more like that of a settler state like South Africa'.[17]

In Asia, too, significant intra-regional agrarian transformations can be observed, due in many instances to the influence of China in the region, especially related to land grabbing, crop booms inside China and other investments in South-East Asia.[18] In this collection, Zhou reveals how Chinese labourers – faced with a scarcity of arable land and labour opportunities – are migrating to the Russian Far East (RFE) where land is cheap and abundant.[19] Chinese investors are also looking to the RFE for business opportunities, investing in farmland, and forming joint ventures with Russian agribusinesses. Zhou argues that both Chinese capital and Chinese labour have revived, in different ways, agricultural production in the RFE, contributing to Russia's food security and offering both capital and labour absorption for otherwise idle or surplus factors of production in China. Zhou illustrates the capitalist dynamics of agrarian change 'from above' and 'from below' in the RFE as Chinese peasants, wage labourers, entrepreneurs, large-scale enterprises, and state-owned farms have looked to their Russian neighbours for farming and investment opportunities.

These papers draw attention to the diverse ways in which agrarian conditions within BRICS countries condition how they influence agrarian dynamics within their respective regions. Intra-regional impacts vary from land and agribusiness deals to labour migration – in fact, transnational shifts are evident in agro-food systems, from inputs to production to processing. The mobility of capital and labour combine in different ways, driven by both pull and push factors, involving multiple actors and stakeholders, and have diverse effects on neighbouring countries. Simplistic narratives of BRICS countries being neo-imperialists within their spheres of influence clearly do not capture the complexities these contributions draw attention to.

New dynamics and multiple centres of power

Beyond national and regional changing dynamics, the rise of BRICS and MICs has led to the emergence of what some scholars are calling a 'polycentric' food regime. This refers to the 'multiple centres of power, and a more diverse range of key international actors within the governance structure of the food-energy complex, both sectorally and geopolitically', in contrast to the North Atlantic-dominated food regimes of the past.[20] Now, not only the traditional powers of the global North but also BRICS and MICs play key roles in the changing dynamics in the patterns of production, consumption, and distribution of the agro-food system. Brazil and China in particular have become key sites for the production and consumption of agro-commodities, as new players (both public and private) have emerged within these countries, reshaping the implicit and explicit rules and regulations which structure agro-food relations on a global scale.[21] Multinationals from the North Atlantic such as ADM, Bunge, Cargill, and Louis Dreyfus (ABCD) still dominate the global grain trade, but Brazilian and Argentinian agribusiness firms are expanding their reach in Latin America largely through *pools de siembra* (sowing pools).[22] Furthermore, China's state-owned national Cereals, Oils, and Foodstuffs Co. (COFCO) has become a new global agribusiness giant, as also discussed by McKay et al. and Wilkinson et al. in this collection.[23]

Also in this collection, Campbell explores new dynamics in Sub-Saharan Africa's agro-food system and the role South African capital is playing in the region.[24] She provides an overview of South Africa's supermarket expansion across the continent – from East Africa, West Africa to Central Africa. This is associated in part with the growth of an urban middle class and growing consumer base. While sub-regional variations are certainly present, Campbell argues that South African supermarket expansion is reshaping relations of production, distribution, and consumption through a model of corporate food retail which excludes or at best marginalises local small-scale farmers. The supermarket revolution is leading to new relations of dependency on cheap manufactured food items from external markets (much of it imported from South Africa), while corporate-controlled value-chains exclude small-scale farmers, even in the fresh produce sector, by means of economies of scale and industry-specific production standards. However, such processes have not gone uncontested, as

Campbell points to forms of resistance to 'supermarketisation' across the region. While South Africa's food retailers may be leading the process of 'supermarketisation', it has also opened the doors to larger multinational corporations and a concentration of control over the food system throughout the region.

Yet, while flows of capital and labour are moving from emerging economies throughout their regions, the implications for agrarian change go beyond capital and labour flows. Milhorance provides insights into the policy coalitions which facilitate the adoption and expansion of the Brazilian agribusiness model, not only across Latin America but also, through South–South cooperation, to the African continent. Policy-makers, bureaucrats, researchers, and corporate actors from Brazil promote the transfer of knowledge and Brazilian expertise in several African countries, which in turn requires financial, technical, and political resources in order to emulate its model of agricultural development. Milhorance asserts that such policy networks indirectly facilitate the expansion of Brazil's agro-industry into foreign markets. The adoption of technologies, new forms of production, norms, and standards based on the Brazilian experience reinforces its position as a global agribusiness power, forming the 'foundations upon which investments and commodity trade are built'.[25] With important insights from key informants, Milhorance points to the underlying motives of the growing South–South agribusiness connections between Brazil and Southern Africa.

These new dynamics in global agro-food relations represent a shift from North Atlantic dominance to a more polycentric food system. Emerging economies have become key sites for agro-commodity production and consumption, no longer dependent on North Atlantic capital or markets. Yet this is not merely a matter of reproducing production systems, value chains, and wider agro-food systems. These are not easily transposed across diverse economic, social, and agro-ecological contexts. As shown by the contributions presented here, such expansion encounters competition and even, at times, failure. Therefore, the outcomes of BRICS and MICs and their expansionary ambitions are uncertain and contingent.

BRICS, MICs, and old hubs of global capital

Lastly, this collection analyses the rise of emerging economies in relation to the old hubs of global capital, represented by North America and Europe. BRICS and MICs are now key players in global trade in food and agro-commodities as new political and economic relations are taking shape around the world. Neoliberal policies and the 'Washington Consensus' which prevailed as the dominant ideology during the last decade of the twenty-first century have been largely discredited as many developing countries (most predominantly in Latin America) seek to distance themselves from US market and policy dependence.[26] The political and economic rise of BRICS and MICs, and the financial crises of the past decade and associated recession in the old hubs, have shifted the global political economy. New alliances and the reassertion of the role of the state in development among these rising powers are now also shaping international development agendas.[27]

Over the past decade, China–Latin America relations have exploded – in terms of trade, finance, and investment. McKay et al. explore the implications of such new economic and political relations in terms of agrarian transformation in Latin America.[28] This contribution analyses China's 'going out' policy and the geopolitical shifts which have led to the growth of Latin America's soy complex. With a focus on Argentina and Brazil, McKay et al. question such emerging partnerships and the notion of South–South cooperation, arguing that the massive expansion of China–Latin America trade in agro-food commodities continues to reinforce similar relations of production and resource control based on a model of extractivism which has plagued the region's industrial development for decades. Rather than BRICS trade presenting a new developmental path, it appears to be reinforcing the old.

Wilkinson et al. similarly analyse the growing agribusiness connections between China, Brazil, and the Southern Cone countries (Argentina, Paraguay and Uruguay) more generally, highlighting China's 'more-than-market' strategy to secure control over raw materials.[29] They show how China has replaced the European Union as Brazil's principal market for agribusiness exports by going beyond trade to more direct negotiation, partnerships, and joint ventures. They contend that China's activity in the Southern Cone can be divided into four phases: (i) land acquisition or 'land grabbing'; (ii) formal negotiations with national- and provincial-level governments; (iii) large-scale infrastructure investments to improve Brazil's export logistics; and (iv) directly competing for control over the global grain trade. This contribution delves into the new strategies and policies which have facilitated relations among these new hubs of global capital, revealing how China is positioning itself as a major player in the global grain trade.

All this suggests that there has been a 'thickening' of trade among BRICS countries themselves, not only due to particular commodity booms but also facilitated by trade deals bilaterally and within the group as a whole. Together and separately, these emerging political and economic powers are increasingly challenging the old hubs of global capital in the North Atlantic as they consolidate themselves as new sites of global capital accumulation, circulation, and consumption, promoted by discourses of 'South-South' cooperation. As the papers in this collection reveal, however, the extent to which such new relations and partnerships challenge, or represent alternatives to, dominant development paradigms regarding the social relations of production, property, and power remains questionable.

Concluding remarks

The emergence of BRICS as a group of emerging economies that are relatively dominant within their regions has seen the reconfiguration of agro-food systems and agrarian relations. This collection shows how this is evident in BRICS themselves, but also increasingly in the MICs and in their respective regions of influence. However, what are often touted as forms of South–South cooperation do not necessarily present alternative development pathways to those promoted by investors from the global North, or from development agencies or international financial institutions. There is, though, a clear pattern of capital from BRICS countries on the move, often seeking to replicate their own models of production, processing, and trade – not always with success. While cooperative relations among the BRICS countries are growing, the pattern of development is not necessarily distinct. Rather, there is a general pattern of extractivism, large-farm development often through contested land deals or 'land grabbing', the expansion of corporate agribusiness and agro-processing, consolidated and vertically integrated value chains, right through to the supermarketisation of food retail. In important ways, then, in order to understand the changing global agro-food system, one needs to engage with the critical ways in which BRICS countries – as states, private capital, and even as a source of labour – are reshaping food systems. This collection aims to provide valuable insights into these changing global dynamics of agrarian change and contributes to the debates regarding the rise of BRICS and its implications for global agrarian transformation.

Disclosure statement

No potential conflict of interest was reported by the authors.

Acknowledgments

This collection is a result of several international conferences organised by BRICS Initiatives in Critical Agrarian Studies (BICAS). We would like to thank all those who participated in the conferences for their input on earlier versions of these papers. We would also like to thank Jun Borras for encouraging us to pursue this collection. Finally, a special thanks to Madeleine Hatfield for her help throughout this process and for going above and beyond her tasks as Journal Manager.

Notes

1. Alden, *China in Africa*; Bond, "BRICS"; Gray and Gills, "South-South Cooperation and the Rise of the Global South".
2. See, e.g. the Institute of Development Studies' 'Rising Powers in International Development Programme'; Scoones, 'New Development Encounters'; Alden, *China in Africas*; Brautigam and Tang, "China's Engagement in African Agriculture"; Carmody and Taylor, "Flexigemony and Force in China's Geoeconomic Strategy in Africa".
3. See www.iss.nl/bicas; www.plaas.org.za/bicas

4. For an analysis on the big picture of BRICS as a group in the international context see Nayyar, "BRICS, Developing Countries and Global Governance".
5. Andrade, "Export or Die".
6. Ibid.
7. World Bank, "Awakening Africa's Sleeping Giant".
8. Nikulin and Trotsuk, "Utopian Visions of Contemporary Rural-urban Russia".
9. See Levien, "The Land Question".
10. Weis, "Accelerating Biophysical Contradictions".
11. See, e.g. Alonso-Fradejas, "Anything but a Story Foretold"; McKay, "Agrarian Extractivism in Bolivia"; Petras and Veltmeyer, "Agro-Extractivism".
12. See Edelman et al., "Global Land Grabs".
13. See Galeano, "Paraguay and the Expansion of Brazilian and Argentinian Agribusiness Frontiers"; Urioste, "Concentration and Foreignisation".
14. Hall, "Land Grabbing in Southern Africa".
15. Martiniello, "Don't Stop the Mill".
16. Ibid.
17. Hall, "Land Grabbing in Southern Africa," 207.
18. See Hofman and Ho, "China's 'Developmental Outsourcing'"; Lu, "Tapping into Rubber"; Thomas, "Going Out"; and Borras et al., "Land Control and Crop Booms".
19. Zhou, "Chinese Agrarian Capitalist".
20. Borras et al., "Land Grabbing in Latin America," 862; see also McKeon, *Food Security Governance*; on food regime analysis see Friedmann and McMichael, "Agriculture and the State System"; McMichael, "A Food Regime Genealogy".
21. Friedmann, "The Political Economy of Food", 30, 31.
22. Oliveira and Hecht, "Sacred Groves, Sacrifice Zones and Soy Production". Pools de siembra refer to the pooling of resources by farm management companies in order to achieve economic of scale through input purchases, storage and processing facilities and to increase bargaining power.
23. See also Wesz, "Strategies and Hybrid Dynamics".
24. Campbell, "South African Supermarket Expansion in sub-Saharan Africa".
25. Milhorance, "Growing South-South Agribusiness Connections".
26. See Ruckert et al., "Post-neoliberalism in Latin America".
27. See Ban and Blyth, "The BRICs and the Washington Consensus".
28. McKay et al., "China and Latin America".
29. Wilkinson et al., "Brazil and China".

ORCID

Ben M. McKay http://orcid.org/0000-0002-5737-5255

Bibliography

Alden, C. *China in Africa: Partner, Competitor or Hegemon?*. London: Zed Books, 2007.
Alonso-Fradejas, A. "Anything but a Story Foretold: Multiple Politics of Resistance to the Agrarian Extractivist Project in Guatemala." *Journal of Peasant Studies* 42, no. 3–4 (2016): 489–515.
Andrade, D. "'Export or Die': The Rise of Brazil as an Agribusiness Powerhouse." *Third World Thematics* 1, no. 5 (2017): 653–672.
Ban, C., and M. Blyth. "The BRICs and the Washington Consensus: An Introduction." *Review of International Political Economy* 20, no. 2 (2013): 241–255.
Bond, P. "BRICS: 'Anti-imperialist' or 'Sub-imperialist'?." *Links International Journal of Socialist Renewal* (2013). https://links.org.au/node/3265.
Borras Jr, S. M., J. C. Franco, S. Gomez, C. Kay, and M. Spoor. "Land Grabbing in Latin America and the Caribbean." *The Journal of Peasant Studies* 39, no. 3–4 (2012): 845–872.

Borras Jr, S. M., J. Liu, Z. Hu, H. Li, C. Wang, Y. Xu, J. Franco, and J. Ye. "Land Control and Crop Booms – Inside China: Implications for How We Think of the Current Global Land Rush." *Globalizations*, Forthcoming.

Brautigam, D., and X. Tang. "China's Engagement in African Agriculture: 'Down to the Countryside.'" *The China Quarterly* 199 (2009): 686–706.

Campbell, M. "South African Supermarket Expansion in Sub-Saharan Africa." *Third World Thematics* 1, no. 5 (2017): 709–725.

Carmody, P., and I. Taylor. "Flexigemony and Force in China's Geoeconomic Strategy in Africa: Sudan and Zambia Compared." *Geopolitics* 15, no. 3 (2010): 496–515.

Edelman, M., C. Oya, and S. M. Borras Jr. "Global Land Grabs: Historical Processes, Theoretical and Methodological Implications and Current Trajectories." *Third World Quarterly* 34, no. 9 (2013): 1517–1531.

Friedmann, H. "The Political Economy of Food: A Global Crisis." *New Left Review* 197 (1993): 29–57.

Friedmann, H., and P. McMichael. "Agriculture and the State System." *Sociologia Ruralis* 29, no. 2 (1989): 93–117.

Galeano, L. A. "Paraguay and the Expansion of Brazilian and Argentinian Agribusiness Frontiers." *Canadian Journal of Development Studies/Revue Canadienne D'études Du Développement* 33, no. 4 (2012): 458–470.

Gray, K., and B. K. Gills. "South-South Cooperation and the Rise of the Global South." *Third World Quarterly* 37, no. 4 (2016): 557–574.

Hall, R. "Land Grabbing in Southern Africa: The Many Faces of the Investor Rush." *Review of African Political Economy* 38, no. 128 (2011): 193–214.

Hofman, I., and P. Ho. "China's 'Developmental Outsourcing': A Critical Examination of Chinese Global 'Land Grabs' Discourse." *Journal of Peasant Studies* 39, no. 1 (2012): 1–48.

Levien, M. "The Land Question: Special Economic Zones and the Political Economy of Dispossession in India." *Journal of Peasant Studies* 39, no. 3–4 (2012): 933–969.

Lu, J. N. "Tapping into Rubber: China's Opium Replacement Program and Rubber Production in Laos." *The Journal of Peasant Studies* (2017): 1–22. doi:10.1080/03066150.2017.1314268.

Martiniello, G. "'Don't Stop the Mill': South African Capital and Agrarian Change in Tanzania." *Third World Thematics* 1, no. 5 (2017): 633–652.

McKay, B. M. "Agrarian Extractivism in Bolivia." *World Development* 97 (2017): 199–211.

McKay, B. M., A. Alonso-Fradejas, Z. W. Brent, S. Sauer, and Y. Xu. "China and Latin America: Towards a New Consensus of Resource Control?" *Third World Thematics* 1, no. 5 (2017): 592–611.

McKeon, N. *Food Security Governance: Empowering Communities, Regulating Corporations*. New York: Rouftledge, 2015.

McMichael, P. "A Food Regime Genealogy." *The Journal of Peasant Studies* 36, no. 1 (2009): 139–169.

Milhorance, C. "Growing South-South Agribusiness Connections: Brazil's Policy Coalitions Reach Southern Africa." *Third World Thematics* 1, no. 5 (2017): 691–708.

Nayyar, D. "BRICS, Developing Countries and Global Governance." *Third World Quarterly* 37, no. 4 (2016): 575–591.

Nikulin, A. M., and I. V. Trotsuk. "Utopian Visions of Contemporary Rural-urban Russia." *Third World Thematics* 1, no. 5 (2017): 673–690.

Oliveira, G. de L. T., and Susanna Hecht. "Sacred Groves, Sacrifice Zones and Soy Production: Globalization, Intensification and Neo-nature in South America." *The Journal of Peasant Studies* 43, no. 2 (2016): 251–285.

Petras, J., and H. Veltmeyer. "Agro-Extractivism: The Agrarian Question of the 21st Century." In *Extractive Imperialism in the Americas*, edited by J. Petras and H. Veltmeyer, 62–100. Leiden: Brill, 2014.

Ruckert, A., L. Macdonald, and K. R. Proulx. "Post-Neoliberalism in Latin America: A Conceptual Review." *Third World Quarterly* 38, no. 7 (2017): 1583–1602.

Scoones, I., L. Cabral, and H. Tugendhat. "New Development Encounters: China and Brazil in African Agriculture." *IDS Bulletin* 44, no. 4 (2013): 1–19.

Thomas, N. "Going out: China's Food Security from Southeast Asia." *The Pacific Review* 26, no. 5 (2013): 531–562. doi:10.1080/09512748.2013.842313.

Urioste, M. "Concentration and 'Foreignization' of Land in Bolivia." *Canadian Journal of Development Studies/Revue Canadienne D'études Du Développement* 33, no. 4 (2012): 439–457.

Weis, T. "The Accelerating Biophysical Contradictions of Industrial Capitalist Agriculture." *Journal of Agrarian Change* 10, no. 3 (2010): 315–341.

Wesz Jr, V. J. "Strategies and Hybrid Dynamics of Soy Transnational Companies in the Southern Cone." *The Journal of Peasant Studies* 43, no. 2 (2016): 286–312.

Wilkinson, J., V. J. Wesz Junior, and A. R. M. Lopane. "Brazil and China: The Agribusiness Connection in the Southern Cone Context." *Third World Thematics* 1, no. 5 (2017): 726–745.

Zhou, J. "Chinese Agrarian Capitalism in the Russian Far East." *Third World Thematics* 1, no. 5 (2017): 612–632.

China and Latin America: towards a new consensus of resource control?

Ben M. McKay ⓘ , Alberto Alonso-Fradejas, Zoe W. Brent, Sérgio Sauer and Yunan Xu

ABSTRACT

The rise of China has provoked changes in global geopolitics, deeply influencing the global economy and trade relations. Of particular importance for agrarian change is China's increased demand for (agro) commodities which has led to new partnerships abroad in order to secure natural resource access. This paper analyses the increasing economic and political relations between China and Latin America and raises questions concerning new trajectories of agrarian change and resource access, asking whether, how and to what extent a new consensus has emerged in reaction to the Washington Consensus which ushered in neoliberal policies to the region from the 1970s onward.

Introduction

As progressive-left governments have swept through Latin America over the past 15 years, a commodities boom has fuelled their economies and social welfare programmes through what has come to be described as a neo-extractivist development model.[1] Chinese demand for raw materials was a key factor in the international commodity price boom of 2007–8 and Chinese capital and diplomacy have gone directly to the source to facilitate and secure such imports through its 'going out' (*zou chuqu*) policy – investing in transport and energy infra-structure, extractive projects, and providing credit without directly interfering with the receiving country's fiscal and trade policies (let alone those regarding social welfare, labour conditions, or environmental protection).

The soybean is a key agro-commodity in China-Latin American relations. China accounts for 64% of the world's soybean imports, nearly 60% of which are produced in Latin America.[2] While the majority of these soybeans originate in Brazil and Argentina, China's influence over the market has important implications for producers worldwide. The protein-rich soy-bean is an important component of China's multi-billion-dollar (USD) grain-feed-meat com-plex, and China is now the largest producer and consumer of pork and second largest poultry producer in the world.[3] For Latin America – which collectively produces more soybeans than any other region – China represents an important and crucial market for its exports.

Chinese direct investment and finance in Latin America has increased substantially over the past decade, particularly in construction and the oil and gas sector. Chinese public finance, through the China Development Bank (CBD) and China Export-Import Bank (Ex-Im Bank), is the largest creditor in Latin America, lending USD $125 billion to the region from 2005 to 2015 in infrastructure (29.5%), transportation (16.5%), hydropower (12.4%), and mining (11.5%).[4] Regarding finance, the story differs from that of North-Atlantic countries and their development finance international institutions. Rather than imposing fiscal or trade conditions on loans, China finances strategic infrastructure and raw material extraction projects accepting payments in commodities and often requiring recipients to contract Chinese construction firms and equipment – dubbed as a form of 'south-south' cooperation.[5]

Such new economic relations should be understood in the context of China's need to not only secure market access for raw materials, but also control distribution channels and ensure transportation infrastructure is adequate and dependable. For the Chinese state, a supply shortage or disruption of their access to soybeans could trigger a price increase for domestic meat producers which would impact millions of Chinese consumers. For Latin America, Chinese demand for raw materials (such as minerals, petroleum and soybeans) facilitates the expansion of their markets and trade opportunities away from US-market dependence while continuing to expand the extractivist development model. As agriculture becomes increasingly industrialised and crops become increasingly flexible in their end use as food, feed, fuel, and industrial material, various economic sectors become integrated in the dynamics of agrarian change.

Over the past two decades, agro-industrial flex crop[6] production has increased dramatically as favourable prices and growing demand from China and India have created a secure market. Just four primary products (iron, copper, soybeans and crude petroleum) make up almost 70% of Latin America's total exports to China; while China's exports to the region are much more diversified, consisting of manufactured goods such as telecommunications equipment, data processing equipment, ships and boats, optical instruments and refined petroleum products.[7] These terms of trade render (once again) Latin America extremely dependent on a few primary commodities highly subject to international market volatility. Nonetheless some of Latin America's progressive-left governments seeking to decrease their dependence on the traditional international financial institutions (IFIs), are looking to China for new political and economic strategic alliances. This raises questions about this new 'Beijing Consensus'[8] and whether, how, and to what extent it differs from the 'Washington Consensus' which ushered in neoliberal policies to the region from the 1970s on.

The focus of this preliminary analysis is to explore the implications of these new economic and political relations for agrarian change in Latin America. As a contribution to the BRICS Initiative for Critical Agrarian Studies (BICAS), we aim to address the new and changing dynamics of the agro-food system in terms of patterns of production, circulation and consumption with the rise of BRICS countries. We seek to provide insights into where and how the concentration of ownership and control over value chains is taking place as well as the new and emerging relations between new and old hubs of global capital. While important research on China's growing influence and relations on agrarian-food issues in Africa is being

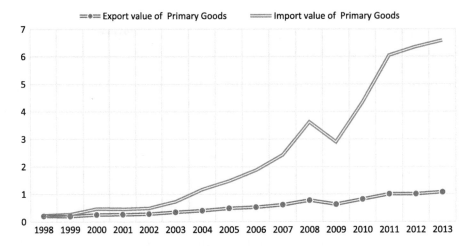

Figure 1. The export and import values of primary goods in China (billion US dollars).
Notes: "China Statistics Yearbook"; Primary goods include food and animals used mainly for food; beverages and tobacco; non-edible raw materials; mineral fuels, lubricants and related materials; animal and vegetable oils, fats and waxes.

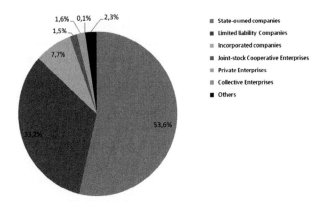

Figure 2. Structure of China's Non-financial Outward FDI Stock, by Domestic Investor Registration Types (2014).
Note: MOFCOM, "Statistical Bulletin".

carried out,[9] we seek to expand and deepen this research agenda in Latin America.[10] In this paper, we point to the need to contribute to these efforts by analysing China's 'going out' policy and some of the geopolitical motivations and dynamics between Latin America and China and their implications for broad trajectories of agrarian change. In grounding the latter analysis, we examine China's role in the shifting geopolitics of the soy complex and particularly in Argentina and Brazil focusing on whether, how and the extent to which new trade, investment, and financial relations with China are shaping trajectories of agrarian change. In the final section, we discuss the implications of these new political-economic relations on the broad trajectories of agrarian change in Latin America and the need to continue to pursue critical research on these emerging relations.

China's 'going out' policy: Emerging dynamics in Latin America

In 2000, the 'going out' strategy was formally introduced in the *Tenth Five Year Plan of China* to encourage outbound investments.[11] Chinese companies are encouraged to invest and operate overseas to get access to international markets, foreign resources and advanced technologies with a range of supports from the Chinese state.[12] Administratively, the state simplifies the examination and approval procedures for foreign investments and loosens control of foreign exchange.[13] Economically, the state offers subsides, venture opportunities, tax reductions and low-interest loans to domestic investors, especially to state-owned companies.[14] Politically, the Chinese state tries to maintain a stable investment environment for Chinese outbound investments through Bilateral Investment Treaties (BIT) and Free Trade Agreements (FTA).[15]

The 'going out' strategy is the result of multiple factors embedded in both the Chinese and global context, at both macro and micro levels. At the macro level, with rapid economic growth, the state is restructuring the economy to make it more outward-oriented considering the following: (i) the 1997 Asian financial crisis, (ii) China's sufficient foreign exchange reserves and (iii) high demand for primary goods/raw materials. First, since the introduction of 'Reform and Opening-Up Policy' (*gaige kaifang*) in 1978, China promoted the 'bringing-in' (*yin jinlai*) strategy, under which inbound foreign investments were highly encouraged and outbound foreign investments were strictly controlled. The 1997 Asian financial crisis rendered export-led growth much more vulnerable, prompting the Chinese government to lessen the country's dependence on exports and start 'going out' to the broader global market.[16] Second, at the start of the 21st Century, China had accumulated a large amount of domestic savings and foreign exchange reserves under the 'bringing-in' strategy. The surplus of savings and foreign exchange not only provided a solid financial base to realise overseas investments, but also posed a lot of pressures (e.g. ever-increasing trade frictions, criticism from foreign countries, pressures to revalue the Chinese Yuan Renminbi, overheating speculation in the domestic market and overcapacity of manufacturing sector), which led to more outward-oriented investments and trade policy reform.[17] Third, the increasing demand for raw materials in China is a major driving force for its 'going out' policy. As shown in Figure 1, the value of primary good imports grew much faster than that of exports, indicating the soaring domestic demand for primary goods in China. Such high demand for primary goods has stimulated Chinese enterprises to invest overseas for easier access to natural resources.

At the micro level, Chinese companies are increasingly investing abroad driven by the need to improve the international recognition of their brands, gain access to advanced technologies, and secure control over natural resources with flexible labour and environmental regulations. These first two points are easier to understand, since Chinese overseas investment can help expand business to foreign markets, increase brand recognition internationally and secure access to advanced technologies. As to the third point, Chinese companies are faced with the ever-growing costs of land and labour domestically, while environmental regulations are increasing due to the country's exorbitant pollution levels. The average annual salary in urban areas, for example (including the wages of peasants who temporarily work in urban areas) increased more than four times from 2001 to 2013. Land is also becoming increasingly scarce and more expensive. In rural areas, land rent increased over three-fold from 2012 to 2016.[18] Environmental regulations have increased with stricter environmental impact assessments, approval procedures and increased fines. In this sense, for Chinese enterprises with intensive demand for labour, a high dependence on natural resources (especially land-based resources), and excessive environmental impacts, it has become more economical and strategic to relocate their production to countries with excess (of cheaper) labour and more flexible social and environmental regulations.

Since the introduction of the 'going out' policy, foreign direct investment (FDI) from China to other countries has increased rapidly, expanding roughly 20 times between 2004 and 2013.[19] China's international trade (import and export) has increased substantially in the global market, from USD $474.29 billion in 2000 to USD $4.16 trillion in 2013.[20] While other Asian countries are still China's main trading partners, the importance of Latin America is rising – with the share of total international trade increasing from 2.66% (USD $12.6 billion) in 2000 to 6.28% (USD $261.4 billion) in 2013.[21] Although the most active investors (in the non-financial sector) are still state-owned companies (53.6%), the share of non-state enterprises among all Chinese outward overseas transactions is rising, from 19% in 2006 to 46% in 2014.[22] Chinese outbound investments have shown certain patterns in terms of their geographic distribution, as noticed by Chen Xiaohong, the director of the Enterprise Research Institute at the State Council's Development Research Center (Figure 2):

> Chinese enterprises choose investment regions based on the industries to which they belong: resource-dependent industries choose to invest in developing countries in Africa and Latin America; technology-seeking industries prefer developed countries especially the U.S. and Western Europe; market-seeking commodity industries choose to invest in Eastern Europe, Africa and also Latin America.[23]

As a region rich in natural resources with a high demand for manufactured and industrialised goods, China has targeted Latin America for its market expansion, and more importantly, for its raw material needs. Seventy-three per cent of China's FDI to Latin America is in extraction and agro-food sectors, with the majority in the form of mergers and acquisitions (M&A) rather than greenfield investments.[24] Such new dynamics are embedded in the restructuring of the world food and agro-commodity system towards a multi-polar regime, with emerging powers such as the BRICS (Brazil, Russia, India, China, South Africa) and some MICs (Middle income countries).

China's 'going out' strategy has certainly increased its investment and trade presence in Latin America. However, as discussed below, rather than direct investments in land, both public and private forms of Chinese capital have penetrated other facets of the value-chain in order to increase their control and access over natural resource flows from the Latin American region.

China-Latin America relations: the political economy of natural resource access

China's economic and political influence is certainly growing across the Latin American region in countries governed by both progressive and conservative regimes. In 2015, Beijing hosted the Community of Latin American and Caribbean States Summit – a 33 country bloc that excludes the United States and Canada – where Chinese President Xi Jinping pledged to invest USD $250 billion over the next 10 years in Latin America, while two way trade is expected to rise to USD $500 billion over the same period.[25] Diminishing economic returns in China, associated with limited natural resource availability and increased social and environmental standards have encouraged new investment, financial, and trade relations abroad.

The so-called 'workshop of the world' is in need of securing access to natural resources and new markets in order to transfer both its surpluses of capital and labour supply abroad.

As much as they have been praised in recent years, current political relations between China and Latin America have not always been comradely. Almost half of the countries worldwide which recognise Taiwan (ROC) are in Latin America. The 'communist menace' that the People's Republic of China embodied from 1949 onward still ignites social imaginaries across the Americas today. This ideological dimension is one of the main reasons for the strengthening of the economic ties between China and the new wave of progressive governments in several Latin American countries since the beginning of the twenty-first century. Economic relations with Bolivia, Brazil, Argentina and Nicaragua reached unforeseen heights since China emerged as a global economic powerhouse facilitated by its 'going out' policy. Even when such economic relations mean an end to the industrial remnants of the import substitution times in countries like Argentina or Brazil, they seem to be outweighed by the benefits of partnering with China, or at least for those controlling exports to and imports from China. Indeed, China became a consistent source of demand for agricultural-, livestock- and natural resource-based raw materials these Latin American countries specialise in. China has even arranged to give loans for oil, which in 2008-2011 reached USD $50 billion – including five loans worth USD $36 billion to Venezuela; one worth USD $10 billion to Brazil; and three worth USD $4 billion to Ecuador.[26] China has also turned out to be a reliable, generous and flexible creditor. In other words, increasing relations with China presented a unique opportunity for these countries to take advantage of the commodity-price boom of the 2000s without the usual economic and political conditionalities of the Washington Consensus.

The traditionally anti-communist and currently conservative governments spreading through Central America have also strengthened relations with China since the turn of the century despite of important ideological differences (in theory). Similar dynamics are taking shape in countries like Peru and Colombia and even most controversially, for national (agri) business elites who seem to set ideology aside in the face of the lucrative economic opportunities with China. Conservative and progressive regimes alike, as well as business elites, seem to believe today more than ever in Deng Xiaoping's famous maxim; 'it doesn't matter whether the cat is black or white, as long as it catches mice'.

China and Latin America's soy complex

One of the most important features of the increased relations between China and Latin America is their interdependencies on the soy complex. Latin America has become the leading soybean producing region with 56% of the global soybean trade, as Brazil (40.3%) and Argentina (7.3%) account for the vast majority of this output.[27] China imports 64% of the global trade, relying heavily on Brazil, the USA, Argentina, and to a lesser extent Uruguay.[28] As indicated in Figure 3, China's share of the global soybean trade has increased dramatically over the past 20 years, while its share of global production has been steadily decreasing.

This vast increase in soybean imports is principally the result of (a) changing dietary patterns in China and (b) the combination of China's reform in 1978, its 'going out' policy and more drastic liberalisation policies introduced in 2001 with China's entry into the World Trade Organization (WTO). Food consumption patterns in China have shifted from a ratio of 8:1:1 (grains:meat:vegetables) in 1980 to 4:3:3 in 2005.[29] In just 20 years per capita meat consumption in China doubled, from 30 kg in 1993 to 62 kg in 2013, and since 2005 there

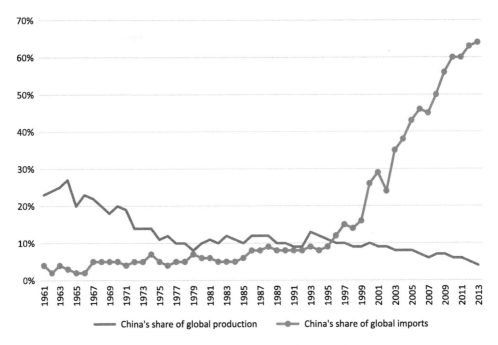

Figure 3. China's share of global soybean production and trade (imports), 1961–2013.
Note: FAOSTAT, "Database".

has been a 25% increase in per capita meat consumption, rendering the food consumption ratio even more 'meaty'.[30] This is not only due to economic growth and rising (upper)middle classes, but the active promotion by both economic and political elites to 'modernize' diets towards higher levels of meat consumption.[31] China is the world's leading meat producer and consumer and access to the protein-rich soybean has become crucial to fuel their industrial livestock complex.[32] Unlike China's 'strategic crops' for food security[33] which include rice, wheat and maize and are more tightly controlled by the state, soybeans were liberalised and redefined as an 'industrial commodity' as early as the 1990s, and with its entry into the WTO import tariffs were drastically cut from 114% to 3%.[34] Due to these conditions, China shifted from the world's leading producer to consumer (and importer) of soybeans (see Figure 3).[35]

For progressive Latin American governments, soybean production offered a gateway out of U.S. dominated trade relations. In the case of Argentina, the Kirchner administration leaned heavily on soy exports to revive the ailing economy after the economic crash of 2001. It should therefore come as no surprise that economic and political relations between the world's leading soybean producing region and China have increased and been reshaped along lines including the 'soybean connection'.

Control over the soy complex has become a mutual priority for economic and political elites on both sides, but claiming a significant stake in this sector is not straightforward and continues to be contested. Even domestically, the Chinese state is vying for control over its own soybean processing industry. In 2004-5, China's soybean industry was in crisis as some 70% of its domestic soybean enterprises collapsed due to unfavourable market conditions as volatile soybean prices resulted many Chinese importers (and crushers) defaulting on their contracts with US suppliers.[36] This crisis presented an opportunity for the ABCD (ADM, Bunge, Cargill, Louis Dreyfus) multinationals which dominate the global grain trade. By 2009, 'nine of the top 10 soy processing enterprises in China were wholly or partly owned by foreign capital' with the ABCD companies controlling 70% of the industry.[37] Both at home and abroad, the Chinese state is using its leverage to support domestic (public and private) companies in order (re)gain control over soybeans and other to natural resources. As part of the state's Strategic Plan for Agricultural 'going out', Chinese enterprises that invest in agriculture, forestry and fisheries abroad can receive up to 30 million yuan (USD $4.3 million) in fiscal and financial support with additional tax and insurance incentives.[38]

While China's 'going out' policy and investment abroad led to some alarmist reports on global land grabbing claiming that 'China is by far the largest investor, buying or leasing twice as much as anyone else',[39] more meticulous research challenged these assumptions finding that such claims are based on speculation rather than supported evidence.[40] In Latin America, Myers and Jie find that Chinese land investments are vastly over-reported or have been suspended for various reasons.[41] They cite reports on Chinese land grabs in Latin America ranging from 300,000 hectares (ha) to 800,000 ha by the International Institute for Sustainable Development (IISD), yet they confirm just over 70,000 ha of land leased or purchased outright by Chinese capital.[42] China has been put under a "global magnifying glass"[43] due in part to its sheer size (population and economy), its politics, and the fact the it represents a new (and perhaps unknown) player in the global food system, challenging the 'old hubs' of transnational agribusiness. Concerning farmland investments in Brazil, for example, Oliveira argues that there is disproportionate media attention given to Chinese investments despite much larger and more substantial investment made by companies from the Global North.[44] Oliveira argues that this type of 'sinophobia' is part of a broader effort by the 'old hubs' of capital to shift attention away from their own investments and suppress rising Chinese competition.[45] Rather than investing directly in farmland, Chinese firms are much more active in the value-chain and have been most active in the two countries which account for almost half of their total soybean imports: Argentina and Brazil. Since only 6% of the world's soy gets consumed as whole beans,[46] economic leverage comes from controlling the processing (crushing and oil refining) facilities. This stage of production is where we see China vying for control. This has geopolitical implications beyond Latin America since old hubs of global capital still have a strong foothold on processing and trade in places like Argentina.

Argentina

Reports on Chinese farmland investments in Argentina have been largely speculative. Myers and Jie for example, find that media reports regarding the following Chinese investments in Argentina cannot be confirmed or have been stalled: a 300,000-ha purchase of soybean farmland in Rio Negro by Heilongjiang Beidahuang Nongken Group Co., and two farmland investments by Chongqing Grain Group of 10,000 ha in Cordoba Province and 130,000 ha in the Chaco region.[47] In their respective works on land grabs in Argentina and by Chinese enterprises, Murmis and Murmis and Hofman and Ho mention the *potential* Rio Negro deal, but at that time it remained uncertain and speculative.[48]

Data published in 2011 shows that 85% of the processing capacity in Argentina is dominated by six companies, only three of which were Argentine – Aceitera General Deheza (AGD), Molinos Rio de la Plata and Vicentín – and three multinationals – Bunge, Cargill (US) and Dreyfus.[49] However, in 2014, China's state-owned national Cereals, Oils and Foodstuffs

Co. (COFCO) purchased majority stakes in the Dutch-based seed and trading company Nidera as well Hong Kong-based agribusiness company Noble Group for an estimated USD$ 2.8 billion.[50] These acquisitions have made COFCO a new global agribusiness giant, challenging the hegemony of the ABCD quartet. Together Nidera and Noble control almost 11% of Argentina's crushing capacity and a significant part of the exports, including 10% of soybean meal, 13% of soybean oil, and 15% soybean grains.[51]

Triggered by internal restructuring of the soy sector and growing industrial pork production in China, since the late 1990s Chinese imports of soy have exploded as shown in Figure 3. The state has also pushed to keep processing on Chinese soil, reshaping the nature of Argentina's export sector. In 1996 exports to China made up 1.96% of Argentina's total trade value. Still, in 1999 China did not import any Argentine soybeans, but did import soybean oil and meal. One year later, in a dramatic reversal, 62% of what China bought from Argentina were unprocessed soybeans, and by 2012 the Chinese share of all soybean exports had risen to 84.42%.[52] Despite Argentina's differential export tax (DET),[53] the growth in China's demand in the soy sector has increasingly favored unprocessed soybeans at the expense of soybean oil and meal, thus creating a 'relative loss of value added within the export basket of the complex'.[54]

As China and Latin America vie for control over the processing sector, northern-based multinational companies have increasingly tried to maintain control by relocating their plants from the US to China and Latin America. ADM, for example, set up new facilities in South America and China, reducing its share in North America to less than 50%. Similarly, Bunge and Cargill have closed processing sites in the US, while expanding their capacity in Latin America and China.[55] It is true that the political context in which these economic trends have taken place has been one of ideological alignment between leftist governments in Latin America and China. However, the decreasing revenues captured by Argentina demonstrate that China may be more politically cooperative than the US, but no less competitive when it comes to controlling export markets.

One of the main strategies China has used to fuel demand for its soy processing sector and create opportunities for Chinese companies abroad is by lending money for investment in production and infrastructure at below market rates in exchange for guaranteed contracts for construction by Chinese companies and/or a commitment to sell the goods produced to China at a set price. In 2010 China loaned Argentina $10 billion under such arrangements.[56] In the midst of Kirchner's protracted dispute with the truckers' union, for example, the Chinese Development Bank proposed a $2.6 billion 10-year loan to revive the railway network connecting much of the soy heartland to Buenos Aires, the country's major port.[57]

While providing alternative rail infrastructure for shipping of goods, which could potentially diffuse the power of other transport unions, Di Paola argues that such political manoeuvres came at an economic price.[58] In the case of two massive dam projects proposed to increase the country's energy capacity by 5% and hydroelectric capacity by 15%, approximately 150 engineering and managerial positions were planned to go to Chinese workers, and the rest of the 5,000 total jobs projected to go to local workers.[59] Importantly, the terms outlined in the Framework Agreement state that works will be 'directly awarded' (Art. 5) to Chinese contractors, provided that 'they are subject to concessional financing from the Chinese side and the award is under advantageous quality and price conditions'. As Di Paola points out, this agreement 'wholly set[s] aside [...] the bidding process as a procedure for the procurement of public works'.[60] Kirchner's policies were permissive of agreements that

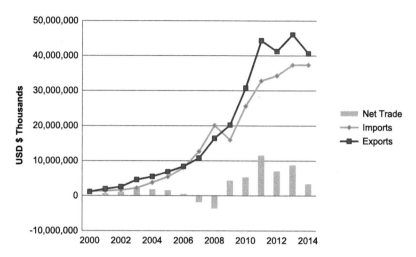

Figure 4. Brazil-China bilateral trade.
Note: Ibid.

did not always contribute to Argentina's competitive advantage *vis a vis* China, in what appears to be an exchange for strategic political alliances, or repositioning both regionally and domestically. However, over time the Kirchner government's ability to capture tax revenues and maintain control over value added processing facilities has waned.

According to China-Argentina economic relations analyst, Ariel Slipak, with the recent change in government, '[president] Macri will remove the ideological element of the relationship with China, turning it into one of pure pragmatism […] With Cristina Kirchner, the alliance was counter-hegemonic and anti-imperialist, but for Macri anything that has ideological content is bad. China will accommodate this new type of connection'.[61] Indeed upon assuming the presidency in December 2015, Macri put these dam projects on hold to examine the costs and benefits. China's response: suspend imports of soybean oil. Although the dam projects are not directly related to the soy sector, the Chinese government is using its soybean oil imports as leverage in broader trade negotiations with Argentina.[62] While under the new Macri presidency the political alliance with China and away from the US is no longer the driving force, it remains to be seen if a desire to ensure exports of soybean oil will encourage Macri to honour the other economic agreements Kirchner made with China.

Brazil

Similar to Argentina, many of the reported Chinese farmland investments in Brazil cannot be confirmed or have been stalled. These include a 200,000-ha farmland investment by Shanghai Pengxin International Group Ltd., a 200,000-ha investment in Bahía by Chongqing Grain Group, and a 200,000–250,000 ha by Pallas International Consultants Group.[63] The only confirmed Chinese investments include a 700-ha and 16,000-ha soybean farmland investment by Zhejiang Fudi Agriculture Group in Rio Grande do Sul and Tocantins, respectively.[64] However, as Oliveira reveals in a recent study of Chinese land grabs in Brazil, Chinese companies have been disproportionately singled-out in Brazil despite having invested far less than other countries, particularly from the Global North.[65] From 2010 to 2013, for example, China ranked 23rd among foreign investors in Brazilian agriculture, investing a total of USD

$21 million compared to the United States' USD $7.6 billion during the same period.[66] There may indeed be a level of 'sinophobia' associated with Chinese investments in farmland as Oliveira suggests, but going beyond a land-centric lens reveals the broader implications of increased Chinese relations for processes of agrarian change and natural resource access.

Brazilian economic growth has been fuelled in recent decades by agro-commodity and mining exports, and China has and continues to play a crucial role in this export surplus.[67] In 2009, China surpassed the United States as Brazil's most important export partner and by 2014 soybeans (41%), iron ore (30%) and crude petroleum (8.6%) represented nearly 80% of Brazil's total export value to China.[68] While Brazil has maintained a trade surplus with China since 2009, it remains dependent on raw material exports and thus volatile commodities markets while China's more diversified industrial and manufactured exports allow for the capture of value-added surpluses and sectoral linkages. As Fearnside and Figueiredo suggest, China has played a major role in shifting Brazil's economy away from manufacturing and towards agricultural commodity exports.[69] While this may weaken the influence of manufacturers/industrialists and labour unions, it has certainly increased the economic and political influence of Brazil's agro-elites 'due to the large amounts of money entering Brazil from the export of soybeans, China being the number one source of these earnings'.[70] For Brazil, the recent commodity price 'bust', will likely result in a trade deficit as occurred in 2008 and 2009 with China (see Figure 4). While Brazilian agro-elites and other extractive sectors have certainly benefitted from these new trade relations, the Brazilian state has failed to foster a more robust, value-added and articulated growth strategy leading to a process of reprimarisation or deindustrialisation of the Brazilian economy as the industrial sector gradually loses ground in the share of Brazilian GDP.[71] For example, 83.6% of Chinese imports from Brazil were primary products, while only 4.7% were 'manufactured products', revealing the existence of an association between China's rise and the reprimarisation of the countries on its export list.[72]

However, even before China's 'going out' policy and its increased presence in global commodity markets, raw material exports in agriculture and mining were a central feature of Brazil's economic strategy, especially after the Kandir Law of 1996 which exempted raw material exports from the Tax on Distribution of Goods and Services (ICMS).[73] This effectively rendered raw agricultural exports much more competitive than industrialised or processed goods. Just two years after the Kandir Law was passed, soybeans increased from just 5% of total exports to 30%, deepening the reprimarization of the economy.[74] From 1999 to 2012, agricultural exports accounted for an average of 40% of total exports with Chinese demand for soybeans gradually becoming the most important export.[75]

While trade relations between the two countries have strengthened, Chinese FDI, particularly in mergers and acquisitions (M&A) has also increased. For example, COFCO, 'now represents the largest and most significant presence of Chinese agribusiness capital not only in the Brazilian soybean complex, but also in its agribusiness sector as a whole'.[76] Furthermore, a recent analysis of shipping data by Reuters reports that 'Asian trading houses, including China's state-owned COFCO, bought 45 percent of [Brazil's] soybean, corn and soybean meal exports last year [2016]. By comparison, the share purchased by the traders known collectively by the acronym "ABCD" was 37 percent'.[77] The report reveals dramatic changes in the control over the Brazilian grain market. In 2003, 57% of Brazilian grains were controlled by the ABCDs, while companies from Asia, collectively, controlled just 9%.[78] On a global scale,

China's share of the total soybean crush has increased from 4% in 1990 to 29% in 2014, signalling an important shift in the geopolitics of the soy complex.[79]

China has also scaled up its financial lending to Brazil, particularly for the energy sector and industrial infrastructure for soybean processing amounting to nearly USD$ 20 billion since 2009.[80] These include the Cuiabá-Santarém railway and the Transcontinental Railway which would link the major soy production area in Mato Grosso to Porto Velho and stimulate soybean expansion with greater access to infrastructure and reduced transportation costs.[81] Now a global leader in processing and trade, China has strategically positioned itself and increased its control over desired natural resources in order to supply its growing domestic industrial and consumer needs.

China-Brazil relations are characterised by industrial, value-added goods flowing into Brazil and primary goods (agricultural and non-agricultural commodities) flowing into China. The current trade relations, aside from the long-term economic implications of these unequal terms of trade, are fuelling a rise of land prices and the expansion of Brazil's agricultural frontiers to the north of Brazil (into the Amazon and Cerrado biome), but also towards Paraguay, Bolivia, Argentina and Uruguay, creating what has been called the 'soybean republic'.[82] This expansion is based on monocrops (mainly soybeans but also sugarcane), changing the use of land, particularly in the Amazon and Cerrado biomes. Fearnside, Figueiredo and Bonjour find that while direct land investments may be marginal, China's rising demand for soybeans and beef products, as well as its direct involvement in infrastructure development, are major drivers of Amazonian deforestation in Brazil.[83] As result of such increased demand for soybeans, frontier expansion and deforestation has led to severe social and environmental consequences, provoking land disputes, conflict and leading to both economic and extra-economic forms of dispossession.[84]

Despite massive public outcry over the recent political turmoil unfolding in Brazil, interim-President Michel Temer has appointed the country's – and perhaps the world's – largest soybean producer, Blairo Maggi, as the new Minister of Agriculture. Not surprisingly, Maggi's first official mission abroad was to China to discuss bilateral trade issues, aiming to increase the export of meat, soy and minerals.[85] He also stated that he and the interim-President are working to eliminate any (formal) barrier for foreign investments in land deals.[86] Despite an approval rating of less than 12%[87], Temer continues to issue executive orders, which has resulted in the dissolution of Brazil's Ministry of Agrarian Development (MDA), responsible for land reform and supporting small-scale family farmers. While a lack of political legitimacy continues at the time of writing, the interim government has made it clear that the growth of agribusiness and relations with China will continue to expand the agricultural frontier.

Conclusion: emerging partnerships or a new imperialism?

China's rapid economic growth and social restructuring require an increasing amount of natural resources – for industry, energy security and its growing meat-complex. However, many Latin American countries with new and increasing economic relations with China are not harnessing the value-added potential through facilitating forward and backward linkages for industrial development.[88] They are pursuing an export-oriented extractivist strategy fuelled and increasingly controlled by Chinese capital. China is 'going out' to fix a potential capital over-accumulation crisis. Surplus capital, less profitable investments, and surplus labour can lead to crises and thus must be put into production, if not at home, then abroad.

While these 'emerging partnerships' may be framed as mutually beneficial 'south-south' cooperation, they continue to reinforce similar relations of production and resource control which have plagued development trajectories throughout the Latin American region for centuries. The main difference, one could argue, is the lack of fiscal and monetary condition- alities imposed by the lender (China), seemingly allowing the borrowing countries to main- tain sovereignty over their economic policies. The new conditionalities of the Beijing Consensus, however, come in the form of Chinese capital and labour requirements. They are accompanied by a more relaxed regulatory framework, which, for the largest Chinese lend- ers,[89] lack industry-specific social and environmental standards, do not require compliance with international environmental regulations, do not have grievance mechanisms, and lack independent monitoring. However, Ray et al., point out that unlike the World Bank, the International Financial Corporation, and the Inter-American Development Bank, only Chinese policy banks require ex-post environmental impact assessments.[90] Evidently, regulatory mechanisms do not guarantee effectiveness or accountability, but the lack thereof eliminates the potential to hold companies accountable – which, for Chinese lenders, implies Chinese companies.

Moreover, the terms of trade between most Latin American countries and China is leading to a combined trajectory of *deindustrialization and reprimarization*, since they continue to extract non-value added raw materials for export, and import heavily industrialised val- ue-added goods. Chinese imports discourage domestic industries in Latin America from producing those goods and jeopardise the ability to diversify their economies. This is, indeed, the nature of global capitalism and requires states to retake control and sovereignty over their natural resources. A focus on primary goods has fuelled the ongoing expansion of corporate-controlled, large-scale agriculture, which favours labour-saving mechanisation and export-oriented production of crops like soybeans. As a result, many Latin American countries are seeing ongoing processes of agrarian transformation that undermine rural working classes' livelihoods, extract wealth from local agrarian economies, and are highly dependent on volatile commodity prices and Chinese demand.[91] So, while the Beijing Consensus may be applauded for its non-interference in the political sphere and respect for 'state sovereignty', it may also erode resource sovereignty and render the economy depend- ent on a 'commodities consensus'[92] heavily influenced by Chinese demand and resource control, even if this control is voluntarily ceded by Latin American governments.

While it is important to recognise that Chinese investors in Latin America or elsewhere are not homogeneous, this important differentiation is beyond the scope of this preliminary analysis. The Chinese state, quasi-state-owned companies, banks, private capital and indi- vidual entrepreneurs have different characteristics and respectively may have different polit- ical and economic arrangements and thus lead to variegated trajectories of agrarian change. While this was omitted in this contribution, these different types of Chinese investments require more detailed analyses in the future.

Across Latin American countries, classes of capital involved (even if partially) in these natural resource-based accumulation projects are still profiting. It seems that, indeed, Deng Xiaoping's maxim about the game of 'cat and mouse' is playing out across Latin America as China continues to finance, trade with, and to a lesser extent invest in land and natural resource-intensive commodity production in countries controlled by both progressive and conservative governments across the region. For resource-rich countries of Latin America, these new and increasing relations are likely to intensify existing dependence on (agro) extractive industries, including soybeans,[93] reinforcing existing relations production, property and power as the Chinese state and private capital collude with the established classes of capital and the state in Latin America. From Washington's neoliberal conditionalities to Beijing's south-south cooperation, it appears that among political and economic elites the consensus remains the same: resource control.

Disclosure statement

No potential conflict of interest was reported by the authors.

Notes

1. See Gudynas, "Diez tesis urgentes sobre el nuevo extractivismo"; Veltmeyer and Petras, "The New Extractivism."
2. FAOSTAT, "Database"; OEC, "Atlas Media Visualization."
3. Sharma, "The Need for Feed."
4. Gallagher and Myers, "China-Latin America Finance Database."
5. Myers et al., "Chinese Finance to LAC."
6. See the Flex Crops and Commodities Special Forum including Borras et al., "The Rise of Flex Crops"; Gillon, "Flexible for Whom?"; Alonso-Fradejas et al., "Inquiring into the Political Economy of Oil Palm"; Oliveira and Schneider, "The Politics of Flexing Soybeans"; McKay et al., "The Political Economy of Sugarcane Flexing"; Hunsberger and Alonso-Fradejas, "The Discursive Flexibility."
7. Ray and Gallagher, "China-Latin America Economic Bulletin."
8. Slipak, "América Latina ante China"; Ramo, "Beijing Consensus."
9. Scoones et al., "A New Politics of Development Cooperations?"; Gu et al., "Chinese State Capitalism?"; Bräutigam and Zhang, "Green dreams"; Buckley, "Chinese Agriculture Development"; Scoones et al., "New Development Encounters."
10. But see Wilkinson et al., "Brazil and China: The Agribusiness Connection," Oliveira, "Chinese Land Grabs in Brazil?" and Slipak, "America Latina ante China."
11. Cheng and Xu, "Review of Domestic Institutions"; Yao and Li, "Overview of the Trends."
12. There are slight changes in the Chinese national plans in terms of the aims of 'going out'. In the Tenth Five Year Plan, the three main aims of 'going out' were clearly described as to increase export, obtain resources and improve technology. While in the Eleventh Five Year Plan, 'to increase export' was replaced by the 'to vary the products', and 'to improve the technological development' was removed from the aims. In the Twelfth Five Year Plan, there was no explanation about the aims of the 'going out'. See Yao and Li, "Overview of the Trends," 132–133.

13. Cheng, and Xu, "Review of Domestic Institutions," 151.
14. In the Official Development Assistance (ODA) programme, the Chinese state required agreements to hire Chinese companies as contractors or material suppliers; Cheng and Xu, "Review of Domestic Institutions," 151–152.
15. Ibid., 152
16. Yelery, "China's 'Going Out' Policy."
17. Nash, "China's 'Going Out Policy'"; Cheng, and Xu, "Review of Domestic Institutions"; Murphy, "China's Going Out."
18. The annual rent of the rural dryland increased from around 300 Yuan/Mu in 2012 to 1000 Yuan/Mu in 2016, from field note of Yunan Xu in Guangxi, China on 10th March 2016.
19. "China Statistics Yearbook."
20. Ibid.
21. Ibid.
22. MOFCOM, "Statistical Bulletin."
23. Murphy, "China's Going Out," 7.
24. Ray et al., "China in Latin America"; Sauer et al., "Ambivalent and Shaky Stance of Brazil."
25. Rajagopalan, "China's Xi Woos Latin America."
26. Gallagher et al., "New Banks in Town."
27. FAOSTAT, "Database."
28. FAOSTAT, "Database"; OEC, "Atlas Media."
29. Huang, "China's New-Age Small Farms."
30. FAOSTAT, "Database."
31. Oliveira and Schneider, "The Politics of Flexing Soybeans."
32. Sharma, "The Need for Feed."
33. As pointed out by Schneider, "In Chinese policy, Food Security is Grain Security, and Grain Security Means Adhering to a 95 Percent Baseline of Domestic Grain Production" (2014, 623).
34. Smaller et al., "Farmland and Water"; Schneider, "Developing the Meat Grab."
35. FAOSTAT, "Database."
36. Schneider, "Feeding China's Pigs"; Hairong et al., "China's Soybean Crisis."
37. Hairong et al., "China's Soybean Crisis," 374.
38. The Ministry of Commerce, Inform (2011) No 76. Accessed March 22, 2017. http://www.mofcom.gov.cn/aarticle/b/bf/201104/20110407525027.html, "Chinese Agriculture goes Global."
39. The Economist, "When Others are Grabbing their Land"; Grain, "Seized!"
40. Hofman and Ho, "China's 'Developmental Outsourcing," 1; Bräutigam and Zhang, "Green Dreams."
41. Myers and Jie, "China's Agricultural Investment."
42. Ibid.
43. Hofman and Ho, "China's 'Developmental Outsourcing.'"
44. Oliveira, "Chinese Land Grabs in Brazil?"
45. Ibid.
46. Oliveira and Schneider, "Politics of Flexing Soybeans," 168.
47. Myers and Jie, "China's Agricultural Investment," 14.
48. Murmis and Murmis, "Land Concentration and Foreign Land Ownership in Argentina"; Hofman and Ho, "China's 'Developmental Outsourcing.'"
49. Tomei and Upham, "Argentina Clustering," 51.
50. Ibid.
51. Wesz Jr. "Strategies and Hybrid Dynamics," 307.
52. Hausmann et al., "Atlas of Economic Complexity."
53. Argentina's DET for soybeans is 23.%; for soybean oil, 19.3% and for soybean meal, 20% (Deese and Reeder 2007, 10)
54. Lopez et al., "A Study of the Impact of China's Global Expansion," 18.
55. Ibid., 22
56. Casas Manzano, "Los préstamos de China."
57. Kotschwar et al., "Chinese Investment," 3.

58. Di Paola, "A Chinese Agreement."
59. Koop, "Kirchner and Cepernic."
60. Di Paola, "A Chinese Agreement," 3.
61. Koop, "New Argentina President."
62. Tambornini, "China bloqueó el ingreso de aceite de soja argentino como represalia por la paralización de las obras destinadas a construir dos represas en Santa Cruz."
63. Myers and Jie, "China's Agricultural Investment," 14.
64. Myers and Jie, "China's Agricultural Investment," 4.
65. Oliveira, "Chinese Land Grabs in Brazil?"
66. Ibid.
67. Sauer et al., "The Ambivalent and Shaky Stance of Brazil."
68. WITS, "Country Profile"; OEC, "Atlas Media Visualizations."
69. Fearnside and Figueiredo, "China's Influence on Deforestation."
70. Ibid., 21.
71. Jenkins, "Chinese Competition Causing Deindustrialization," 72.
72. Curado, "China Rising"; (2015), Jenkins, "Chinese Competition." However, even acknowledging 'a growing deficit in manufactured goods', which has been compensated by commodity exports, Jenkins and Barbosa (2012, p. 71) see this as a positive since it shows the '…ability to supply more primary products, adding crude oil to the basket of Brazilian exports to China', generating trade surplus to Brazil.
73. Wesz, "Strategies and Hybrid Dynamics," 292.
74. Ibid, 292.
75. Ibid.
76. Ibid.
77. Bonato, "New Titans on the Block."
78. Ibid.
79. Oliveira, "The Geopolitics of Brazilian Soybeans"; Oliveira and Schneider, "The Politics of Flexing."
80. Gallagher and Myers, "China-Latin America."
81. Fearnside and Figueiredo, "China's Influence on Deforestation," 26.
82. Wesz, "Strategies and Hybrid Dynamics."
83. Fearnside et al. "Amazonian Forest Loss and the Long Reach of China's Influence."
84. Wesz, "Strategies and Hybrid Dynamics"; Sauer et al., "Ambivalent and Shaky"; Fearnside, "Land-tenure Issues."
85. MAPA, "Ministro Blairo Maggi viaja a China."
86. Valor Econômico, "Novo Ministro define suas prioridades"; O Globo, "Temer quer liberar venda."
87. WSJ, "Interim Brazilian Government."
88. See for e.g. McKay, "Value-chain Agriculture."
89. From 2005–2015, Chinese loans to Latin America were from China Development Bank, CBD (USD $100.6 billion) and China's Export-Import Bank (USD $24.1 billion) (Gallagher and Myers, 2014)
90. Ray et al., "China in Latin America."
91. See Alonso-Fradejas, "Anything but a Story Foretold"; McKay and Colque, "Bolivia's Soy Complex"; and on Argentina see Brent, "Territorial Restructuring."
92. Svampa, "Consenso de los commodities."
93. See McKay, "Agrarian Extractivism in Bolivia."

ORCID

Ben M. McKay http://orcid.org/0000-0002-5737-5255

Bibliography

Alonso-Fradejas, A., J. Liu, T. Salerno, and Y. Xu. "Inquiring into the Political Economy of Oil Palm as a Global Flex Crop." *Journal of Peasant Studies* 43, no. 1 (2016): 141–165.

Alonso-Fradejas, A. "Anything but a Story Foretold: Multiple Politics of Resistance to the Agrarian Extractivist Project in Guatemala." *Journal of Peasant Studies*. 42, no. 3–4 (2015): 489–515.

Bonato, G. 2016. *New Titans on the Block: ABCDs Lose Top Brazil Grains Spot to Asian Rivals*. Reuters. Accessed March 1, 2017. http://www.reuters.com/article/us-brazil-grains-idUSKCN0WP19V

Borras, S., J. Franco, R. Isakson, L. Levidow, and P. Vervest. "The Rise of Flex Crops and Commodities: Implications for Research." *Journal of Peasant Studies* 43, no. 1 (2016): 93–115.

Bräutigam, D., and H. Zhang. "Green Dreams: Myth and Reality in China's Agricultural Investment in Africa." *Third World Quarterly* 34, no. 9 (2013): 1676–1696.

Brent, Z. W. "Territorial Restructuring and Resistance in Argentina." *The Journal of Peasant Studies* 42, no. 3–4 (2015): 671–694.

Buckley, L. "Chinese Agriculture Development Cooperation in Africa: Narratives and Politics." *IDS Bulletin* 44, no. 4 (2013): 42–52.

Casas Manzano, A. 2015. "Los Préstamos De China a América Latina Crecieron 22.000 Millones." *EL PAÍS*, February 27.

China Statistic Yearbook. 2014. Accessed March 24, 2016. http://www.stats.gov.cn/tjsj/ndsj/2014/indexch.htm

Cheng, S., and M. Xu. 2011. "The Review of the Domestic Instituions on the Chinese Foreign Direct Investment (Zhongguo Duiwai Zhijie Touzi De Guonei Zhidu Pingxi)." *Inquiry into Economic Issues (Jingji Wenti Tansuo)* 10: 149–154.

Curado, M. 2015. "China Rising: Threats and Opportunities for Brazil in Latin American Perspectives." Issue 205. 42, no. 6: 88–104, November.

Deese, W., and J. Reeder. 2007. "Export Taxes on Agricultural Products: Recent History and Economic Modeling of Soybean Export Taxes in Argentina." *United States International Trade Commission Journal of International Commerce and Economics*, Web version. Accessed April 22. https://www.usitc.gov/publications/332/journals/export_taxes_model_soybeans.pdf

Di Paola, M. M. *A Chinese Agreement*. Buenos Aires: Fundación Ambiente y Recursos Naturales (FARN), 2015.

Ellis, R.E. 2016. *Is Bolivia Outsourcing Too Much to China?* Open Democracy. Accessed April 22. https://www.opendemocracy.net/democraciaabierta/r-evan-ellis/is-bolivia-outsourcing-too-much-to-china

FAOSTAT. *Database*. Rome: FAO, 2014.

Fearnside, P. M. "Land-Tenure Issues as Factors in Environmental Destruction in Brazilian Amazonia: The Case of Southern Pará." *World Development* 29, no. 8 (2001): 1361–1372.

Fearnside, P. M., and A. M. R. Figueiredo. *China's Influence on Deforestation in Brazilian Amazonia: A Growing Force in the State of Mato Grosso*. Boston, MA: Discussion Paper, Global Economic Governance Initiative, Boston University, 2015.

Fearnside, P. M., A. M. R. Figueiredo, and S. C. M. Bonjour. "Amazonian Forest Loss and the Long Reach of China's Influence." *Environment, Development and Sustainability* 15, no. 2 (2013): 325–338.

Gallagher, K. P., and M. Myers. *China-Latin America Finance Database*. Washington, DC: Inter-American Dialogue, 2014.

Gallagher, K. P., A. Irwin, and K. Koleski. *The New Banks in Town: Chinese Finance in Latin America*. Washington, DC: Inter-American Dialogue Report, 2012.

Gillon, S. "Flexible for Whom? Flex Crops, Crises, Fixes and the Politics of Exchange Use Values in US Corn Production." *Journal of Peasant Studies* 43, no. 1 (2016): 117–139.

Gu, J., C. Zhang, A. Vaz, and L. Mukwereza. 2016. "Chinese State Capitalism? Rethinking the Role of the State and Business in Chinese Development Cooperation in Africa." *World Development* 81: 24–34.

Gudynas, E. 2009. "Diez Tesis Urgentes Sobre El Nuevo Extractivismo. Contextos Y Demandas Bajo El Progresismo Sudamericano Actual." In *Extractivismo, Política Y Sociedad*, edited by CAAP and CLAES. 187–225. Quito: Centro Andino de Accíon Popular (CAAP) y Centro Latino Americano de Ecología Social (CLAES).

Grain. *Seized! GRAIN Briefing Annex*. Barcelona: GRAIN, 2008.

Hairong, Y., C. Yiyuan, and K. H. Bun. "China's Soybean Crisis: The Logic of Modernization and Its Discontents." *Journal of Peasant Studies* 43, no. 2 (2016): 373–395.

Hausmann, R., C. Hidalgo, S. Bustos, M. Coscia, S. Chung, J. Jimenez, A. Simoes, and M. Yildirim. *The Atlas of Economic Complexity*. Cambridge, MA: Puritan Press, 2011.

Hofman, I., and P. Ho. "China's 'Development Outsourcing': A Critical Examination of Chinese Global 'Land Grabs' Discourse." *Journal of Peasant Studies* 39, no. 1 (2012): 1–48.

Huang, P. C. C. "China's New-Age Small Famrs and Their Vertical Integration:Agribusiness of Co-Ops?" *Modern China* 37, no. 2 (2011): 107–134.

Hunsberger, C., and A. Alonso-Frajedas. "The Discursive Flexibility of 'Flex Crops': Comparing Oil Palm and Jatropha." *Journal of Peasant Studies* 43, no. 1 (2016): 225–250.

INE. *Comercio Exterior*. La Paz: Instituto Nacional de Estadisticas, 2016.

Jenkins, R. 2015. "Is Chinese Competition Causing Deindustrialization in Brazil?" *Latin American Perspectives*, Issue 205. 42, no. 6: 42–63. November.

Jenkins, R., and A. F. Barbosa. "Fear for Manufacturing? China and the Future of Industry in Brazil and Latin America." *The China Quarterly* 209 (2012): 59–81.

Koop, F. 2015a. "Kirchner and Cepernic: Two Dams Mired in Environmental Conflict." *Dialogo Chino*. Accessed May 8. http://dialogochino.net/kirchner-and-cepernic-two-dams-mired-in-environmental-conflict/

Koop, F. 2015b. "New Argentina President to Put Deals with China under the Microscope." *Dialogo Chino*. Accessed May 8. http://dialogochino.net/new-argentina-president-to-put-china-deals-under-the-microscope/

Kotschwar, B., M. H. Theodore, and J. Muir. *Chinese Investment in Latin American Resources: The Good, the Bad and the Ugly*, 12–13. Washington DC: Peterson Institute for International Economics, No. WP, 2012.

Lopez, A., D. Ramos, and G. Starobinsky. 2008. *A Study of the Impact of China's Global Expansion on Argentina; Soybean Value Chain Analysis: Final Report*. Buenos Aires: Centro de Investigaciones para la Transformación (CENIT), Working Paper No. 2.

MAPA. 2016. "Ministro Blairo Maggi Viaja à China Em Sua Primeira Missão Oficial Ao Exterior." *Noticias, Ministerio Da Agricultura*. Accessed June 9. http://www.agricultura.gov.br/comunicacao/noticias/2016/05/ministro-blairo-maggi-viaja-a-china-em-sua-primeira-missao-oficial-ao-exterior

McKay, B. M. "Agrarian Extractivism in Bolivia." *World Development* 97 (2017): 199–211.

McKay, B. 2017. "Value-Chain Agriculture and Control Grabbing: BRICS, MICs and Bolivia's Soy Complex." *Globalizations*, forthcoming.

McKay, B., and G. Colque. "Bolivia's Soy Complex: The Development of 'Productive Exclusion.'" *Journal of Peasant Studies* 43, no. 2 (2016): 583–610.

McKay, B., S. Sauer, B. Richardson, and R. Herre. "The Political Economy of Sugarcane Flexing: Initial Insights from Brazil, Southern Africa and Cambodia." *Journal of Peasant Studies* 43, no. 1 (2016): 195–223.

MOFCOM. *2014 Statistical Bulletin of China's Outward Foreign Direct Investment*. Beijing: MOFCOM, 2015.

Murmis, M., and M. R. Murmis. "Land Concentration and Foreign Land Ownership in Argentina in the Context of Global Land Grabbing." *Canadian Journal of Development Studies* 33, no. 4 (2012): 490–508.

Murphy, M. 2008. *Issue in Focus: China's 'Going Out' Investment Policy*. http://csis.org/files/publication/080527_freeman_briefing.pdf.

Myers, M., K. Gallagher, and F. Yuan. *Chinese Finance to LAC in 2015: Doubling down*. Washington, DC: China-Latin America Report, Inter-American Dialogue, 2016.

Myers, M., and G. Jie. *China's Agricultural Investment in Latin America: A Critical Assessment*. Washington, DC: Inter-American Dialogue, 2015.

Nash, P. 2012. *China's 'Going Out' Strategy*. Retrieved from Diplomatic Courier http://www.diplomaticourier.com/china-s-going-out-strategy/

O Globo. 2016. "Temer Quer Liberar Venda De Lotes De Terra a Estrangeiros." Accessed June 8. http://oglobo.globo.com/economia/temer-quer-liberar-venda-de-lotes-de-terra-estrangeiros-19372079

OEC. 2016. "Atlas Media Visualizations." The Observatory of Economic Complexity, MIT Media Lab. Accessed June 9. http://atlas.media.mit.edu/en/

Oliveira, G. de L.T. 2017. "Chinese Land Grabs in Brazil? Sinophobia and Foreign Investments in Brazilian Soybean Agribusiness." *Globalizations*, forthcoming.

Oliveira, G. de L.T. "The Geopolitics of Brazilian Soybeans." *Journal of Peasant Studies* 43, no. 2 (2016): 348–372.

Oliveira, G. de L.T., and M. Schneider. "The Politics of Flexing Soybeans: China, Brazil and Global Agroindustrial Restructuring." *Journal of Peasant Studies* 43, no. 1 (2016): 167–194.

Oya, C. "Methodological Reflections on 'Land Grab' Databases and the 'Land Grab' Literatura 'Rush." *Journal of Peasant Studies* 40, no. 3 (2013): 503–520.

Rajagopalan, Megha 2015. "China's Xi Woos Latin America with $250 Bln Investments."

Reuters. Accessed April 25, 2016. http://www.reuters.com/article/2015/01/08/us-china-latam-idUSKBN0KH06Q20150108

Ramo, J. C. *The Beijing Consensus*. London: Foreign Policy Centre, 2004.

Ray, R., K. P. Gallagher, A. Lopez, and C. Sanborn. *China in Latin America: Lessons for South-South Cooperation and Sustainable Development*. Boston, MA: Global Economic Governance Initiative, Boston University, 2015.

Ray, R., and K. Gallagher. *China-Latin America Economic Bulletin: 2015 Edition*. Boston, MA: Global Economic Governance Initiative, Boston University, 2015.

Sauer, S., M. Balestro, and S. Schneider. 2017. "The Ambivalent and Shaky Stance of Brazil as a Regional Power in Latin America." *Globalizations* (forthcoming).

Schneider, M. "Developing the Meat Grab." *Journal of Peasant Studies* 41, no. 4 (2014): 613–633.

Schneider, M. *Feeding China's Pigs: Implications for the Environment, China's smallholder farmers and food security*. Minneapolis and Washington, DC: Institute for Agriculture and Trade Policy, 2011.

Scoones, I., K. Amanor, A. Favareto, and Q. Gubo. "A New Politics of Development Cooperation?" *Chinese and Brazilian Engagements in African Agriculture, World Development* 81 (2016): 1–12.

Scoones, I., et al. "'New Development Encounters: China and Brazil in African Agriculture." *IDS Bulletin* 44, no. 4 (2013).

Sharma, S. *The Need for Feed: China's Demand for Industrialized Meat and Its Impacts*. Minneapolis, MN: Institute for Agriculture and Trade Policy, 2014.

SIECA. 2016. *Database*. Accessed May 20. http://estadisticas.sieca.int/

Slipak, A. "América Latina Ante China: ¿Transición Del Consenso De Washington Al Consenso De Beijing?" Presented at the Jornadas de Economía Crítica, Facultad de Ciencias Económicas, La Plata, Argentina, 2014, 1–21.

Smaller, C., Q. Wei, and L. Yalan. "Farmland and Water: China Invests Abroad." *IISD Report*. Winnipeg: International Institute for Sustainable Development, 2012.

Svampa, M. 2013a. "'Consenso De Los Commodities' Y Lengajes De Valoración En America Latina' [The 'Commodities Consensus' and Valuation Languages in Latin America]." *Nueva Sociedad*, no. 244 marzo-abril, 30–46.

Tambornini, E. 2016. "China Bloqueó El Ingreso De Aceite De Soja Argentino Como Represalia Por La Paralización De Las Obras Destinadas a Construir Dos Represas En Santa Cruz." *Valorsoja.Com*, October 6. http://www.valorsoja.com/2016/10/06/china-bloqueo-el-ingreso-de-aceite-de-soja-argentino-como-represalia-por-la-paralizacion-de-las-obras-destinadas-a-construir-dos-represas-en-santa-cruz/#.WNfjZBJ95mN.

The Economic Observer. 2012. "Chinese Agriculture Goes Global." Accessed March 1, 2017. http://www.farmlandgrab.org/post/view/20030

The Economist. 2011. "When Others Are Grabbing Their Land." Accessed March 1, 2017. http://www.economist.com/node/18648855

Tomei, J., and P. Upham. "Argentine Clustering of Soy Biodiesel Production: The Role of International Networks and the Global Soy Oil and Meal Markets." *Open Geography Journal* 4 (2011): 45–54.

USDA. *'Guatemala Sugar Annual', GAIN Report Number: 2014004*. Washington, DC: USA Government, 2014.

Valor Economico. 2016. "Novo Ministro Define Suas Prioridades." Accessed June 8. http://www.valor.com.br/agro/4576627/novo-ministro-define-suas-prioridades

Vasquez, W. "Cada Préstamo Tendrá Dos Tipos De Tasas De Interés." La Razon. Accessed April 22, 2016. http://www.la-razon.com/suplementos/financiero/prestamo-tipos-tasas-interes-financiero_0_2367963320.html

Veltmeyer, H., and J. Petras. *The New Extractivism: A Postneoliberal Development Model or Imperialism of the Twenty-First Century?*. London: Zed Books, 2014.

Wesz Jr., V.J. 2016. "Strategies and Hybrid Dynamics of Soy Transnational Companies in the Southern Cone." *Journal of Peasant Studies* 43, no. 2, March.

Wilkinson, J., V.J. Wesz Jr., and A. Lopane. 2016. "Brazil and China: The Agribusiness Connection in the Southern Cone Context." *Third World Thematics.* doi:10.1080/23802014.2016.1259581.

WITS. 2016. *Country Profiles.* World Integrated Trade Solution, World Bank. Accessed June 6. http://wits.worldbank.org/Default.aspx?lang=en

WSJ. 2016. "Interim Brazilian Government Has Approval Rating of 11.3%." *Wall Street Journal.* Accessed June 9. http://www.wsj.com/articles/interim-brazilian-government-has-approval-rating-of-11-3-1465403619

Yao, Z., and Z. Li. "The Overview of the Trends and Policies of Chinese Foreign Direct Investment (Zhongguo Duiwai Zhijie Touzi De Fazhan Qushi Yu Zhanwang)." *International Economic Review (Guoji Jingji Pinglun)* 2 (2011): 127–142.

Yelery, A. *China's 'Going Out' Policy: Sub-National Economic Trajectories.* Delhi: Institute of Chinese Studies, 2014.

Chinese agrarian capitalism in the Russian Far East

Jiayi Zhou ⓘ

ABSTRACT

Chinese actors have been actively engaged in agriculture in the Russian Far East since border liberalisation, from agriculture labourers, independent farmers with small- and medium-sized plots, to capital-rich agribusinesses that cultivate farmland on a much larger scale. With the use of wage labour and other capitalised production inputs, the occurrence of economic differentiation among producers and strong profit-seeking drivers, this stands in contrast to the situation within China itself – where institutional and structural constraints still limit the development of full-blown capitalist agriculture. This article presents the first case study of this phenomenon, in comparative perspective.

Beginning in the early 1990s, Chinese farms and greenhouses began to be spotted along the countryside and near urban centres in the Russian Far East (RFE), along its increasingly liberalised border with China. Chinese workers were first hired by Soviet state and collective farms to compensate for the local labour shortage. But these workers soon began to lease their own plots of farmland on which they cultivated vegetables, and which they sold back onto the deprived RFE market. As profits were made, word-of-mouth and active corporate recruitment began to occur in China, setting off a chain of migration and a 'farming rush' (*zhongdi laojin*) for Russian land, as Chinese media outlets reported it.

Idle soil on the land-abundant but demographically thin territory of the RFE presented an opportunity for those on the opposite side of the Amur River, where labour is abundant but land is scarce. In addition to differing structural circumstances, there are also regulatory policies that constrain farm expansion inside China. Thus, over the past two decades, Chinese peasants and migrants – primarily from Heilongjiang Province – have headed to the RFE in search of opportunities unavailable in China. In one Heilongjiang county, it has even been reported that up to 10 per cent of its population is perennially engaged in agriculture on Russian territory.[1] With cheap and abundant Russian land available for lease, Chinese who have set up farms and vegetable greenhouses there have been able to quickly expand their capital inputs, buying more machines and hiring more labour to keep up with their ever increasing acreages. Working underneath them are very often fellow Chinese that have left their own plots in rural Northeast China to become essentially itinerant farm workers. Chinese media have referred to these agriculturalists as 'peasants' turned 'farmers' (*nongchang zhu*), with reported profits even warranting titles of 'peasant millionaires.'[2]

Starting in the 2000s, Chinese corporations and state-owned farms have also joined these counterparts. With the added benefit of greater access to finance and often implicit or explicit Chinese (as well as Russian) Government support, these more capital-rich entities lease larger scales of agricultural land, often from the local Russian Government's land funds and have formed joint ventures with Russian companies and agribusinesses. Rather than growing higher value crops in vegetable greenhouses, these corporate actors, with larger acreages and more machinery, produce more grain and pulses. They engage as well in animal husbandry, dairy production and increasingly in industrial processing. Increasingly, such actors have embarked in vertical integration, with value chains stretching across the border.[3]

This article digs into these Chinese agricultural actors, both with small- and large-scale landholdings. It details their motives, accumulation processes and the economic relations between them. But their activities speak to broader dynamics: Chinese agriculture in the RFE, with large-scale production bases by agribusiness, mechanisation, the use of hired wage labour, as well as economic differentiation among producers, and driven by profit-making motives at almost all levels – is by all appearances robustly capitalist. An important foil to this story, however, is the slower rise of agrarian capitalism within China itself. Despite a reform process that has seen the market's penetration into nearly every segment of the economy, agriculture to an extent remains the 'last bastion of socialism,' in what has been referred to as a 'country of small peasants.'[4] This is changing, and new dynamics of capitalisation in agricultural production are reshaping the countryside both from above and from below.[5] Nevertheless, the contrast with the forms and social relations of production of Chinese agriculture in Russia is still quite stark.

In Chinese overseas investment in agriculture, more external attention has been focused on China's food security drivers, but analyses of cases show that in countries of Africa, South-East Asia and even in Central Asia, it is often commercial rather than national strategic imperatives that motivate Chinese investors.[6] The RFE case is not in unique in this regard. However, it is rather unique among the various cases, in that Chinese serve as primary producers, not only investors but also farmers and labourers. This substantial human dimension allows for a richer examination of the production relations among specifically Chinese actors, and thus a comparison with agrarian change in China itself. Put differently, it offers an opportunity to examine how different agrarian pathways can emerge under different structural and institutional conditions. At the same time, Chinese agrarian transformation itself needs to be more greatly situated within a regional and global context, as political borders become increasingly irrelevant to the movement of capital. These dynamics cannot be divorced from the Chinese domestic context, including resource and policy constraints for Chinese enterprises especially in relation to agricultural land. But this also means that a part of China's agrarian transformation is manifesting itself outside of its own borders.

The first section will briefly and broadly describe key elements of agrarian transition inside of China. This is followed by the history, modalities of production and production relations that characterise Chinese agriculture in the RFE, and motivating factors. The paper concludes with some broader comparative analysis. Interactions with Russians – both rural residents and governmental authorities – are not addressed here, but it must be stressed Russia is by no means a neutral backdrop by which these processes take place. The paper is informed by secondary data analyses based on available academic literature as well as Chinese news stories that are more anecdotal in nature. It seeks to lay the groundwork for further empirical studies on this topic by researchers in the future; it is necessarily exploratory rather than explanatory. Nevertheless, there is added value in that Chinese agricultural activity in Russia has so far not been examined as its own separate topic in any academic- or policy-related studies.

Transition in China

Agrarian capitalism generally refers to a system of commercialised production through active markets of labour, land and capital. In the prevalent neoliberal economic narrative, this is commonly thought to result in large-scale agriculture, utilising wage labour and highly mechanised production. But as Lenin posited, 'infinitely diverse combinations of the elements of capitalist evolution are possible.'[7] Case studies of the development of agrarian capitalism in various countries point to the fact that unique national institutions, structures and conditions shape divergent historical pathways and outcomes regarding forms of agriculture transition.[8]

In the People's Republic of China, overall market liberalisation was sparked from peasant experiments with de-collectivising in the 1970s. Under the subsequent Household Responsbility System (HRS), first adopted in the early 1980s, rural land is owned by village collectives, and distributed to village residents in long-term land-use arrangements. While HRS helped unleash market forces in rural China, but also now works dually to shield agricultural production from full liberalisation. Under normal circumstances, it is allocated to a given village's rural residents on the basis of equity, rather than efficiency or productivity. No true land factor market exists, and the institutional difficulty in wrestling plots of land from peasants and their collectives – land that is also often non-contiguous, fragmented and unsuitable for scaled-up operations – hampers capital involvement in the production side of agriculture to a great extent.

There are of course myriad ways in which China's agriculture is *capitalised* if not outright capitalist.[9] As Yan and Chen (2015) put it, 'except for the absence of outright private property rights in farmland, conditions for farming today are almost completely commodified and marketed.'[10] Market forces as well as state policies have led to rural differentiation, increasingly unequal holdings and capitalist dynamics from below and from above. For instance, the legalised land-lease market that emerged has allowed for differentiation among rural producers, precipitating the emergence of what has been deemed in Chinese literature a 'middle peasant' (*zhongnong*) group.[11] Larger scale farms and so-called 'family farms'[12] that employ much more wage labour have also emerged. Penetration of urban as well as foreign capital into the countryside has also influenced China's agrarian evolution.

While agribusinesses and urban actors are strong players in higher parts of the agrifood industry and value chain, their ability to form agricultural production bases has been much more limited.[13] This is also shifting, however. Statistics from the Ministry of Agriculture showed that at the end 2012, agribusinesses accounted for 10.3% of all transferred land, a growth of 115% from 2009.[14] Farmers' cooperatives have also emerged as an alternate means of increasing scale, providing production technology and helping overcome barriers of market access for small producers. These cooperatives have grown substantially in connection with government support policies, more than doubling from being in 6.7% of villages in 2006 to 20.8% in 2008.[15] Emphasising the need for agricultural modernisation, increased production scale and vertical integration, political authorities have been providing various financial subsidies and incentives to designated 'dragon-head enterprises.'[16] Vertically integrated households linked to these companies by formal contract or informal arrangements have spread across China.

China's agriculture is without a doubt 'capitalizing': so-called 'peasants' (*nongmin*) are moving away from subsistence agriculture, differentiating in the light of varying ascriptive or achieved endowments, producing higher value agricultural products for commercial profit and becoming more linked with markets and non-local actors to a greater extent than ever before. But there remain structural limits to scaled-up, industrialised and non-household-based agriculture. China's arable land to population ratio is exceedingly tight, estimated at 0.08 ha per capita in 2010.[17] This ratio is also squeezed by urban expansion, land degradation and other pressures on China's agricultural and natural resources. In fact, average farm size in China over the past decades has even decreased from the average of 0.7 ha after HRS was fully implemented in 1985, to 0.5 ha.[18] These structural constraints of limited land availability also affect issues of rural livelihoods and social order. Wen Tiejun (2000), for instance, has argued that for a country like China, with high population to land ratio, small plots continue to serve a subsistence more than a production function: 'under conditions of severe shortage of (land and water) resources, there is no room for China's small peasant economy to engage in Western-style privatization.' He Xuefeng similarly writes, 'economic efficiency should be second to equality under these national structural conditions.'[19] The rural–urban dual structure is part of this: without the security, services and benefits of urban *hukou* or registration, land continues to serve a safety net function for households that might otherwise choose to (more permanently) transfer their land. While it is debated, there are also arguments that collective vs. individual ownership has afforded village communities 'a base for stronger collective action and resistance' against dispossession.[20]

Recognising the sensitive social implications of rural reform, the central government, at the same time that it actively promotes so-called modern agriculture, has so far refrained from wholesale systemic reform such as land privatisation, and continues to call for preservation of rural residents' rights and interests.[21] Finally, China's agricultural system is mostly marked by extremely low levels of proletarianisation. Philip C. C. Huang et al.'s (2012) analysis found the upper limits on hired agricultural labour input to be about 5–8%, with a more probable lower limit estimate of 3%.[22] While metrics of this have been disputed, and while various emergent large-scale farms are hiring labour at a much greater level, the family nevertheless remains to a large extent the primary unit of labour in Chinese farming.[23] Due to these factors, China often continues to be referred to as a 'small peasant economy' (*xiaonong jingji*).

There are of course significant variations in the extent of agrarian capitalisation across the country, owing not only to regional economic disparities, but differences in natural resource endowments and topography, and local developmental models that may vary across even adjacent municipalities. In fact, in Northeast China – where the majority of actors relevant to RFE agriculture hail – lower population density and the geographical flatness of the Northeast and have allowed for farms of larger scales and which are mechanised to greater degrees than in the rest of China. In Heilongjiang province, per capita arable land is three times the national average, with crop production patterns of soybean, corn and rice that are also much more heavily mechanised. Also relatively unique to Northeast China are the prevalence of state-owned farms, which account for a third of crop production in

Heilongjiang.[24] In such farms, in contrast to the rest of China, land was not allotted on an egalitarian basis during de-collectivisation, but rather based on 'each family's capital endowment, which resulted in highly unequal holdings.' The state-owned farms have much more control of production vis-à-vis 'farm employees'; land tenure is less secure for the latter. State-owned farms also provide market access, and facilitate commercialisation and industrial processing. Zhang's (2010) research in Northeast China found that in these state-owned farms, none of the 'farm employees' were engaged exclusively in subsistence-oriented farming.[25]

Capitalist agriculture seems to have advanced much more within these state-farm structures, though it is not clear if this spills over to non-state farms and rural villages in the Northeast. Many of these state-owned farms are now no longer engaged exclusively in agriculture, and have diversified their portfolios into other sectors of the economy. They are in many respects analogous to state-owned enterprises (SOEs). Some of these state-farms are also actively encouraging these 'farm employees' to go abroad to Russia. These factors may well have great influence on the particularities of Chinese agriculture in Russia, and could account for some of the forms of production among and social relations between Chinese farming there. Indeed, it is perhaps a local political economy perspective that is more relevant than broad-brush stroke national comparisons. However, the above summary nevertheless describes an overall framework of agriculture that is still markedly different from what the next section describes, and the contrast may still be illustrative.

Transition in the RFE

In contrast to village ownership in China, early 1990s land reform in Russia privatised 108 million hectares of agricultural land. These lands, which had been managed by large Soviet collective and state farms (*kolkhozes* and *sovkhozes*), were distributed to their former workers as ownership rights to unspecified plots.[26] Unlike in China, where de-collectivisation led to massive 're-peasantization,' these workers for a variety of reasons mostly left these plots unclaimed. Private family farming languished, while Soviet-era farms in most cases stayed structurally intact, while simply being re-labelled into large-farm enterprises.

Since the early 2000s, Russian state support to agriculture, including loans, tax breaks and other policy incentives and resources, has overwhelmingly focused on large-scale entities. It also explicitly encourages capital investment into rural Russia from domestical and international. In an effort to the latter, the Farm Land Bill was signed into law in 2002, which allows foreigners to lease Russian agricultural land for up to 49 years, and the purchase of land by Russian-majority shareholder companies (one major factor in the increase in the scale of Chinese activity starting in the 2000s). While nearly more half of Russia's output in many agricultural products comes from household subsidiary farming that uses mostly family labor, such smallholders still depend substantially on large-scale farms for a range of inputs and services, in a relationship 'resembling to some extent a (semi)feudal, patrimonial, or Prussian form of agriculture.'[27] And although current the Russian agriculture structure is dualistic in many regards, it is 'at the 'forefront' of financialisation and large-scale global commodification of agriculture and land.'[28]

In addition to differences in state policies at a national level, natural resource endowments and land availability starkly differ in Russia. Russia has one of the world's highest per capital arable land rates, at 0.85 ha compared to 0.08 ha for China.[29] This has been coupled with 'land abandonment of monumental proportions' in the post-Soviet era, as the economy declined and governmental support for agriculture and interest in farming waned in the 1990s.[30] In the RFE, the impact was even more pronounced, with sown area decreasing by nearly a half between 1995 and 2007.[31] Heavily disadvantaged in terms of demographics, infrastructure and transportation, RFE agriculture had depended on the support and subsidies of the central state to a greater degree than in European parts of Russia. Though the RFE it comprises one-third of Russia's territory, in 2009 it held only 4.6% of the country's population. Population fell 19.8% between 1991 and 2008, both as a result of outmigration and natural loss.[32] This demographic crisis exacerbated the labour shortage, which fed back into the agricultural as well as general economic decline. In addition, approximately 40% of the agricultural land in Russia that went into private ownership in the 1990s went to pensioners. Though three-fourths of this land was expected to have been passed down through inheritance by 2010, in the RFE (as well as in the rest of Russia), 'many heirs simply [did] not claim inherited land shares or plots.'[33]

But in contrast to the rest of Russia, however, the majority of arable land in the RFE remained un-privatised and was held in the hands of the state's *raion* (regional) land distribution funds. This was in principle to be redistributed to peasant farmers after the 1991 land reform, but this did not occur. For example, in 1999, Amur Oblast's land committee held over 900,000 hectares of arable land in its land fund, but that same year leased out only 700 hectares to peasant farmers, while leasing over 250,000 hectares to agricultural enterprises.[34] It is not clear whether this was necessarily due to lack of interested local individual or smaller scale local applicants, but the Russian Government has shown consistent policy preference and even bias for large-scale farming since state support re-emerged.[35] Furthermore, it has been noted that in the 1990s, the state allocated it to 'almost anyone who applie[d] for it,' including 'immigrant farmers from China, Korea, Holland, and the United States.'[36]

Of relevance for this case study, it is only the RFE's southernmost provinces that have any substantial arable land: Amur Oblast (where some 60% of this land is concentrated), Khabarovsk Krai, the Jewish Autonomous Oblast, Primorsky Krai and Zabaikalsky Krai. All share a border with China. As mentioned, sown area in these provinces decreased throughout the 1990s, falling 45% between 1995 and 2005, while increasing by nearly 23% over the same period in the three bordering Northeast Chinese provinces.[37]

Chinese Agriculture in the RFE

Immediately following the normalisation of Sino-Russian relations and the liberalisation of the border, Chinese workers began to fill the labour demand in the RFE, primarily in the construction and agriculture sector. In 1988, the Suifehe Municipal government signed the first contract for vegetable growing with Baranovsky state farm in Primorsky Krai.[38] Similar formal agricultural labour arrangements in the 1990s were arranged by Chinese SOEs or local governments as 'a form of foreign economic cooperation' with the active support of Chinese authorities.[39] These workers were often comprised of surplus labour from Northeast China's countryside, or underemployed urban workers.[40] According to many reports, it was largely from this pool of agricultural workers, already engaged in reviving agriculture for the region that the first more independent Chinese farmers emerged on Russian soil. Such farm labourers, as well as vegetable traders, peasants and other Chinese individuals began to directly rent land on former collective farms, under sharecropping and other contractual arrangements with Russians which allowed them use of agricultural machinery, transportation and other render services.

With backgrounds as *nongmin* in China, they brought to Russian farms their own agricultural techniques and expertise, including for cultivating crops like soy and melons, and greenhouse cultivation for vegetables.[41] Along with shuttle traders and cross-border peddlers, they helped provide the RFE with fresh produce, even some that had previously been completely unavailable such as watermelons.[42] The availability of fallow land at significantly cheaper than rental rates than in China, and the much more profitable market for agricultural products in the RFE, led to a 'farm rush' (*zhongdi laojin*) by Chinese. These labourers, small traders and peasants took advantage of opportunities to expand their scale and make commercial profit on the RFE market. In a few cases, as described later, 'peasants' were able to massively enrich themselves and become capitalist farmers.

Such Chinese farmers and farm labourers, as pointed out by some Russian authors,

> considerably surpass locals in terms of the culture of agricultural work and professionalism … in those areas of the RFE where Chinese work in agriculture, they do not simply satisfy the vegetable needs of the population, but create a surplus.'[43]

Their extra harvest was generally sold locally, as transportation costs to China were exorbitant, and the price point for fresh vegetables much higher in Russia.[44] Some negative impacts on local Russian producers has been noted, but the effects on consumers have been to, within a decade, lower costs for products such as cucumbers and tomatoes from 50 times that of sale price in the early 1990s. Indeed, Chinese capitalised so heavily so robustly on this market that some reports were that they had captured anywhere from two-thirds to up to even 90% of the vegetable markets in the RFE.[45] A researcher at Vladivostok State University even remarked that the region had become 'totally dependent on [Chinese].'[46]

In the 2000s, these arrangements shifted towards private labour-exporting firms, self-organised and self-financed businesses, and individual entrepreneurs.[47] Larger scale agriculture and agricultural investments began to emerge through agribusinesses, as well SOEs and state-owned farms from Northeast China. The timing corresponds to aforementioned legislative changes in Russia allowing foreigners to lease Russian agricultural land. Chinese agricultural investments were therefore in tandem with other international and transnational actors that became increasingly Russian agriculture, mostly on the western part of Russia. The timing also corresponds with China's Going-Out strategy, through which Beijing strongly encouraged and incentivised domestic enterprises to invest abroad.

Over the past decade and a half, Chinese have begun to shift from extensive to intensive farming, and have begun to form 'leaner' production teams which sometimes hire local Russians to make up for the shortfall, and for cost-saving purposes. Their leases have also increased from short one-year contracts to five-year, 20-year or to the maximum 49-year lease arrangements. While smaller plots of land can be obtained directly through contract negotiations with local former collective farms or the local government, large-scale investments in land often entail establishing joint venture with Russian companies (which allows indirect land ownership), or authorisation by higher up Russian authorities.[48] Unlike the aforementioned Chinese farmers who produce greenhouse vegetables, these large-scale grow mainly soybean and grains, but also engage in livestock projects, and increasingly are involved in agro-processing. Many Chinese farmers in Russia now sub-lease on land acquired by larger Chinese or partially Chinese-owned agribusinesses and corporations, in a nested farming structure.

There is a fluid mix of actors at all levels, from individuals to SOEs, with much cooperation between them – not only in land but also in labour-sharing arrangements. State-owned farms have sub-contracted or obtained land concessions from private Chinese enterprises already operating in Russia, while private enterprises have gained the clout of state-affiliated enterprises in support of exporting and licencing. Corporations have utilised state-owned farm employees labour on their private company-held (or rather, leased) land.[49] Overall, however, private companies have been a driving force in most of the large-scale ventures. According to the Xinjiang Academy of Social Sciences, in terms of Heilongjiang's overall agricultural investments in Russia, the lion's share of the capital – at least in 2012 – was coming from individual and private sources, with government investment accounting for only about 30% of funds.[50]

According to Qu Wei, President of the Heilongjiang Academy of Social Sciences, because of the dual state-/enterprise-nature of China's state-owned farms system, Russia prefers private company investment, and therefore Chinese state-owned farms usually engage Russian agriculture in a subordinate position to private companies.[51] But more recently, national SOEs such as China National Cereals, Oils, and Foodstuffs Corporation (COFCO) are also showing interest in the Russian agricultural market. The COFCO Vice President in 2015 announced plans for constructing two grain warehouses, each of 100,000 MT capacity, in the RFE, expressing also that the company's strategy was to establish control over the full production chain, from farm to table.[52] Higher level and larger agricultural deals by corporate and state actors in Russia and China have been accelerating. In May 2015, during a state visit by Xi Jinping to Moscow, a 2 billion USD investment fund was announced for financing agricultural projects between the two countries.[53] The RFE's Primorsky Krai is now also home the first agricultural industrial park China has established abroad, with 68,000 ha.[54]

Scale of involvement

There is no precise data on the number of Chinese nationals engaged in agriculture, or the amount of hectares that they lease; such information is not compiled by the central government. Municipalities or county governments in Northeast China have in some reports provided data on numbers of hectares leased by their residents, but this information is piecemeal. Listing this fragmented data would probably not provide a precise or holistic picture of the involvement, epitomising what Edelman refers to as 'messy hectares,' and potentially distracting from analysis of the broader processes.[55]

In terms of larger scale land deals, data provided by the recently established China and Russia Agricultural Cooperative Association (CRACA) show that members' cultivation area or holdings across Russia and Siberia total 380,000 ha. There are nearly one hundred member companies in this association, each of which holds at least 500 ha of agricultural land. According to the CRACA, this covers approximately 80% of cultivation area by Heilongjiang-based actors in Russia. At an official forum in 2013, it was estimated that actors from Heilongjiang province were cultivating 500,000 ha in the RFE.[56] This may still represent a low estimate, as data collection on more moderate-sized or independent farms is made difficult by the existence of informal arrangements, including underreporting by Russian lessees for tax evasion purposes.[57] However, as the RFE's peak arable land only stood at around 3.21 million hectares in the late 1980s, half of a million hectares constitutes a substantial amount proportionally.[58]

Notably, many of the actors hail from Heilongjiang's Dongning County, which has become the top county involved in Russian agricultural development, and the distribution hub for imports of Russian agricultural products linked to Chinese production bases. It reportedly has thousands of people perennially engaged in grain cultivation, fruit and vegetable cultivation, livestock breeding, forest harvesting, fishing and other such work in Russia, 'accounting for 10% of the county's population.'[59] Dongning actors were also estimated to be involved in developing over 210,000 ha of arable land in the Russia, which amounts to nearly five times the farmland of the county itself.[60] The magnitude of this involvement is not likely to be representative of other Northeast China counties or cities, so it remains unclear whether the types of engagement described are related to very localised dynamics. However, the dispersed geographical base of agribusinesses and corporations in the CRACA means that it is likely that at least some of the dynamics related to actors are applicable to other parts of the region.

Actors and dynamics

This section provides illustrations of the capital dynamics that are at play both 'from above' and 'from below' in Chinese agriculture in the RFE. They represent what are the most extreme or news-worthy cases, but as well speak to more generalisable dynamics that have been described above. Interacting with many of these market-led or accumulation dynamics are also local state actors, with imperatives that are both economic and political in nature.

Village-based recruitment

Taiyangsheng Village in Daduchuan Town of Dongning County had a very high concentration of residents going abroad to Russia to farm in 2012. Out of a population of about 420 households, one of its residents estimated that there were 50–60 households with farms in Russia and another 70–80 individuals going to Russia as farm workers and wage labourers. The village itself only has a total of 1000 mu (67 ha) of land, amounting to around 2–3 mu (0.13–2 ha) for each household. The first three villagers to attempt farming in Russia left in 1998. Eventually, the profits they made inspired others in the village to participate, particularly after domestic food prices dropped around the year 2000. In Russia, the farms set up by villagers were more than 10 ha.[61]

In Yongli Village in Harbin County, a villager who was once, as the journalist puts it, an 'insignificant peasant' from the village became a 'big boss' in Russia (*eluosi da laoban*), attributed with raising the living standards his once poverty-ridden village. Yongli, with about 5 mu (0.3 ha) per capita, had already surpassed household needs for agricultural land with 'none left to be divided among newborns.' In 1994, when the township government organised a group of farmers to grow vegetables in Russia, the villager participated as a technician and later seized upon profit-making opportunities. He negotiated a greenhouse vegetable contract in Russia, and began to finance and recruit seasonal farm labourers from his village, bringing a total of 11 production groups into Russia between 1996 and 2005. The earliest villagers who left for Russia under his direction nearly all became 'bosses' (*laoban*) of their own. In other cases of labour recruitment, peasants have often been recruited by someone from the same village or hometown. This type of behaviour is not limited to the so-called peasantry; the importance of social capital, and very close-knit migrant communities are prevalent in Chinese transnational economic migration patterns. Finally, also incentivising Yongli villagers to make this leap into the unknown was the fact that the all expenses related to their foreign work: travel, visa, food and housing, are usually covered by the recruiters.[62]

In another case, a peasant from Harbin's Bin County had been farming in China for 20 years when his few hectares were struck by pests. He therefore took a chance farming abroad when a fellow villager seeking recruits for Russian farming. As the report frames it, in his 15 years in Russia, he not only became a 'farmer' (*nongchang zhu*) with 300 ha of land, but also a 'boss' (*laoban*) who has successively led over 100 peasants as labourers to Russia. His expected revenue for 2011, the date of the article, was four million yuan. According to the article, Bin County's 'bosses both big and small' owned or managed nearly 3,000 vegetable greenhouses in Russia.[63]

Agricultural wage labourers

Basic wage labourers constitute the bulk of the Chinese who go to Russia for agriculture.[64] All documented cases of Chinese farmers in Russia show prevalent use of farm labourers, on smaller scale farms and vegetable greenhouses, as well as larger scale ventures. In the 1990s, Chinese Government authorities were often closely connected to labour exporting to Russia. It is unclear what the motives were, but the problem of rural surplus labor was one which at the time, and perhaps continues to be 'a top priority for all levels of the [Heilongjiang provincial] government.'[65] As mentioned, state-owned farms are also actively involved in this kind of surplus labour transfer, and have in some cases actively encouraged their 'farm employees' to go abroad. However, these labourers are also recruited by fellow rural villagers in more private networks of chain migration, as has described earlier.

Chinese sources have noted very often the exploitative work conditions that many of these farm workers face in terms of housing and work hours. This is revealed in the increased difficulty of labour recruitment. Despite the appeal of better earnings, a consulting firm manager from Dongning noted that finding those interested in labouring in Russia has become more difficult as local Chinese now believe that 'farming abroad is even more fatiguing that at home.'[66] One former farm labourer from the city of Heihe detailed working in a greenhouse for 15 hours a day, in a 'slavish life,' with no entertainment, food consisting mostly of potatoes except for special occasions when he ate instant noodles. Housing conditions can be equally stark, with workers kept together in shared spaces sometimes without electricity, gas and toilets, 'with no minutes of free time.' He noted that income from this work, however, did considerable exceed what would be able to make in China.[67] The Bin County Labor Office Deputy Director, quoted in 2006, stated that there was an attrition rate of around 30% of peasants who 'cannot endure the hardship, and return home to farm.'[68]

In one of the more extreme cases, 61 Chinese agricultural workers – mostly hailing from one small town in Heilongjiang – fled into the mountains in Kemerovskaya after suffering wage deductions and suffering physical threats from their management, despite 14- hour work days of hard labour. Resolving the issue and returning the workers required the involvement of Chinese local consulate, and made national headlines.[69] Of course while in the context of Russia, such cases of persons may be considered as being divorced from the means of production, and fully proletariat by the sense of the term, their rural *hukou* or registration status within China usually means that they do retain certain land holdings and rights at home, even as they are strictly labourers abroad. They may perhaps be considered a transnational type of 'semi-proletariat farm worker,' according to Zhang and Donaldson's (2008) typology.[70] But insofar as the transition to labourers on farms in Russia follows more generalisable dynamics of proletarianisation both to urban areas within China and labour migration abroad, it perhaps should not be considered a distinctly agrarian phenomenon.

Entrepreneurial farming

Interestingly, many of the more independently operating farms in the RFE have been called 'family farms' (*jiating nongchang*). This term refers not to the use of family-based labour, but to a neologism in Chinese policy terms, one that refers to more professionalised, modern, and entrepreneurial farms of a moderate to large scale that became targets for state support in 2013.[71] Though used informally, the use of the term in describing similar farms in Russia denotes to some extent the internationalisation of those domestic shifts. A number of noted cases of such farms.

One resident of Xinli Village of Dongning, who was a vegetable market vendor in Ussurisky, took up farming when a fellow villager convinced him of its profitability. He hired six Chinese employees and invested 210,000 yuan for planting basic vegetables such as onions and turnips, as well as watermelons. Profits fluctuate very much depending on prices. Independent farmers such as himself usually cultivate dozens of hectares with greenhouses, mostly to grow vegetables. Though crops like soybeans, barley and other grains are more stable in their selling prices, these require much greater capital investment, which is not within the capacity of the 'self-employed' (*geti hu*).[72] According to him, there is in fact much exit by Chinese who make losses, unable to make up the initial capital investment in machinery, water infrastructure and other things necessary to manage large acreages.

Not all such entrepreneurial farmers have rural backgrounds. One farmer, in the Leninsky district of the Jewish Autonomous Oblast, originally worked as a Russian translator on a Chinese pig farm, but acquired an initial 20 ha for himself, to 'begin a career as a landlord (*dizhu*).' Through connections, he leased farmland through a Chinese company specialising in land-lease. This Chinese company rents from the Russian Government and then sub-leases this land to other actors. With a rental cost of 300 yuan per ha annually, the farmer by his fourth year had expanded to 400 ha, and was reinvesting all his profits into labour or capital inputs. He employed five workers, all of which were peasants from Heilongjiang, and which could with machinery – each overseeing 100 ha. He said he paid each of these workers about 30,000 yuan annually. His crops, primarily soybeans, are sold entirely on the Russian market.[73]

Other profiled cases include a Chinese who had originally been engaged in labour export to Russia, but himself began to operate a farm in 2000, and now has more than 16,000 ha in Primorsky Krai's Pogranichny District, planting mostly soy and corn. His operations are highly mechanised.[74] Another farmer, with 2000 ha in development, half of which was dedicated to soybeans, was reportedly able to take out a 3.5 million yuan local at a low interest from a Chinese Government bank, with which he purchased combines and tractors. Working under him were 10 Chinese labourers.[75]

Large-scale enterprises

One of the more often referenced cases of large-scale private enterprises in the RFE is Dongning Huaxin Group (Dongning Huaxin Industry and Trade Group). The company is not strictly an agribusiness, but a rather private company that has a wide variety of investments in trade, transportation, construction and real estate, much of which is in Russia. [76] Included in their portfolio is one of the largest Chinese agricultural investment projects in Russia; the Armada farm – a joint venture – was established in 2004, and has 50,000 ha in Primorsky Krai's Sino-Russian Agricultural Economic Cooperation Zone. For some perspective, the arable land in Dongning County itself only amounts to about 50,000 ha. [77]

Dongning Huaxin Group in fact spearheaded the formation of the Sino-Russian Agricultural Economic Cooperation Zone in 2010, as well as the CRACA in 2012. Its dominance in the RFE agriculture has led to a mode of production what one Chinese analyst referred to as the 'Huaxin model' (huaxin moshi). [78] Besides large-scale crop and livestock farming, livestock farming, dairy and cattle, Dongning Huaxin also has three grain (liangshi, including soybean) processing centres, an oilseed crushing plant and an animal feed mill. [79] According to its chairman, the company tries to implement a policy of 60% local workforce out of their total workforce of 600. [80] The company also engages in contract farming along two models. The first is where the company contracts out land at a fixed price, but where the contractor is responsible for machinery, management and subcontracting its own labor force. The entirety of the crop and harvest is sold back to and exclusively the right of the Dongning Huaxin Group, which bears the brunt of price volatility. A second contracting model is where the Dongning Huaxin not only distributes land to Chinese contractors, but also provides more active assistance in the form of seeds, fertilizser, visa support, machinery and customs support. The output belongs to the contractor, but is sold back to Huaxin under specified contract conditions, which then sells the product. Similar contract farming forms may extend to other Chinese investment projects or agribusinesses in Russia. Such production modalities are necessary because, according to the company's Planning Director, the company simply has acquired too much land. For instance, in 2011, Armada had only developed 10,000 ha, or a fourth of their total agricultural land holdings. [81]

This is just one of many large-scale Chinese agricultural investment projects in Russia. The CRACA, whose members are engaged in cultivation, livestock breeding or agricultural processing in Russia at a scale of at minimum 500 ha each, has almost a hundred members distributed across Siberia and the RFE. [82] These larger scale investments and production areas are becoming more actively engaged in industrial processing and the entire agricultural value chain, both in Russia and across the border.

State-owned farms

In 2004, Baoquanling Land Reclamation Bureau's Far East Agricultural Development Company, a local state-farm agribusiness corporation and branch of the Heilongjiang Land Reclamation Administration, set up its first subsidiary company in the Jewish Autonomous Oblast engaged in agricultural development. It established a second subsidiary in the same oblast in 2008. The company has now has a land-lease contract with the local government for 10,000 ha. The parent Beidahuang Group, China's largest agribusiness company, had by 2008 already all of its nine branches operating in Russia, with 28 farms, three dragon-head enterprises and over 30 projects – ranging from grain production and processing, livestock breeding, to timber harvesting. Its labour export to Russia had reached 4720 persons.[83]

Other subsidiaries of state-owned farms have also been extremely active in Russia. Some have been making arrangements with local Russian governments, as above. But others are also engaging through cooperative arrangements with private Chinese enterprises who act as a land-leasing intermediary. Wutong River Farm from Heilongjiang for instance, which had 'surplus labor, idle machinery, advanced planting technology – but no more available land [in China] on which to plant' signed an land concession agreement with Dongning Huaxin Group in 2010, for 3000 ha of land near the city of Ussuriysk.[84]

State-owned farms in China have become very powerful commercial agents in their own right, sharing parallels to SOEs in other sectors of the economy. Their push to invest in Russian agriculture, whether as financial investment or for more sociopolitical reasons, undoubtedly still connects to domestic accumulation dynamics. As one case in point, an farm employee on one of the state-owned Beidahuang Group's subsidiary companies had had his land expropriated by farm authorities in his home village. He was thereafter encouraged to engage in Russian agriculture, and was planting soybeans in Russia for a monthly wage of 3000 yuan.[85]

Motivations

There are a variety of motivations at work in the above developments. Solving the issue of surplus labour has been a component of both labour export and the transfer of farm employees to Russian soil – at the level of local government or state-owned farms.[86] Where the state is involved, it is mostly local- or provincial-level government that facilitates these Sino-Russia exchanges, and provincial SOEs in Northeast China. But these activities are still deeply connected with the 'pressure to make profits' and are 'commercially oriented.'[87] Local governments encourage migrating farmers as well as a means of increasing rural incomes. With leasing costs only a fraction of the cost to lease or 'transfer' land within China, in cases 10 times lower than in China, or only 'symbolic' rental costs of for instance 10–100 yuan a hectare per annum, farmers can make substantially more than in China, even accounting for the various transit, visa costs and taxes paid towards the local Russian Government.[88]

However, a substantial if not majority of the farming actors in the RFE have in fact been private entities, whether individuals or enterprises. Disparate and unorganised, and smaller scale in terms of capital intensity and in terms of hectares leased – the motives again essentially to make profit rather than support any national or provincial food security goals. Most clearly, this is revealed in the fact that the vast majority of production is for the local Russian market. As Dongning Huaxin Group's Planning Director said of the company's activities in 2011: 'This is pure business; as of now it has nothing to do with China's food security strategy.'[89] Importantly, these capitalist drivers parallel other cases of Chinese agricultural engagement in Central and Southeast Asia.[90]

Since its 2001 WTO ascension, China has become increasingly dependent on international markets for soybeans and animal feed. Soybeans are in fact the only major agricultural crop for which China is less than 50% self-sufficient.[91] But while this is a major output of the Chinese large-scale farms in Russia, until very recently, much of what was produced again had been crushed and sold locally. Reasons that have been cited for this were poor transportation infrastructure and tariff costs (which also hamper transportation of and export to

Western destinations), imports affecting the soy market in China and negatively impacting Heilongjiang domestic producers, and import quotas being dominated by large national players rather than the smaller corporate actors who are operating in Russia.[92]

But indeed, in 2015–2016, the vast majority the soybeans exported from the RFE did go to China.[93] And some of the policy bottlenecks regarding imports have since been resolved. The CRACA was granted an import licence by the provincial government when it was established in 2012. With the support of the provincial government bodies, their members now enjoy national preferential tariff policies.[94] Shipments of agricultural products from Russia to China are in fact growing, with 430,000 MT of grain (including soybean) imported back to China from members of the CRACA in 2015. Cross-border vertical integration is also proceeding apace.[95] And as noted, national SOEs such as COFCO are now also becoming more interested and involved in tapping the Russian market.

Comparisons and reflections

While there are many cases of Chinese land acquisitions abroad, the case of Russia is particularly unique in the significant presence of Chinese as producers, labourers and farmers – in addition to being corporate investors. For this reason, the labour and human dimension lends itself particularly well to a comparison of agriculture as it stands and is evolving within the China itself – where institutions and structural conditions still (though increasingly smaller) limit on the extent to which farming is a commercial industry as opposed to serving livelihood functions. The emergence within China of what at one point in history would have been referred to as 'rich peasants' – once subjects of violent elimination campaigns in revolutionary China (as well as Russia) – is one example of how modern Chinese social relations have transformed, stratified and become 'capitalised' within even the hallowed sector of agriculture. But placed in juxtaposition to Chinese agrarian capitalism in the RFE, which is marked if not characterised by economic differentiation, mechanisation, proletarianisation and large-scale urban-based capital, the case of Russia and RFE still remains starkly outside of the domestic norm.

The Russia and the RFE thus offers one lens into Chinese agrarian transition under less binding institutional and structural constraints. This is not to suggest that these developments are 'spontaneous,' or the natural product of a freer market. Pre-existing political and economic power structures within China, as well as in Russia, have their shaping hands in both labour export and land allocation. Just as agrarian change inside China is being shaped by the state, so it is in Russia, where the local and national decision-makers, and state imperatives of accumulation play a role in land distribution.[96]

In addition, certain caveats apply to broad national-level comparisons. As mentioned, more analysis at the more localised political economy level is necessary. Furthermore, it is a self-selected group of the entrepreneurial-minded Chinese that have become capitalist farmers in Russia, agribusinesses or other enterprises within China that have accumulated capital within China to be able to invest in Russia, and (mostly) rural or migrant workers already driven by economic circumstances to hire themselves out as labourers in Russia. In other words, capitalising dynamics exist already inside of China that have resulted in this outflow that is increasingly restructuring Russian territory. And beyond comparisons with Chinese domestic national or provincial-level dynamics, the case study of Chinese in the RFE also needs to be situated among other cases, for instance, investments in other bordering regions such as Central Asia and Southeast Asia, in further geographic locales, as well as looking at it in tandem with more generalisable dynamics of 'land grabbing' by capitalist actors globally. Further research and fieldwork is needed, but to the extent that Chinese land acquisitions since the 1990s have contributed to a revival of agricultural production and local RFE food security, without the displacement and dispossession that so marks other more clear cut cases of 'land-grabbing,' this case could potentially nuance further the rich debate on the specificities of land acquisitions globally, as well as diverse impacts on rural populations.[97]

However, as the first preliminary scoping study of this phenomenon, and one that is based on grey literature, this paper errs on the side of description rather than trying to draw definitive causal lines or conclusions on what may be 'messy' processes and dynamics not well revealed by the current data. What this case study does clearly suggest is that while particular and unique national circumstances do matter in shaping the form and trajectory of a given society's agrarian transition, 'context' under conditions of globalised capital and liberalised borders can no longer be seen as only domestic in scope. The case of the RFE should must be included as part of the broader narrative of Chinese agrarian change, a story that quite clearly already has important transnational dimensions and implications.

Funding

This work was supported by BRICS Initiative for Critical Agrarian Studies.

Notes

1. Lu and Chen, "Dongning is the National Leader."
2. China Russia Information Network, "Villages of Chinese."
3. Liu, "Investigation of Heilongjiang Peasants."
4. Wen, "Will 21st China."
5. Huang, "China's Hidden Agricultural Revolution"; Gui, "Not Becoming Capitalist"; Yan and Chen, "Agrarian Capitalization without Capitalism?"
6. Thomas, "Going Out"; Hofman, "Politics or Profits."
7. As quoted in Bernstein, "V.I. Lenin and A.V. Chayanov: Looking," 59.
8. Byres, "Paths of Capitalist Agrarian Transition."
9. See: Zhang and Donaldson, "Rise of Agrarian Capitalism"; Huang, "China's Hidden Agricultural Revolution"; Yan and Chen, "Agrarian Capitalization without Capitalism?"
10. Yan and Chen, "Agrarian Capitalization without Capitalism?" 375.
11. See: Chen, "Small Peasants"; Lu, "Peasant Differentiation"; Gui Hua, "Not Becoming Capitalist"; Yuan, "Subsistence Agriculture." Interestingly, there is also evidence that land transfers have in fact stimulated more equalised distribution of land, and have benefitted those farms that are smaller in terms of area or household size. See: Jikun et al., "The Effect of Off-farm Employment."

12. The term family farms (*jiating nongchang*) in this case refers not literally to family farms that are managed or run by household labour, but a relative policy neologism refers to entrepreneurial and professionalised farms of a well-above average scale, as referred to in the Chinese Communist Party's No. 1 Document of 2013. See: Ministry of Agriculture, "China's First Family Farm."

13. Qian and Donaldson, "The Rise of Agrarian Capitalism," 44.

14. Li and Chen, "Need for Regulations on Businesses."

15. Jikun et al., "Small-scale Farmers," 28.

16. Dragon-head enterprises are agribusinesses that are recognised by the state and receive a number of policy supports, to further the aim of increasing production scale and integrating production processes In short – to help modernise agriculture.

17. World Bank Databank, "Arable Land (Hectares per Person)."

18. Huang et al., *Small-scale Farmers*, 20; Ministry of Agriculture, "China's First Family Farm." http://www.moa.gov.cn/zwllm/zwdt/201306/t20130604_3483252.htm (accessed 31 Dec 2014).

19. Day, *The Peasant in Postsocialist China*, 151.

20. Zhang and Donaldson, "China's Agrarian Reform," 264.

21. Xinhua News, "Li Keqiang Calls for Modern Agriculture Development."

22. Huang et al., "Capitalization without Proletarianization."

23. Yan and Chen, "Agrarian Capitalization without Capitalism?" 383.

24. USDA, "Northeast China."

25. Zhang, "Reforming China's State-owned Farms," 374.

26. Duncan and Ruetschle, "Agrarian Reform and Agricultural Productivity," 205.

27. Spoor et al., "Food Security in a Sovereign State."

28. Visser et al., "Oligarchs, Megafarms, and Land Reserves,"917.

29. See note 17 above.

30. Ioffe, et al., 'Land Abandonment in Russia,' 529.

31. Lotspeich, "Economic Integration of China and Russia," 130.

32. Motrich and Naiden, "The Social-demographic Situation," 554.

33. Duncan and Ruetschle, "Implementing Agrarian Reform," 108.

34. Duncan and Ruetschle, "Implementing Agrarian Reform," 103.

35. Visser et al., "Oligarchs Megafarms, and Land Reserves."

36. Duncan and Ruetschle, "Agrarian Reform," 200–1.

37. Lotspeich, "Economic Integration," 130.

38. Larin, "Chinese in the Russian Far East."

39. Wang, "China's Export of Labor."

40. Qilu Weekly, "Chinese people farming in Russia"; Shkurkin, "Chinese in the Labour Market," 88; Nyriri, *Chinese in Eastern Europe and Russia*, 78.

41. Alexseev, "Chinese Migration in the Russian Far East."

42. Nyiri, *Chinese in Eastern Europe*, 78.

43. Shkurkin, "Chinese in the Labour Market."

44. Brooke, "New Face of Farming."

45. Tencent Finance, "Going to Russia"; 360doc.com, "Siberia's Chinese."

46. Lintner, "Is China the Future of Russia's Far East?"

47. See note 3 above.

48. See note 2 above.

49. Heilongjiang Government Website, "Mudanjiang's Dongning County."

50. Xinjiang Academy of Social Sciences, "Research on Heilongjiang Province."

51. See note 2 above.

52. The Investigator, "Chinese Enterprises Will Build."

53. The Moscow Times, "Russia and China to Launch $2 Billion."

54. China Daily, "Dongning People."

55. Edelman, "Messy Hectares."

56. Russian Federal Service for Veterinary and Phytosanitary Surveillance, "Rosselkhoznadzor Participates."

57. Lee, "The Russian Far East and China."
58. Minakir and Freeze, *The Russian Far East*, 55.
59. Lu and Chen, "Dongning."
60. China Daily, "Opportunities and Risks."
61. See note 2 above.
62. Tencent Finance, "Going to Russia."
63. See note 3 above.
64. See note 2 above.
65. Tencent Finance, 'Going to Russia' to plant vegetables!"
66. See note 2 above.
67. Agroxxi.ru, "Chinese Vegetable Business in Siberia."
68. See note 62 above.
69. The Investigator, "Heilongjiang Farm Workers."
70. Zhang and Donaldson, "Rise of Agrarian Capitalism," 32.
71. Xinhua News, "CPC Central Committee and State Council views."
72. See note 2 above.
73. Jiao, "去俄罗斯种地 Going to Russia to Farm."
74. See note 60 above.
75. See note 67 above.
76. Stanway, "Insight: For Chinese Farmers."
77. See note 2 above.
78. Ma, "Study of Heilongjiang-Russia agricultural trade."
79. Website of the CRACA.
80. Stanway, "Insight: For Chinese Farmers."
81. See note 2 above.
82. Website of the CRACA.
83. Heilongjiang Province Land Reclamation Bureau, "Heilongjiang Province," 44.
84. See note 2 above.
85. See note 3 above.
86. Xinjiang Academy of Social Sciences, "Research on Heilongjiang."
87. Hofman and Ho, "China's 'Developmental Outsourcing.'"
88. China Russia Information Network, "From Abject Guy"; Hu, "Overseas Farming Getting Hot."
89. See note 2 above.
90. Thomas, "Going Out: China's Food Security"; Hofman, "Politics or Profits."
91. Clever and Wu, *China – Oilseeds and Products Annual.*
92. Yang, "Returning Grain'; Ma, "Agricultural 'Going Out'".
93. USDA, "Russian Federation, Oilseeds and Products Annual 2016."
94. Heilongjiang Government Website, "Mudanjiang's Dongning County."
95. Ministry of Commerce of the PRC, "Heilongjiang's Agricultural Development."
96. Zhou, "Beyond 'Natural Pressures.'"
97. Borras and Franco, "Global Land Grabbing."

ORCID

Jiayi Zhou http://orcid.org/0000-0003-1173-3114

Bibliography

350doc.com. 2012. "鲜卑利亚(西伯利亚)的中国人." September 10. Accessed March 13, 2017. http://www.360doc.com/content/16/0628/02/1188133_571271070.shtml

Agroxxi.ru. 2013. "Китайский овощной бизнес в Сибири Chinese vegetable business in Siberia." Accessed August 10. http://www.agroxxi.ru/gazeta-zaschita-rastenii/zrast/kitaiskii-ovoschnoi-biznes-v-sibiri.html

Alexseev, Mikhail. "Chinese Migration in the Russian Far East: Security Threats and Incentives for Cooperation in Primorskii Krai." In *Russia's Far East: A Region at Risk*, edited by Judith Thornton and Charles E. Ziegler, 319–347. Seattle, WA: University of Washington Press, 2013.

Bernstein, Henry. "V.I. Lenin and A.V. Chayanov: Looking Back, Looking Forward." *Journal of Peasant Studies* 36, no. 1 (2009): 55–81.

Borras, Saturnino M., and Jenny C. Franco. "Global Land Grabbing and Trajectories of Agrarian Change: A Preliminary Analysis." *Journal of Agrarian Change* 12, no. 1 (2012): 34–59.

Brooke, James. 2004. "New Face of Farming in Russia's Far East." *New York Times*, July 8

Byres, Terence J. "Paths of Capitalist Agrarian Transition in the Past and in the Contemporary World." In *Agrarian Studies: Essays on Agrarian Relations in Less Developed Countries*, edited by V. K. Ramachandran and M. Swaminathan, 54–83. New Delhi: Tulika Books, 2003.

Chen, Ling 陈玲. "小农、中农抑或大户:中国农业的发展战略选择." [Small Peasants, Middle Peasants or Large Ventures: Strategic Choices in China's Agricultural Development.] 农村经济 [Rural Economy] 10 (2013): 3.

China Daily. 2012. "俄罗斯远东农业开发的机遇与风险." [Opportunities and Risks of Agricultural Development in the RFE.] Accessed December 5. http://www.chinadaily.com.cn/zgrbjx/2012-12/05/content_15989310.htm

China Daily. 2015. "东宁人赴俄罗斯种地揽金 建起中国首个国家级境外农业产业园." [Dongning People in Russian Farming, Established China's First State-level Foreign Agricultural Industrial Park.] Accessed August 24. http://cnews.chinadaily.com.cn/2015-08/24/content_21686248.htm

China Russia Agricultural Cooperative Association in Heilongjiang Province Website. http://www.hljdeny.com/cn_public_html/index.Asp

China Russia Information Network. 2012. "赴俄务农村"造就数百个百万富翁: 收成比打工翻好几倍." [Villages of Chinese Laborers in Russia Have Created Several Hundred Peasant Millionaires.] Accessed June 15. http://www.chinaru.info/huarenhuashang/eluosihuaren/14615.shtml

China Russia Information Network. 2011. "俄罗斯的中国村庄: 从卖菜到种地 耕种在俄罗斯土地上的中国农." [Chinese Villages in Russia: Peasants Who Went From Selling Vegetables to Farming on Russia's Land.] Accessed November 24. http://www.chinaru.info/huarenhuashang/eluosihuaren/9957.shtml

China Russia Information Network. 2012. "从落魄小子到俄罗斯地主—东北人在俄罗斯种地." [From Abject Guy to Russian Landlord – Northeasterns Farming in the RFE.] February 15.

Clevel, Jennifer, and Wu Xiping. *China – Oilseeds and Products Annual*. USDA GAIN Report, 2015.

Day, Alexander F. *The Peasant in Postsocialist China*. Cambridge: Cambridge University Press, 2013.

Duncan, Jennifer, and Michelle Ruetschle. "Implementing Agrarian Reform in the Russian Far East." *Comparative Economic Studies* 43, no. 4 (2001): 95.

Duncan, Jennifer, and Michelle Ruetschle. "Agrarian Reform and Agricultural Productivity in the Russian Far East." In *Russia's Far East: A Region at Risk*, edited by Judith Thornton and Charles E. Ziegler. Seattle, WA: University of Washington Press, 2003.

Edelman, Marc. "Messy Hectares: Questions about The Epistemology of Land Grabbing Data." *Journal of Peasant Studies* 40, no. 3 (2013): 485–501.

Gui, Hua 桂华. "Not Becoming Capitalist – China's Agricultural Development Pathway." ["没有资本主义化的中国农业发展道路."] 战略与管理 [Strategy and Management] 11 (2013): 8–36.

Heilongjiang Government Website. 2013. "Mudanjiang's Dongning County has Become the Nation's Largest Distribution Center for Russian Grain Imports." ["牡丹江市东宁县成为我国最大俄罗斯进口粮食集散地."] Accessed December 31. http://www.mofcom.gov.cn/article/resume/n/201312/20131200446395.shtml

Heilongjiang Province Land Reclamation Bureau. "黑龙江省农垦:实施 "走出去"战略成效显著." [Heilongjiang Province Land Reclamation: Implementing the Going-Out Strategy with Remarkable Results.] 广东农垦 [Guangdong State Farms] no. 3 (2013): 44–45.

Hofman, Irna. "Politics or Profits Along the "Silk Road": What Drives Chinese Farms in Tajikistan and Helps them Thrive?" *Eurasian Geography and Economics* 57, no. 3 (2013): 457–481.

Hofman, Irna, and Peter Ho. "China's 'Developmental Outsourcing': A Critical Examination of Chinese Global 'Land Grabs' Discourse." *Journal of Peasant Studies* 39, no. 1 (2012): 1–48.

Hu, Junhua. 2009. "海外种地渐热." [Overseas Farming Getting Hot.] *Panorama Network*, February 26. http://www.p5w.net/news/cjxw/200902/t2189425.htm

Huang, Jikun, Xiaobing Wang, and Huanguang Qui. *Small-scale Farmers in China in the Face of Modernization and Globalization*. London: IIED/HIVOS, 2012.

Huang, Jikun, Gao Liangliang, and Scott Rozelle. "The Effect of Off-farm Employment on Household's Decisions to Rent Out and Rent in Cultivated Land in China." *China Agricultural Economic Review* 4, no. 1 (2012).

Huang, Phillip C.C. "China's Hidden Agricultural Revolution." *Rural China* 8, no. 1 (2010): 1–10.

Huang, Phillip C. C., Gao Yuan, and Yusheng Peng. "Capitalization without Proletarianization in China's Agricultural Development." *Modern China* 38, no. 2 (2012): 139–173.

Ioffe, Grigory. "Nefedova, Tatyana and De Beurs, Kirsten. (2012). "Land Abandonment in Russia"." *Eurasian Geography and Economics* 53, No. 4 (2012): 529–549.

Jiao, Hongyan 焦红艳. 2012. "去俄罗斯种地." [Going to Russia to Farm.] 法治周末 [Legal Daily]. Accessed February 15. http://www.chinaru.info/huarenhuashang/eluosihuaren/11642.shtml

Larin, Victor. "Chinese in the Russian Far East: Regional Views." In *Crossing National Borders*, edited by Tsuneo Akaha and Anna Vassilieva, 47–67. Tokyo: United Nations University Press, 2005.

Lee, Rens. *The Russian Far East and China: Thoughts on Cross-Border Integration*. Philadelphia, PA: Foreign Policy Research Institute (FPRI), November 2013.

Li, Yongshen 李永生, and Chen Hongfei 程鸿飞. 2013. "工商企业租赁农户承包耕地要监管——农业部农村经济体制与经营管理司负责人解读中央1号文件." [Need for Regulations on Businesses Leasing Farmland – The MOA is Responsible for Interpreting Central Document No.1.] *Website of PRC Ministry of Agriculture*, Accessed February 4. http://www.moa.gov.cn/ztzl/yhwj2013/xwbd/201302/t20130204_3215159.htm

Lintner, Bertil. 2006. "Is China the future of Russia's Far East?" *The Hankyoreh*, November 29. http://www.hani.co.kr/arti/english_edition/e_international/175005.html

Liu, Jiawen 刘佳雯. 2011. "黑龙江农民俄罗斯"种地淘金"调查." [Investigation of Heilongjiang peasants' 'farm rush' in Russia], 华夏时报 [China Times], Accessed July 15. http://www.chinatimes.cc/hxsb/news/zhengce/110715/1107152023-24920.html

Lotspeich, Richard. *"Economic Integration of China and Russia in the Post-Soviet Era."* In *The Future of China-Russia Relations*, edited by James A. Bellacquia. Lexington: University Press of Kentucky, 2010.

Lu, Rui 刘锐. "农民阶层分化与乡村治理转型." [Peasant Differentiation and the Transformation of Rural Governance.] 中州学刊 [Zhongzhou Journal] 12, no. 6 (2012): 89–93.

Lu, Xiaoming 吕晓明, and Chen Yang 陈洋. 2013. "东宁对俄农业开发"全国领先 [Dongning is the National Leader of Agricultural Development in Russia.] *Northeast News* (republished by: Heilongjiang Economy), Accessed December 31. http://hlj.ce.cn/sy/gd/201312/31/t20131231_1283433.shtml

Ma, Lin 马琳. "黑龙江省对俄农业经贸合作模式创新研究." [Study of Heilongjiang-Russia agricultural Trade Cooperation Models.] 对外经贸 [Foreign Trade] 1 (2014): 42–44.

Ma, Yuzhong 马玉忠. "农企"走出去"遭遇"成长的烦恼"." [Agricultural 'Going Out' is Experiencing 'Growing Pains'.] 中国经济周刊 [China Economic Weekly] 29 (2014): 80–81.

Minakir, Pavel A., and Gregory L. Freeze, eds. *The Russian Far East: An Economic Handbook*. New York, NY: M.E. Sharpe, 2004.

Ministry of Agriculture Information Office. 2013. "我国首次家庭农场统计调查结果显示." [China's First Family Farm Statistical Survey Results.] *Ministry of Agriculture of the PRC Website*, Accessed June 4. http://www.moa.gov.cn/zwllm/zwdt/201306/t20130604_3483252.htm

Motrich, Ekaterina L., and S. N. Naiden. "The Social-demographic Situation and Labor Migration: The Far Eastern Sector." *Studies on Russian Economic Development* 20, no. 5 (2009): 554–562.

Nyriri, Pal. *Chinese in Eastern Europe and Russia*. London: Routledge, 2007.

Qilu Weekly. 2012. "在俄罗斯种地的中国人." [Chinese People Farming in Russia.] Accessed March 11. http://www.qlweekly.com/News/Topics/201203/115788.html

Russian Federal Service for Veterinary and Phytosanitary Surveillance. 2014. "Rosselkhoznadzor Participates in the First Russia-China Agricultural Forum 'Condition and Prospects of Russian-Chinese Cooperation in Agriculture.'" Accessed July 6. http://www.fsvps.ru/fsvps/news/10348.html?_language=en

Shkurkin, Anatolii M. "Chinese in the Labour Market of the Russian Far East: Past, Present, Future." In *Globalizing Chinese Migration*, edited by Pal Nyiri and Igor Saveliev. Burlington, VT: Ashgate Publishing Company, 2002.

Spoor, Max, Natalia Mamonova, Oane Visser, and Alexander Nikulin. "Food Security in a Sovereign State and 'Quiet Food Sovereignty' of an Insecure Population: The Case of Post-Soviet Russia." Conference Paper #28. Paper presented at International Conference 'Food Security: A Critical Dialogue' at Yale University, New Haven, CT, September 14–15, 2013.

Stanway, David. 2013. "Insight: For Chinese farmers, a rare welcome in Russia's Far East." *Reuters News*, Accessed December 22. http://www.reuters.com/article/2013/12/22/us-china-russia-agriculture-insight-idUSBRE9BL00X20131222

Tencent Finance. 2006. "到俄罗斯种菜去!中国农民握远东 90%菜市." [Going to Russia to Plant Vegetables! Chinese Peasants Capture 90% of the Far East Vegetable Market.] Accessed August 18. http://finance.qq.com/a/20060818/000287.htm

The Investigator. 2013. "黑龙江民工在俄打工被殴不实 钱被扣想逃回家." [Heilongjiang Farm Workers in Russia Were Not Beaten, Had Wages Deducted and Wanted to Flee Home.] Accessed July 15. http://m.guancha.cn/society/2013_07_15_158368

The Investigator. 2015. "中企将在俄远东投建两个10万吨存储仓." [Chinese Enterprises Will Build Two 100,000 ton Storage Warehouses in the RFE.] Accessed October 19. http://www.guancha.cn/economy/2015_10_19_338047.shtml

The Moscow Times. 2015. "Russia and China to Launch $2 Billion Fund to Boost Farming." Accessed May 8. http://www.themoscowtimes.com/business/article/russia-and-china-to-launch-2-billion-fund-to-boost-farming/520388.html

Thomas, Nicholas. "Going Out: China's Food Security from Southeast Asia." *The Pacific Review* 26, no. 5 (2013): 531–562.

United States Department of Agriculture (USDA). "Northeast China: Prospects for U.S. Agricultural Exports." *International Agricultural Trade Report*, April 2014.

USDA. "Russian Federation, Oilseeds and Products Annual 2016." *Global Agricultural Information Network Report*, March 2016

Wang, Shengjin. "China's Export of Labor and its Management." *Asian and Pacific Migration Journal* 4, no. 2–3 (1995): 429–447.

Wen, Tiejun 温铁军. "21 世纪的中国仍然是小农经济?" [Will 21st China Still be a Small-peasant Economy?] 国际经济评论 [International Economic Review] 6 (2000): 29–29.

World Bank Databank. "Arable Land (Hectares Per Person)." 2016. Accessed October 6. http://data.worldbank.org/indicator/AG.LND.ARBL.HA.PC?year_high_desc=false

Xinhua News. 2013. "Li Keqiang Calls for mOdern Agriculture Development." November 6. http://news.xinhuanet.com/english/china/2013-11/06/c_132865217.htm

Xinhua News. 2015. "中共中央 国务院关于加快发展现代农业进一步增强农村发展活力的若干意见." [CPC Central Committee and State Council, Views on on Accelerating the Development of Modern Agriculture and Enhancing the Vitality of Rural Development.] January 31. Accessed January 5. http://www.gov.cn/jrzg/2013-01/31/content_2324293.htm

Xinjiang Academy of Social Sciences. 2012. "黑龙江省对俄东部地区农业合作升级问题研究." [Research on Heilongjiang Province's Upgraded Agricultural Cooperation with Russia's Eastern District.] Accessed May 17. http://www.xjass.com/zy/content/2012-05/17/content_232575.htm

Yan Hairong and Chen Yiyuan. "Agrarian Capitalization Without Capitalism? Capitalist Dynamics from Above and Below in China." *Journal of Agrarian Change* 15, no. 3 (2015): 366–391.

Yuan, Mingbao 袁明宝. "生计农业: 中国小农的现实表达与发展转型." [Subsistence Agriculture: The Expression and Transformation of China's Small Peasant.] 南京农业大学学报 [Journal of Nanjing Agricultural University] 6 (2013): 21–24.

Yang, Hong 杨虹. 2013. "海归"粮食:农业"走出去"呼唤国家战略." [Returning Grain: Agricultural 'Going Out' is Calling for a National Strategy.] 中国经济导报 [Chinese Economic Herald], Accessed February 7. http://www.ceh.com.cn/cjpd/2013/02/171247.shtml

Zhang, Qian Forrest, and John A. Donaldson. "The Rise of Agrarian Capitalism with Chinese Characteristics: Agricultural Modernization, Agribusiness and Collective Land Rights." *The China Journal* 60 (2008): 25–47.

Zhang, Qian Forrest, and John A. Donaldson. "China's Agrarian Reform and the Privatization of Land: A Contrarian View." *Journal of Contemporary China* 22, no. 80 (2012): 255–272.

Zhang, Qian Forrest. "Reforming China's State-owned Farms: State Farms in Agrarian Transition." Paper presented at the 4th Asian Rural Sociology Association (ARSA) International Conference, Legazpi City, Philippines, 2010.

Zhou, Jiayi. "Beyond 'Natural Pressures': Chinese Agriculture in the Russian Far East." In *Handbook of Asian Borderlands*, edited by Alexander Hostmann, Martin Saxer, and Alessandro Rippa. Routledge, (forthcoming 2017).

'Don't stop the mill': South African capital and agrarian change in Tanzania

Giuliano Martiniello

ABSTRACT

South African corporate agribusiness and large-scale commercial farmers have been major players in the current acquisitions of large tracts of very fertile land in southern and eastern Africa through massive investments in large-scale commercial farming, food processing, the production of biofuels and eco-tourism. By emphasising the significance of analysing the changing capital smallholder relationship in historical perspective, the paper explores continuity and change in the agrarian social structure and the land use dynamics of the Kilombero valley. It argues that smallholders are differentially and adversely integrated within agribusiness-led vertically organised agri-food chains consolidating and widening existing patterns of social inequality.

Introduction: land enclosures, agribusiness and smallholders' integration

The recent wave of large-scale land acquisitions in Africa, that international development and financial institutions, see as a 'development opportunity'[1] and critics as 'land grabbing',[2] has given renewed vigour to debates over land, food and agricultural issues. The term 'land grabbing' generally refers to large-scale, cross-border commercial land deals carried out by transnational corporations or initiated by food-insecure foreign governments.[3] This consolidated an already existing trend in which questions of control, access, use and governance of land had returned to the core of development discourses among international development institutions.[4] Yet large-scale land deals are not epiphenomenal if seen from the perspective of countries in the Global South, entailing both historical continuities and discontinuities with colonial and post-colonial patterns of land acquisitions. The African continent seems to have been the epicentre of the new wave of land acquisitions. The World Bank estimated that 45 million hectares of land have been involved in commercial deals in Africa between 2008–2009 and 2009–2010.[5] The re-emergence of large-scale land deals in the context of triple and mutually reinforcing financial, food and energy crises brings to the fore the question of renewed competition for natural resources, not simply within the traditional north/south dichotomy, but within a wider geographical spectrum that this time includes BRICS (Brazil, Russia, India, China, South Africa). The involvement of both northern powers and BRICS has led to charges of a 'new scramble for Africa'.[6]

South African corporate agribusiness and large-scale commercial farmers have been key players in the current acquisitions of large tracts of very fertile land in Africa.[7] Agricultural deregulation and trade liberalisation, that characterised the transition to democratic rule in post-apartheid South Africa, created the preconditions for the consolidation of land and agricultural resources among fewer large-scale producers, which decreased from 60,000 in 1996 to 30,000 in 2014,[8] though these statistics are under question. Expanding concentration of ownership in food and agricultural sectors rapidly ensued after the removal of state support, price controls, grants and marketing boards, and the abolition of quota systems. Capital concentration also went along major value chains: input industries; processing, packaging and logistic industries; agricultural finance; commercial banks; investment funds; and food giants, such as Tiger Brands and supermarkets like Shoprite.[9] Trends of 'financialization' and 'supermarketization' of the food sector underpin the expanding interpenetration of different segments and fractions of capital into complex assemblages of global interests, and underscore increased concentration and power within the changing international food regime.[10]

Increased concentration within the corporate food sector and the challenges of land reforms in South Africa, coupled with new opportunities created by waves of agricultural restructuring and land privatisation in southern African countries, pushed many important players to expand their acquisitions in the region. Often encouraged by Pretoria, South African agribusiness investments, though by no means the dominant players in most southern and eastern African economies, are shaping agrarian relations in ways that are reminiscent of prior waves of dispossession experienced in the region's settler-colonial societies but this time in collaboration with (democratically elected) African governments giving it a different spin to openly violent settler colonialism. The rush for biofuels, mining extraction, forestry, tourism and agricultural deals, which are major drivers of the current wave of acquisitions, are creating the conditions for the 'South Africanization' of the region,[11] and the consolidation of oligopolistic power of South African sugar giants and other processing industries.[12] Indeed, South African companies were dynamic agents of socio-economic transformations and new regional contradictions in the late apartheid years[13] and during the first democratic decade.[14] The rapid expansion of both large-scale commercial farmers and corporate players and their consequent move in the southern African region, was labelled as the 'Second Great Boer Trek'.[15]

This brief historical exegesis is relevant as some critics have pointed to some theoretical and methodological limitations in the 'literature rush' about 'global land grabbing': the ahistorical[16] and epiphenomenal character of its narratives; the unrigorous methodologies often based on data collected by agitprop organisations[17]; the Manichean and dualistic constructions, which ignored the socially diversified character of rural populations[18]; the lack of attention to intermediate levels of analysis at the regional, national and local levels, often neglecting the role of the state and national elites.[19]

This paper explores the socio-ecological implications of large-scale agricultural investments using as a case study the 1998 acquisition by Illovo of the Kilombero Sugar Company Limited (KSCL) in the Morogoro region of Tanzania. The deal predates the current land grabs and literature rush, it therefore represents a privileged entry point to analyse past and present, global and local, dynamics and trajectories of agrarian change. The focus on a single investment needs, however, to be both historicised and situated in the larger global political and economic context of accelerating industrialisation of agriculture. In this way, the case study methodology offers the possibility to move beyond the conjunctural focus contained in the current land rush literature, and to understand the linkages between earlier and current trends and trajectories of agrarian change through the years of structural adjustment and neoliberalism.

As an assemblage of nucleus estate plus outgrowers schemes, KSCL has been framed in policy-oriented literature and corporate discourses as an example of a collaborative and inclusive business model, characterised by the virtuous combination of business imperatives with human and social development.[20] This paper aims to explore these claims, by trying to understand how agricultural investments differentially affected particular geographical areas and social groups or classes. It will do so by analysing the implications of agricultural commercialisation on a group of outgrowers in the Msolwa-Rwembe area. This research trajectory acquires further relevance in the face of the current re-emergence of contract farming and outgrowers' schemes among governments and global development institutions' interventions often framed as an alternative to 'land grabbing'.[21] In this sense, it contributes to the already widespread literature and debate on agricultural modernisation and smallholders' integration within global commodity chains,[22] deagrarianisation and diversification of livelihood strategies,[23] and class differentiation of petty-commodity producers[24] or commercially oriented smallholders.[25]

By proposing to historicise contemporary dynamics of displacement and development and appreciate the historical sedimentation of place in assessments of debate on agribusiness–smallholder relationship, the paper argues that livelihoods of rural Tanzanians have become heavily influenced by the exigencies of maximisation of capacity utilisation of the sugar mill. The strategies of social reproduction of rural populations have been affected, to quote Marx, by the 'dull compulsion of economic relations',[26] not merely by the coercive means of state violence. This is further revealing of the ways in which the capital–smallholder relationship can be restructured in terms of the social structures set in place by particular formations of fixed capital and the way these condition everyday life. This case study gains further significance, as the Kilombero valley has been in the last few years the centre of large-scale land acquisitions for conservation, tourism and agricultural purposes,[27] and was recently targeted for the further expansion of sugar and other agricultural investments under the Southern Agricultural Growth Corridor of Tanzania initiative.[28]

The political economy of South African sugar

The expansion of South African capital has been the subject of significant debates as the politico-economic relations of African countries with BRICS expanded. The debate, mostly grounded within international relations, has been extensively dualistic in character. Critics have argued that South African investments in Africa have increasingly assumed a sub-imperialist character, playing the role of a hub or bridge between international capital and the continent and amplifying some of the worst characteristics of capitalism.[29] To some observers of the south–south solidarity persuasion, economic and political exchanges between BRICS and the rest of the continent are mutually beneficial in helping to reclaim Africa from the fringes of the global economy where powerful globalisation forces had pushed it.[30] South Africa is instead still playing its characteristic but contradictory role of semi-periphery in the world system, assuming a Janus-faced position that generates relations of subordination with northern countries, and unequal power relations with its southern partners.[31] The analytical focus on BRICS as a block of power, however, tended to downplay inter-capitalist rivalries in accessing natural resources and international markets – as showed in the case of dumped Brazilian sugar and chicken imports in southern Africa, or the development of the 6 million ha ProSavanna mega-project by Brazil in Mozambique[32] – and significant differences in existing patterns of social inequalities, social structures, development strategies, political histories. Interpreting BRICS in general and South Africa in particular as a node for capital expansion and as new sites of expanded production, circulation and consumption of agricultural commodities, instead allows us to ask how changes in the dynamics of the agro-food system affect the regional agrarian structures.[33]

We can also infer differences with respect to agribusiness models of production and the character of investments. Chinese investments, for example, are mostly state-led and target mineral-rich and fertile agricultural areas and promote forms of agricultural (technical) cooperation such as in Tanzania, Ethiopia and Uganda. Indian investments are instead based on private capital, and their significance in the region is the result of political and economic ties forged by Indian capital during colonialism and re-energised in the late neoliberalism. The Brazilian public–private partnership in sugar production, experimented in the Cerrado and, currently, exported to Mozambique, is characterised by large-scale mechanisation projects, and increased reliance on migrant workers.[34] Other investments in sugarcane cultivation, mainly driven by South African capital, opted for a business model based on the integration of large-scale nucleus estates with outgrowers or contract farming schemes.[35]

Starting in the democratic transition period, Illovo, whose first presence in South Africa can be traced back to 1891 in KwaZulu-Natal, expanded agricultural estates and built 16 manufacturing sites across 6 southern African countries making it the largest sugar producer in the continent. In 2005 Associated British Foods purchased majority shares followed by more recently full ownership. These events allow us to capture increased concentration in the global agro-food value chains, the role of South Africa as a hub and the increased global dimension to South African capital. In 2013, Illovo Group's ownership structure included: 100% of Illovo Sugar SA; 76% of Illovo Sugar in Malawi; 90% of Maragra Acucar in Mozambique; 60% of Ubombo Sugar in Swaziland; 82% of Zambia Sugar; and 55% of Kilombero Sugar in Tanzania. In doing so, Illovo progressively acquired quasi-monopolistic control of significant shares of sugar industry production: 100% in Malawi; 93% in Zambia; 40% in Tanzania; 35% in Swaziland; 30% in South Africa; and 21% in Mozambique.[36] Changes in the pattern of commercialisation and marketing underpin the current expansion and location of agribusiness in the continent as Illovo's marketing strategy is in fact increasingly based on growing domestic markets, which represent 63% of total sugar sales.[37] Interestingly, the countries where Illovo is expanding its operations are also ranked as those with the highest per capita consumption rates at a global level: South Africa (6th); Swaziland (10th); Malawi (11th); Tanzania (13th); Zambia (14th); and Mozambique (15th). Another driving factor may have been the growth of domestic retail sugar prices. In 2012–2013, the SADC domestic retail prices were among the highest when compared with global standards: Zambia (4th); Mozambique (7th); Tanzania (10th); Malawi (12th); Swaziland (14th); and South Africa (15th).

Though domestic prices, and global levels of consumption, explain to a significant extent the boom of sugar in the region, growing ethanol markets and the development of biomass economy have played an important role too. In a context of growing socio-ecological concerns about climate change and search for renewable sources of energy, multipleness and flexibleness of selected crops and commodity use allow companies to diversify their products portfolio, reduce risks associated with price oscillations and volatility and exploit the conjunctural market opportunities.[38] The combined effect of improved production methods, the sustained application of science into technological innovations that suit agribusiness' exigencies in exploring potential new terrains of accumulation, and the changing commercial and marketing strategies, severely restructured the agricultural sector simultaneously expanding the fungibility of certain crops and widening the spectrum of opportunities that the agricultural sector presents in the region.

In southern Africa, the politics of flex crops is still in its infancy as only 7% came from downstream production and energy co-generation.[39] Yet the dynamics of investment in the sugarcane bioeconomy are shaping the current possibilities for companies to combine the production of refined sugar with other non-food products. The downstream operations are concentrated in South Africa – namely, at the Sezela complex and the Merebank plant in Durban, and the Glendale Ethanol Distillery on the KwaZulu-Natal north coast, though new plants have also been developed in Malawi where molasses is supplied for fuel and potable alcohol[40]; in Swaziland in projects of co-generation of electricity; in Zambia in an ethanol plant to serve the domestic fuel market,[41] in Tanzania where a new ethanol distillery has been operating since October 2013 in the production of extra neutral alcohol.[42]

By further investing in value addition to its core products of fibre, sugar and molasses Illovo is simultaneously expanding sugar production and differentiating its arrays of downstream products, which now include ethanol, flavouring products, syrups, furfural alcohol,[43] agribusiness products,[44] extra neutral alcohol and power co-generation. As the Illovo's chairman Don MacLeod put it, the objective of the company is 'to optimize return on every stick of cane'.[45] Yet the fact that the majority of the company's revenues come from sugar sales is both an indicator of high margins profitability within the sugar sector, especially in countries which present optimal agro-ecological conditions such as Tanzania where sugarcane yields are among the highest in the world.[46]

Large-scale plantations and peasants' commercialisation in historical perspective

The great agro-ecological potentialities of this lowland, enhanced by its fertile alluvial soils, attracted attention as long ago as 1909 when the Germans surveyed a possible railway route through the valley.[47] In colonial accounts, the Kilombero valley in the region of south–central Tanganyika was pictured as an agricultural zone of high potential where sustained large-scale irrigated cultivation on a scale unprecedented in Tanganyika would have been technically possible and economically advantageous.[48]

The first large-scale sugar commercial plantation was established in the 1930s by an Indian landowner who used to cultivate sugarcane, extract juice, concentrate and process it into slices of coarse sugar and market it as 'sukari-guru'.[49] Sugarcane had been cultivated on a very small scale and generally processed into beer or chewed for the juice in the northern part of the Kilombero Valley before the colonial period though it remained marginal among subsistence-oriented smallholders crops.[50] Millet and as the century progressed rice and maize were the main crops grown in the area on an individual basis through practices of shifting cultivation and by combining fallow with traditional irrigation.[51] Apart from two or three acres cultivated with sugar or cotton, peasants were self-sufficient in food crops like rice, groundnuts, maize and cassava.[52] By the 1950s, the number of plants producing 'suka-ri-guru' managed by Arabs and Asians had greatly expanded, thanks to privileged access to bank loans under colonial rule.

At national level, the incorporation of peasants within the commercial circuits of the colonial economy was enhanced in the 1950s when several large-scale settlement projects with African settler tenant farmers had been initiated by the Tanganyika Agricultural Corporation.[53] The general aim of the colonial state was to transform the traditional African cultivator into a modern smallholder by separating him from his traditional environment and integrating him into production systems 'under close supervision'[54] as a response to grievances and protests emerged to enforced agricultural programmes or institutions which lately fuelled resentments into nationalist demands.[55]

In August 1960, the Kilombero Sugar Company Limited (KSCL) was officially formed under joint private ownership by the International Finance Corporation, the Commonwealth Development Corporation, the Standard Bank of East Africa and the Netherlands Overseas Finance Co managed its operations.[56] The sugar estate was located close to the Great Ruaha River, a tributary of the Kilombero. The total concession was 25,000 acres but only 2200 ha were initially planted under cane, providing jobs for 3000 people.[57] Four other privately owned sugar estates, plus three government-sponsored land settlement schemes, were located in close proximity. The policy of KSCL was to encourage and assist outgrowing of cane by African smallholders providing them with inputs and services on credit. In 1962, the first milling season, a few large Indian and European plantations, the settlement scheme with 250 smallholders and a group of 14 African farmers provided sugarcane.[58] The company operated under the pattern of nucleus estate plus outgrowers, with the former producing 70% of the cane and the latter 30%.[59] The Msolwa-Ruembe zone in the Kilombero Valley can be conceived, as a 'frontier area',[60] characterised by the penetration and settlements of European (and other foreign) farmers, increased capitalist production methods, ensuing needs for labour and the integration of smallholders within the circuit of agribusiness.

Integrating smallholders within the circuits of production of the company, as an outgrowing operation, arguably among the first experiments in sub-Saharan Africa, had three major aims: (a) expand the production of sugarcane in the area both to maximise the processing capacities of the milling plant and as a shield against the risks of poor harvests; (b) closely supervised settlements in particular were meant to isolate peasants from the larger politics of protest which had animated the country in the 1950s; (c) supporting 'progressive' farmers was also meant to generate an emulation effect by wider segments of the population once the superior results generated by the adoption of modern agricultural techniques would have been visible.

The political scenario was radically altered by the adoption of the Arusha declaration in 1967 which included nationalisation, villagisation[61] and collective farming. As a consequence all the shares of KSCL were sold to the government and entrusted to the Tanganyika Agricultural Corporation, a parastatal set-up by government to manage the affairs of the rapidly expanding sugar industry (among other agricultural export crops). Yet the government did not possess the management skills needed, and so it left management to a Dutch firm, Handels Vereniging Amsterdam.[62] In parallel, the area was further tied to the national trade circuits through the development of new TAZARA railway, which was designed to pass in close proximity to KSCL.

Msolwa Ujamaa, as its name indicates, was a newly created village with its own village authorities. Its establishment was the result of government efforts aimed at consolidating settlements and opening up of the area for sugarcane production. Land previously owned by a TANU party official was given out in small parcels of two acres (0.8 ha) for about 60 people to settle complemented in 1976 by a further 400 ha of his estate which were nationalised representing the totality of village land.[63] Village authorities allocated land to private cultivators after a formal application. Slowly but steadily, the village grew as a result of a constant inflow of settlers attracted by the potential economic opportunities and social infrastructure the area provided.

The second step of Ujamaa involved collective farming in which residents were requested to farm communal land and share the proceeds according to labour involvement. In Msolwa Ujamaa collective farming began in 1969 and involved crops such as paddy, maize and sugarcane.[64] Fuelled by the Lomé Convention which allocated sugar quotas at favourable prices to Tanzania as part of the agreement between Africa, Caribbean and Pacific (ACP) group of states and European Economic Community, the government gave substantial stimulus to sugar industry. In 1974, the building of a new plant, Kilombero II (Ruembe), just three kilometres away from Kilombero I (Msolwa), had started with the support of the Dutch Government (20%), the Danish Government (31%), IDA/IBRD (32%) and the Government of Tanzania (17%).[65] They assumed that sugar production would rapidly increase with the injection of fresh capital investments for the purchase of technologically advanced machinery used for cane harvesting and transporting to the factories.

However, the 3000 ha of land targeted for the new estate was entirely inhabited. The process of relocation of the local population (mainly composed of local inhabitants, workers of Kilombero I, and workers who settled in the area in the period of construction of the new railway), resulted in serious confrontations with the special armed police, known as Field Force Unit,[66] which played a vigorous role in the massive dislocations of millions of poor peasants and nomadic populations into 'development' villages.[67]

The government initiated renewed campaigns in the Msolwa-Ruembe zone to stimulate outgrowers' participation in sugarcane cultivation who reached 1000 units, and accounted for 42% of the total cane delivered to KSCL in 1978.[68] At that time, the work of planting, harvesting and loading of produce was done by hand and money accruing from the sale of cash crops was returned to the grower, less costs for seeds, transport and fertilizers. Simultaneously, it stimulated the role of outgrowers associations which, established in the aftermath of the Arusha Declaration as result of farmers' initiatives, maintained relationships with KSCL and coordinated the use of machineries.

Allegedly, to respond to a growing mismatch between domestic demand and supply, increased sugar production found instead its way onto international markets, particularly between 1975 and 1980.[69] By the end of the 1970s, the plantation/estate sector produced nearly 50% of total sugar export value and 25% of total domestic value.[70] Government expenditure on milling expansion was about 30% of the total net industrial investments during the Third Five-Year Plan, making sugar processing the most expensive single food industry investment. The result, however, was an excess capacity of about 57% in the country's sugar-processing factories.[71]

Polarisation and class differentiation among outgrowers

The export-oriented strategy in relation to sugar sector development was premised upon loans and high imports of agricultural machineries which rendered the economy vulnerable to adverse development in the world market.[72] Rapid increase in the price of oil, decreasing terms of exchange for agricultural commodities, the war with Uganda and droughts increased the country's exposure to foreign debt. Government had in fact become increasingly dependent on external funding for agriculture, largely from global financial institutions and from bilateral institutions like USAID and CIDA. Structural adjustment plans drastically affected government spending and de-structured the organisation of collective farming.[73]

The decline of collective farming can also be ascribed to government policies, which started to promote more individualised forms of farming. Communal work was not properly implemented and supported by adequate leadership and education, and gave way to more individualised forms of agricultural production or block farms, which mostly benefited the best positioned agricultural entrepreneurs, who retained that agricultural initiatives including packages of improved seeds and fertilizers which characterised the large agricultural World Bank projects of the 1970s, would be consistent with villagisation since they implied intensive cultivation of small areas by large numbers of individual farmers.[74]

In Msolwa Ujamaa outgrowers experienced a serious decline in farm income, along with the non-availability of farm equipment, inputs and credit. Rural credit once channelled through the Cooperative Bank of Rural Development became mainly oriented to big growers: loans to parastatals and private companies grew from 6.4 to 70.7%, while loans to individuals for food production dropped from 6.7 to 5.1% between 1972 and 1980.[75] Money formerly advanced to cooperatives – which received a substantial portion of credit and benefited kulaks and large producers, but provided marketing and other services to small producers as well – was shifted to the corporate sector.[76]

Such trends enhanced the crystallisation of diverse social groups in the Msolwa-Rwembe area: (a) 10 large-scale private estates harvesting a total of 83,340 ha, which represented 38.5% of cane delivered to the company with a productivity of 32.5 tons of cane per ha; (b) 8 Ujamaa villages harvesting 24,318 ha (7.5% of total cane delivered to KSCL) with a productivity of 21.3 tons per ha; (c) 13 associations of small-scale cane farmers, whose members amounted to 500 individuals with an average acreage of cultivated cane of 1.63 ha per farmer (representing 37.5% of total cane to KSCL); and (d) 30 group farms, with a total area of harvested cane of 22,250 ha, representing 13.0% of cane to KSCL, and with the highest productivity per ha of 40.6 tons of cane.[77] Overall, outgrowers boosted in numbers and in terms of cane cultivation, reaching a peak in 1978–1980, and then declined as a result of cost-price squeeze in the years of structural adjustment.[78] In 1986 as a result of the changing land use dynamics (from food crops to sugarcane), 70% of total land was under cane and 30% under food crops.[79]

In the following decade Tanzania followed a path of liberalisation and privatisation. Illovo Sugar LTD (55%), and Ed&F MAN, a British commodity trader (20%), and the Tanzanian Government (25%)[80] took over the Kilombero Estates in 1998. The privatisation era further accentuated existing instances exponentially projecting dynamics of class differentiation, land use and agrarian change. Both new owners and government once again stimulated a larger involvement of outgrowers. Campaigns of sugarcane promotion were launched in the area and credits were allocated along with free seeds for the first year. There existed basically no legal constraints nor minimal acreage endowment to participate in outgrowers schemes. Preparing the ground for privatisation, the government supported these initiatives by providing residents in Msolwa Ujamaa with 2 acres of land between 1990 and 1995.[81] Before Illovo's acquisition there were no incentives and little motivation to grow sugar, as

Table 1. Typical outgrowers expenditures.

Tractor hire	60,000Tsh[a] per acre
Soil spinning and softening	40,000Tsh per acre
Lines for cane planting	40,000Tsh per acre
Seeds	200,000Tsh per acre
Seeds transport	40,000–80,000Tsh according to distance
Fertilizers	60,000Tsh per acre
Seasonal labour (weeding)	50,000Tsh per acre
Migrant labour (harvesting)	6,500Tsh per ton
Loader	3,000Tsh per ton
Sugarcane transport to factory	6,000Tsh per ton

[a] 1 US dollar = 1500 Tanzania shillings. Source: Author.

previous initiatives experienced major limitations in terms of access to inputs, transport services, skill and technology. Interviews with a group of outgrowers in Msolwa Ujamaa revealed that company officials started to actively campaign after privatisation of KSCL, parading the virtues of sugarcane cultivation and promising the construction of new infrastructures and social services such as roads, schools and hospitals, and access to electricity.

As one outgrower put it: 'they motivated the people to grow more cane inside and outside the plantations and factories, the more you produce more money you will get'.[82] In this way, a new wave of farmers joined the ranks of outgrowers, which increased from 3384 small, 8 medium and 3 large outgrowers in 2002 to 5718 small, 56 medium and 11 large out growers in 2005/2006, respectively, accounting for 59, 17 and 24% of total outgrower production.[83] If we compare these data with those provided by Sprenger in 1986, we can notice that: (a) that the numbers of outgrowers sensibly increased; (b) the share of cane provided to the company by large outgrowers substantially increased moving from 38.5 to 59%; (c) in relative terms the portion of sugarcane provided by smallholders drastically deteriorated. These are symptoms of both an increase in smallholders' commercialisation, enhanced social polarisation and concentration of sugarcane production in the hands of large and medium outgrowers, but also of the rampant social differentiation and inequalities.

Overall outgrowers' production also rapidly increased from 100,000 tons of cane a year before privatization to 500,000 by 2004/2005.[84] The company succeeded in increasing sugar output from less from 29,000 tons in 1998 to 127,000 tons in 2002–2003.[85] It successively expanded its milling capacity to crush 250–70 tons of sugarcane every hour.[86] This was considered to be the major achievement of KSCL restructuring, as it brought the rate of mill capacity utilisation to 97%, the highest within the Illovo Group.[87]

Outgrowers adverse incorporation

The cane supply agreement signed between KSCL and sugarcane growers associations, which today include approximately 8000 members, establishes the distribution of cane quotas, with relative schedules for cane harvesting and factory delivery, and the cane price per ton (at an average level of sucrose content) among associations and the different groups of farmers. Spurred by increasing global prices in the early years of privatisation, KSCL used to buy all the cane produced by outgrowers and demanded further expansion of land areas. Associations also stimulated expanded sugarcane cultivation as privatisation had basically transformed them into services providers and contract managers. The most influential social groups therefore drew plenty of opportunities for capital accumulation by the uncontrolled expansion of sugarcane production. The result was a further rush for sugarcane cultivation and its related set of capital-intensive activities (see Table 1), an inflow of settlers in the area, the development of rental land markets and generalised cane over-cultivation.

Revenues to the outgrowers are calculated through the system of *rendements*, after sugarcane is weighed, the sucrose content measured, sugar processed and sold. The company establishes an average theoretical level of sucrose at 10%, against which it calculates the price per ton. Ten per cent of the outgrower's payment is retained until the end of the season when variations of the actual market price are factored. It generally takes 45 days to receive payment but there have been several cases in the community where it has taken up to two months.

Yet after the initial boom of sugarcane prices, increased international competition and cheap importation from Brazil and Indonesia, spurred by the liberalising vein of the world trade regime, have resulted in reduced tariffs in the East Africa Community lowering the price on the domestic market. This is the reason why, the company argues, it has been unable to collect substantial portions of sugarcane previously commissioned to outgrowers for a number of years. In 2012/2013, the company estimated that 65,000 tons of outgrowers' cane could not be harvested.[88] The Msolwa Ujamaa Cane Growers Association (MUCGA) in fact harvested a total of 29,000 tons of sugarcane in 2009–2010 though the target was 45,000, leaving 16,000 tons of sugarcane in the field. Conditions for outgrowers have since deteriorated as a result of simultaneously increasing prices for inputs and energy, below average sucrose content, and decreasing sugarcane price per ton, which decreased from 68,000Tsh in 2011, to 65,000Tsh in 2012, and 58,750Tsh in 2013.[89]

The case of MUCGA, formed on 1 December 2008, is revealing as in the face of decreasing revenues from cane the number of hectares of land under cane increased from 3190 acres in 2010/2011 to 5416 in 2012/2013 and association members increased from 410 to 1152. In the face of enduring decrease of sugarcane revenues, the harvested tons of sugarcane went from 29,000 in 2009 to 50,850 in 2013.[90] In the same year, the company reached its record estate cultivation of 726,000 tons.[91]

How do we explain the company's apparent paradox of simultaneously refusing to accept some portions of outgrowers' sugarcane maintaining that low prices prevent it to do so, while simultaneously maximising sugarcane cultivation on its estates? How do we further understand why a reduction of revenues from sugarcane has been matched by an increase of acreage under cane?

The first question clearly represents a key contradiction for the company. As its production in absolute terms increases, it will unavoidably need less and less outgrowers sugarcane if the mills' processing capacity are left unaltered. This is revealing of the position of subordination of outgrowers *vis-a-vis* the the productive choices of the company, as they represent the weak ring of the buyer-driven vertically structured commodity chain. They are the most exposed to the risks and oscillations of global market prices and low harvests. Within this group, however, the quotas system allows the burden of the crisis to be externalised to small outgrowers who got much less bargaining power in the negotiation of cane quotas.

I suggest that these dynamics can be best interpreted as coterminous manifestations of adverse incorporation of smallholders within agribusiness-led value chains,[92] and differential impact on various outgrowers categories of large-scale initiatives of agricultural industrialisation[93] in a context of systemic overproduction. Outgrowers have indeed been integrated into the production process to carry out extra-production as a guarantee against low harvests and poor deliveries. In this sense, outgrowers have been used as an instrument to optimise the capacity utilisation of mills and as a buffer against risks of underproduction. Monson sees the promotion of outgrowers' schemes as linked to the reduction of labour costs per unit.[94] Mbiliny and Semakafu refer to them as proletarian labourers working for the company.[95] Others highlight the emergence of small-scale capitalist entrepreneurs.[96] For Bernstein they are petty commodity producers, a contradictory combination of capital and labour, which paved the way for social differentiation and the commoditisation of subsistence.[97] The last definition is particularly useful as it captures the tension of commercially oriented smallholder agriculture: partly entrepreneurs and partly labourers. Yet in the case of cane cultivation, capital-intensive activities greatly outpace the working activities performed by family members. Outgrowers are left with minor chances to internalise the costs involved in cane cultivation through extra labour efforts. The outcome is an amplification of the overall exposure to, and dependence on, market forces and imperatives.

In the period between 2010–2013, the combination of rising costs for inputs and loans, poor harvests and low sucrose content dramatically affected the social reproduction strategies of small-scale commercially oriented smallholders. Debt spread in the area, pushing some outgrowers to leave the sugar business. In some cases, small outgrowers have lost access to land, as it was used as collateral to guarantee credit from local banks. In these cases, growers' associations act as solicitors of the payment. Land currently lost by smallholders is re-purchased by larger growers, further stimulating dynamics of land concentration and selection of the most productive producers. Large and medium outgrowers expand their landholdings and differentiate between sugar and other crops, such as maize and rice elsewhere in the valley, and/or re-invest part of their profits into lucrative initiatives. In this way, a crisis for the majority is simultaneously translated into opportunities of expansion for a few.

As a result of the unrestrained expansion of sugar cultivation, further fragmentation of landholdings ensued. In Msolwa Ujamaa, we found many outgrowers with very limited access to land starting from 0.1 ha. Interviews with small-scale outgrowers revealed that rural households suffer periodically from food insecurity as sugarcane almost entirely extinguished land availability for food crops in the area. Today only very limited food production is found in the area, as evidenced by the growth of house gardens as farmland is increasingly being dedicated to sugarcane. Consequently, poor outgrowers are unable to produce enough food to fully reproduce rural households and heavily depend on local markets to access food which is simultaneously becoming more expensive as it comes from more distant areas. The spread of thievery and lack of supervision made food cultivation increasingly problematic, engendering further shifts in land use from food crops for local consumption to cash crops (sugarcane) for national consumption and export to regional and global markets.

Small outgrowers seem to be caught in a contradictory condition, as in the face of decreasing revenues from sugarcane, they have no option but to remain in the business because of the absence of alternatives. Consequently, they find it very difficult to move away from sugarcane, as crop diversification has become basically impossible, because access to credit, inputs and social services (including school access for the children) can only be obtained through association membership, and because escalating pressures over land have reduced the options for crop diversification.

An inclusive business model?

Nowadays, the entire complex of KSCL includes large-scale irrigated plantations totalling 10,445 ha, two sugar factories (KI and KII) and a recently built 12 million litre distillery, which started to produce extra-neutral alcohol from molasses in October 2013. As an intermediate product to produce cognac and other beverages, this is sold mainly to Tanzanian distilleries, Tanzanian breweries and to the medical and health sector. With an annual income of 240 billion Tsh and production estimated at 129,737 tons of sugar per year – a 15% increase over that produced in the previous year[98] – the complex is recognised by the Illovo Group as combining high levels of productivity, full-capacity utilisation, energy efficiency and corporate social responsibility.[99] The system of large-scale estates plus nucleus outgrowers has been defined as an 'inclusive business model'.[100] This argument is resonant with pro-inclusion donor-driven and policy-oriented analysis based in new institutional economics, which argue that outgrowers' schemes protect small-scale farmers against market risks, as companies provide farmers with reliable access to input supply and guaranteed market access.[101] Outgrowers' schemes have found increased political legitimisation among transnational corporations and governments, as claims of inclusivity allow them to repel allegations of 'land grabbing' by advocacy and civil society groups. Though it is indisputable that KSCL has been increasingly sharing profit opportunities with local propertied and entrepreneurial classes, it is equally important to underscore that the exposure to market risks, especially in relation to price volatility and cost-price squeeze, similarly increased.

The preoccupation of corporate and donor discourses is extremely biased towards how to make markets work for the poor,[102] silencing questions of how markets have been historically and asymmetrically constructed. This perspective of enquiry is extremely ahistorical and ideological, as the focus of the question is devoid of political content and ignores the uneven power relations in which these schemes are embedded. It in fact neglects the ways in which risks have been externalised by companies to smallholders who have been increasingly bearing the costs of an increasingly over-subsidised and distorted global sugar market.

In this context, the proposition that the crisis of sugar revenues in Tanzania is merely the result of illegal sugar imports or low import duties in the East African Community,[103] which engendered a flow of cheap sugar from Brazil and Indonesia, ignores the systemic trends of global overproduction, the proliferation of financial speculative influences, and the wider dynamics of power and accumulation on a global level within which Tanzania is implicated. Changes in sugar and other food prices cannot be simply explained through market fundamentals. Similarly, changes in the EU trade governance with developing countries substantially reduced the price paid for sugar established in the frame of ACP.[104]

Though in condition of quasi-monopoly the company has, in theory, the power to impose lower sugarcane prices to outgrowers, an alternative explanation can be found in gradually increasing costs involved in the cultivation and processing of sugarcane. Where land and labour are fixed, costs of production are not constant. In order to maintain certain levels of production and profitability, the industrial model of mechanised agriculture needs growing quantities of energy, in the form of machines and fertilizers at any new agricultural cycle.[105] According to the second principle of thermodynamics each time that energy is converted from a state to another one, we witness a 'penalization' which consists of energy lost which cannot be recovered. Entropy is the measure of this loss of energy which cannot be again transformed in labour.[106] In the long run, the constant application of rising quantities of fertilizers, herbicides and anti-parasites greatly contributes to the reduction of soil fertility and the deterioration of the eco-system.[107] Heavy dependence on high-technology agricultural machines and petrochemical fertilizers, which generates massive emissions of CO_2 and nitrogen oxides, highlights the biophysical contradictions of industrialised agriculture.[108] I argue that the recent establishment of a distillery for ethanol production, or the recently denounced and contested attempts by the company to get more land in the valley,[109] can be seen as responses by capital to raising processing and cultivation costs and as an attempt to by-pass the limits to profitability, imposed by volatile markets, and reduce risks connected to large-scale monocultures. Raising costs of production also represent a challenge for outgrowers, who have faced rampant input and transport costs.

Specifically to sugarcane deleterious ecological implications can be inferred. The highly water- and energy-intensive character of the sugar industry, based on a fossil fuel economy, contributes to the already devastating impact of agricultural industrialisation on climate change, causing the deterioration of the material basis on which production is built. Sugar production requires huge amounts of water for irrigation and for sucrose extraction. Residents lamented that the level of the Ruaha River, from which the company draws its water, has often gone below one metre in the last few years jeopardising their agricultural livelihoods.[110] Whether this has to be attributed to illegal water channels set up by desperate small-scale farmers, as KSCL argues, or to worsening environmental conditions exasperated by droughts and other environmental shocks, the impact on food production will affect one million people dependent on the water resources downstream of the Great Ruha River.[111] Furthermore, the sugar agro-industry generates air pollution, mainly from pre-harvest burning and effluent from sugar mills, which have elevated levels of carbon monoxide and ozone in the atmosphere. Burning itself has been found to be a major cause of the decline in the soil's microbial activity and the deterioration of its physical and chemical properties, which in part explain persistent low sucrose content in outgrowers' cane. The widespread use of fertilizers, which exert higher concentrations of ammonia in the soil, list among their undesired effects that of retarding the soil of its natural fertility.

Rather than sustainable, the model is further problematic from a social point of view, as it replicates the same migrant labour system which characterised the colonial era because the company still relies on this exploitive labour form for cane cutting. The massive exploitation of migrant labour by cane outgrowers represents in this context a further insight into the dynamics of class differentiation and fragmentation. These trends in social differentiation and intra-class relations illuminate the social and political instabilities of the class compromise around sugar production.[112] Social fractures and frictions, which have progressively emerged, question the reliability of win–win narratives. Already in 1998 widespread protests emerged, especially as a result of forced displacement. In 2007, cane cutters organised a strike for better working and wage conditions. The police did not authorise the strike and repressed the demonstration killing five people. In 2009 a land NGO reported serious conflicts in the area of Ruipa and Namawala southward in the valley, as Illovo had approached village officials to obtain further land access. Villagers organised and mobilised. State repression ensued and arrests of 'troublemakers' followed. Recently the company reported several 'malicious fires' on its own estates. In 2014, the leaders of growers' associations formally protested in Dodoma about declining revenues from sugar, and asked the government to build a new mill in the area to absorb the excess cane production. The government refused as a new mill in the radius of 40–50 km would have represented a challenge to KSCL monopoly. These events signal the emergence of a multiplicity of political responses from below which, though fragmented, express the lineages of hidden and/or confrontational struggles against dispossession and over the terms of market incorporation.[113] They expose the fractures in the socio-economic structures that regulate the production, circulation and consumption of sugar in the context of deregulation, liberalisation and privatisation of land and agricultural resources under Kilimo Kwanza (Agriculture First), Tanzania's Green Revolution to transform agriculture into a modern and commercial sector.

Conclusions

South African capital long-term interests in the region actively promoted large-scale agricultural projects in less saturated markets as strategies to reinforce capital accumulation driven by growing global demand for sugar, power and ethanol. In doing so it contributed to mould specific social structures of accumulation and agrarian relations in the region. The paper argued that the expansion of large-scale agricultural initiatives in sugarcane cultivation, and the ensuing forms of smallholders' integration into capitalist markets, stimulated the creation of a class of small-scale commercially oriented smallholders adversely incorporated within vertically organised and corporate-driven transnational value chains which enhance the vulnerability of the weak segments of the productive chain to the risks and price oscillations of the market.

This study emphasised the significance of analysing the unfolding of the agrarian political economy and of the capital–smallholder relationship in the *longue durée* in order to decrypt the dynamics of agrarian change, the development of the agrarian structure and the rural power relations. Understanding endurance and change in new capital–smallholder assemblages help us to understand them in the context of capital strategies aimed at by-passing the limits to accumulation and expanding its reach in the countryside. These schemes do not signal a declining interest of agribusiness in direct production. Rather they express an increase in agribusiness control of smallholders productive and marketing activities which paves the way to new forms of integration within the circuits of agribusiness accumulation not simply as commodity-providers but as commodity/services purchasers. Such trends are reinforced by the increasingly extractive character of agribusiness productive activities spurred by the economic opportunities provided by flexi-crops and agricultural commodities in the context of growing biomass economies. The maximisation of the crushing capacity of the mill, embodied in the injunction 'Don't stop the mill' that I noticed on several no entry signposts during my first visit to Illovo industrial cluster, has become the dominant economic imperative around which agrarian social relations in the Kilombero valley have been organised. The proliferation of these schemes expanded and re-created uneven geographies of class relations and differentially impacted on rural communities, by transforming patterns of land use, intensifying food insecurity, promoting social polarisation and profoundly affecting the environmental landscape. Pro-inclusion narratives increasingly focused on the positive impact of organisational, institutional and marketing innovations promoted through contract farming. The paper instead conceived it as the site of intense social, political and economic struggles, where different interests of landowners, large-scale capitalist farmers, agribusiness and smallholders have historically been articulated.

Disclosure statement

No potential conflict of interest was reported by the author.

Funding

This work was supported by the BICAS (BRICS Initiative in Critical Agrarian Studies).

Acknowledgements

I wish to thank Lucy Misinzo for her precious fieldwork assistance in the Kilombero valley. I also need to acknowledge the support of Illovo managers who provided me with vital statistics on Illovo and KSCL. Last but not least, I need to thank the numerous outgrowers I had the opportunity to interview during fieldwork who spent time and shared their knowledge with me.

Notes

1. FAO et al., *Principles for Responsible Agricultural Investments*.
2. GRAIN, *Seized* and La via Campesina, "Conference Declaration."
3. Zoomers, "Globalization and the Foreignization of Space," 429.
4. Amanor and Moyo, *Land and Sustainable Development*.
5. World Bank, "Rising Global Interest in Farmland," vi.
6. Moyo et al., "Imperialism and Primitive Accumulation."
7. Hall, "Land Grabbing in Southern Africa."
8. Hall and Cousin, "Commercial Farming and Agribusiness in South Africa."
9. Greenberg, "Agrarian Reform and South Africa's."
10. McMichael, "A Food Regime Genealogy."
11. Hall, "The Next Great Trek?"
12. Richardson, "Big Sugar."
13. Chossudovsky, *The Globalization of Poverty*.
14. Miller, "New Regional Imaginaries."
15. Shivji, "South Africa's Second Primitive Accumulation," 38.
16. Moyo et al., "The Agrarian Question."
17. Edelman, "Messy Hectares" and Oya, "Methodological Reflections."

18. Borras and Franco, "Global Land Grabbing."
19. Peters, "Conflicts over Land."
20. Sulle, "A Hybrid Business Model."
21. Cotula and Leonard, *Alternatives to Land Acquisitions*.
22. Daviron and Gibbon, "Global Commodity Chains"; Gibbon and Ponte, *Trading Down*.
23. Bryceson, "Deagrarianization."
24. Bernstein, *Class Dynamics*.
25. Cousin, "Smallholder Irrigation Schemes."
26. Marx, *Capital*.
27. Chacage, *Land Acquisition*.
28. Sulle and Hall, *Reframing a New Alliance*.
29. Bond and Garcia, *BRICS: Anti-Capitalist Critique*.
30. Cheru and Modi, "Introduction."
31. Martin, "South Africa," 180.
32. Borras, et al., "Politics of Agrofuel."
33. Hall and Cousins, "Commercial Farming."
34. Sauer and Pietrafesa, "Cana de Açugar."
35. Smalley et al., "The Role of the State."
36. Illovo, *Integrated Report*, 6.
37. Ibid., 46.
38. Borras et al., "The Rise of Flex Crops," 2.
39. McKay et al., "The Politcal Economy," 20.
40. Illovo, *Integrated Report*, 96.
41. McKay et al., The Political Economy, 21.
42. Interview, KSCL Corporate Manager, 5 June 2014.
43. Furfural is an organic compound derived from a variety of agricultural by-products and used as an extractive solvent in the purification of base oils.
44. Phytofortifiers/soil improvers, fertilizers, fungicides and agricultural nematicides.
45. Illovo, *Integrated Report*, 27.
46. Nkonya and Barrero-Hurle, *Analysis of Incentives*.
47. Beck, "The Kilombero Valley," 37.
48. East African Royal Commission, *1953–55 Report*.
49. Sprenger, *Sugarcane Outgrowers*, 11.
50. Kopoka, *Acquisitions and Utilization*, 8.
51. Baum, "Land Use."
52. Beck, "The Kilombero Valley," 39.
53. Cliffe and Cunningham, "Ideology."
54. Huizer, "The Ujamaa Village," 3.
55. Cliffe, "Nationalism."
56. Kopoka, *Acquisitions and Utilization*, 18.
57. Sprenger, *Sugarcane Outgrowers*, 11.
58. Baum, "Land Use," 23.
59. Kopoka, *Acquisitions and Utilization*, 19.
60. see Cliffe, "Rural Class Formation," 206.
61. The policy of territorial (re)organisation which prescribed the creation of new administrative entities and villages in which local population were often coercively assembled allegedly in order to facilitate services provision.
62. Sprenger, *Sugarcane Outgrowers*, 11.
63. Smalley et al., "The Role of the State," 7.
64. Ibid.
65. Kopoka, *Acquisitions and Utilization*, 20.
66. Sprenger, *Sugarcane Outgrowers*, 12.
67. Coulson, "Agricultural Policies."
68. Sprenger, *Sugarcane Outgrowers*, 13.

69. Kopoka, *Acquisitions and Utilization*, 15.
70. Tibajuka and Msambichaka, "The Role of Large-scale Farming," 68.
71. Kopoka, *Acquisitions and Utilization*, 17.
72. Wuyts, "Accumulation, Industrialization and the Peasantry," 160.
73. Bernstein, "Agricultural 'Modernization'."
74. Coulson, *Tanzania: A Political Economy*, 257.
75. Dinham and Hines, *Agribusiness in Africa*, 120.
76. Mbilinyi, "Agribusiness and Casual," 115.
77. Sprenger, *Sugarcane Outgrowers*, 16.
78. Mbilinyi and Semakafu, *Gender and Employment*.
79. Sprenger, *Sugarcane Outgrowers*, 25.
80. Though it later sold government shares.
81. Smalley et al., "The Role of the State," 7.
82. Interview, Msolwa Ujamaa outgrower, 15 June 2014.
83. Smalley et al., "The Role of the State," 12.
84. Interview, company official, 9 June 2014.
85. Smalley et al., "The Role of the State," 12.
86. Interview, company official, 10 June 2014.
87. Illovo, *Integrated Report*.
88. Interview, company official, 10 June.
89. MUCGA, Historia.
90. Interview, Msolwa Ujamaa Chairman, 13 June 2015.
91. Illovo, *Integrated Report*, 43.
92. Hickey and du Toit, "Adverse Incorporation."
93. Borras and Franco, "Global Land Grabbing."
94. Monson, *Africa's Freedom Railway*.
95. Mbiliny and Semakafu, Gender and Employment.
96. Smalley et al., "The Role of the State."
97. Bernstein, *Class Dynamics*.
98. Illovo, *Integrated Report*, 43.
99. Interview, Illovo Communication Manager, 16 November 2013.
100. Sulle, "An Hybrid Business Model."
101. Oya, "Contract Farming."
102. World Bank, *Agriculture for Development*.
103. Smalley et al., "The Role of the State" and Illovo, *Integrated Report*.
104. Richardson-Ngwenya and Richardson, "Aid for Trade."
105. Rifkin, *Entropia*.
106. Rifkin, *Entropia*, 77.
107. Altieri, "Ecological Impacts of Industrial Agriculture."
108. Weis, "The Accelerating Biophysical Contradictions."
109. HAKIARDHI, *Facts Finding*.
110. Interview, Msolwa Ujamaa outgrower, 1 July 2014.
111. Mwakalila, "Vulnerability of People's Livelihoods."
112. O'Laughlin, "Burning Cane."
113. Borras and Franco, "Global Land Grabbing."

Bibliography

Altieri, M. A. "Ecological Impacts of Industrial Agriculture and the Possibilities for Truly Sustainable Farming." In *Hungry for Profit, the Agribusiness Threat to Farmers, Food and the Environment*, edited by Henry Magdoff, John Bellamy-Foster, and Frederick Buttel, 77–92. New York: Monthly Review Press, 2000.
Amanor, Kojo, and Sam Moyo, eds. *Land and Sustainable Development*. London: Zed Books, 2008.

Baum, Eckhard. "Land Use in the Kilombero Valley: From Shifting Cultivation towards Permanent Farming." In *Smallholder Farming and Smallholder Development in Tanzania: Ten Case Studies*, edited by Hans Ruthenberg, 21–50. Munich: Weltforum Verlag, 1968.

Beck, A. D. "The Kilombero Valley of South-Central Tanganyika." *East African Geographical Review*, no. 2 (1964): 37–43.

Bernstein, Henry. "Agricultural 'Modernization' and the Era of Structural Adjustment: Observations on Sub-Saharan Africa." *The Journal of Peasant Studies* 18, no. 1 (1990): 3–35.

Bernstein, Henry. *Class Dynamics of Agrarian Change*. Halifax: Fernwood Publishing, 2010.

Bond, Patrick, and Ana Garcia, eds. *BRICS: An Anticapitalist Critique*. Chicago, IL: Haymarket Books, 2015.

Borras, S. M., David Fig, and Sofia Suárez. "The Politics of Agrofuels and Mega-Land and Water Deals: Insights from the ProCana Case, Mozambique." *Review of African Political Economy* 38, no. 128 (2011): 215–234.

Borras, Saturnino M., and J. C. Franco. "Global Land Grabbing and Political Reactions 'from Below.'" *Third World Quarterly* 34, no. 9 (2013): 1723–1747.

Borras, J. S., J. C. Franco, S. R. Isakson, Les Levidow, and Pietje Vervest. "The Rise of Flex Crops and Commodities: Implications for Research." *Journal of Peasant Studies* 43, no. 1 (2015): 93–115.

Bryceson, D. F. "Deagrarianization and Rural Employment in Sub-Saharan Africa: A Sectoral Perspective". *World Development* 24, no. 1 (1996): 97–111.

Chacage, Chambi. *Land Acquisition and Accumulation in Tanzania: The Case of Morogoro, Iringa and Pwani Regions*. Pelum Tanzania: Dar es Salaam, 2010.

Chossudovsky, Michael. *The Globalization of Poverty: Impacts of IMF and World Bank Reforms*. London: Zedbooks, 1997.

Cliffe, Lionel. "Nationalism and the Reaction to Enforced Agricultural Change in Tanganyika during the Colonial Period." In *Socialism in Tanzania*. Vol. I, edited by Lionel Cliffe and John Saul, 17–24. Dar es Salaam: East African Publishing House, 1972.

Cliffe, Lionel. "Rural Class Formation in East Africa." *The Journal of Peasant Studies* 4, no. 2 (1977): 195–224.

Cliffe, Lionel, and G. L. Cunningham. "Ideology, Organization and the Settlement Experience in Tanzania." In *In Socialism in Tanzania*. Vol. II, edited by Lionel Cliffe and John Saul, 131–140. Dar es Salaam: East African Publishing House, 1973.

Cheru, Fantu, and Renu Modi. "Introduction: Peasants, the State and Foreign Direct Investment?" In *Agricultural Development and Food Security in Africa* edited by Fantu Cheru and Renu Modi, 1–11. New York: Nordic African Institute, 2013.

Cotula, Lorenzo, and Rebeca Leonard, eds. *Alternative to Land Acquisitions: Agricultural Investment and Collaborative Business Models*. London: IIED/SDC/IFAD/CTV, 2010.

Coulson, Andrew. "Agricultural Policies in Mainland Tanzania." *Review of African Political Economy* 4, no. 10 (1977): 74–100.

Coulson, Andrew. *Tanzania: A Political Economy*. Oxford: Clarendon Press, 1982.

Cousins, Ben. "Smallholder Irrigation Schemes, Agrarian Reform and 'Accumulation from above and from below' in South Africa." *Journal of Agrarian Change* 13, no. 1 (2013): 116–139.

Daviron, Ben, and Paul Gibbon. "Global Commodity Chains and African Export Agriculture." *Journal of Agrarian Change* 2, no. 2 (2002): 137–161.

Dinham, Barbara, and Colin Hines. *Agribusiness in Africa*. London: Earth Resources Research, 1983.

East African Royal Commission. *1953–55 Report*. London: H.M.S.O, 1955.

Edelman, Marc. "Messy Hectares: Questions about the Epistemology of Land Grabbing Data." *Journal of Peasant Studies* 40, no. 3 (2013): 485–501.

FAO, IFAD, UNCTAD, and World Bank. *Principles for Responsible Agricultural Investments That Respect Rights, Livelihoods and Resources. A Note for Discussion*. Washington, DC: World Bank, 2010.

Gibbon, Peter, and Stefano Ponte. *Trading Down. Africa: Value Chains, and the Global Economy*. Philadelphia, PA: Temple University Press, 2005.

GRAIN. *Seized: The 2008 Land Grab for Food and Financial Security*. Barcelona: GRAIN, 2008.

Greenberg, Stephen. "Agrarian Reform and South Africa's Agro-Food System." *The Journal of Peasant Studies* 42, no. 5 (2015): 957–979.

HAKIARDHI. *Facts Finding Mission Report on the Prevailing Land Dispute at Namawala Village in Kilombero District, Morogoro Region*. Dar es Salaam: Land Rights and Resources Institute, 2009.

Hall, Ruth. "Land Grabbing in Southern Africa: The Many Faces of the Investor Rush." *Review of African Political Economy* 38, no. 128 (2011): 193–214.

Hall, Ruth. "The Next Great Trek? South African Commercial Farmers Move North." *The Journal of Peasant Studies* 39, nos. 3–4 (2012): 823–843.

Hall, Ruth, and Ben Cousins. "Commercial Farming and Agribusiness in South Africa and their Changing Role in Africa's Afro-Food System." Paper presented at the International Conference "Rural Transformations and Food Systems: The BRICS and Agrarian Change in the Global South", University of Western Cape, Cape Town, April 20–22, 2015.

Hickey, Sam, and Andries du Toit. "Adverse Incorporation, Social Exclusion and Chronic Poverty." Chronic Poverty Research Centre Working Paper 81. Manchester, NH: Institute for Development Policy and Management, 2007.

Huizer, Gerrit. "The Ujamaa Village Programme in Tanzania: New Forms of Rural Development." Institute of Social Studies, Occasional Papers 11. The Hague: ISS, 1971.

Illovo Sugar Limited. *Integrated Report*. Mount Edgecombe: Illovo Sugar, 2013.

Kopoka, P. A. *Acquisitions and Utilization of Technological Skills for Industrial Development: A Case Study of the Sugar Industry in Tanzania*. Dar es Salaam: University of Dar es Salaam, 1989.

La via Campesina. "Conference Declaration: Stop Land Grab Now." International Peasant Conference, Nyeleni, November 17–19, 2011.

Martin, W. G.. "South Africa and the 'New Scramble for Africa': Imperialist, Sub-imperialist, or Victim?" *Agrarian South: Journal of Political Economy* 2, no. 2 (2013): 161–188.

Marx, Karl. *Capital*. Vol. I. New York: Penguin Books, [1867] 1976.

Mbilinyi, Marjorie. "Agribusiness and Casual Labor in Tanzania." *African Economic History*, no. 15 (1986): 107–141.

Mbilinyi, Marjorie, and Maria Semakafu. *Gender and Employment on Sugarcane Plantations in Tanzania*. Geneva: ILO, 1995.

McKay, Ben, Sergio Sauer, Ben Richardson, and Roman Herre. "The Political Economy of Sugarcane Flexing: Initial Insights from Brazil, Southern Africa and Cambodia." *Journal of Peasant Studies* 43, no. 1 (2015): 195–223.

McMichael, Philip. "A Food Regime Genealogy." *The Journal of Peasant Studies* 36, no. 1 (2009): 139–169.

Miller, Darlene. "New Regional Imaginaries in Post-Apartheid Southern Africa: Retail Workers at a Shopping Mall in Zambia." *Journal of Southern African Studies* 31, no. 1 (2005): 97–125.

Monson, Jamie. *Africa's Freedom Railway: How a Chinese Development Project Changed Lives and Livelihoods in Tanzania*. Bloomington: Indiana University Press, 2009.

Moyo, Sam, Paris Yeros, and Praveen Jha. "The Agrarian Question: Past, Present and Future." *The Agrarian South: A Journal of Political Economy* 1, no. 1 (2012): 1–10.

Moyo, Sam, Paris Yeros, and Praveen Jha. "Imperialism and Primitive Accumulation: Notes on a New Scramble for Africa". *The Agrarian South: A Journal of Political Economy* 1, no. 2 (2012): 181–203.

Msolwa Ujamaa Cane Growers Association. 2013. *Historia Fupi Kuhusu Chama Cha MUCGA* [A Brief History of MCGA Association]. Msolwa Ujamaa.

Mwakalila, Shadrack. "Vulnerability of People's Livelihoods to Water Resources Availability in Semi Arid Areas of Tanzania." *Journal of Water Resource and Protection* 3, no. 9 (2011): 678–685.

Nkonya, Nganga, and Jesus Barrero-Hurle. *Analysis of Incentives and Disincentives for Sugar in the United Republic of Tanzania*. Technical Notes Series, MAFAP. Rome: FAO, 2012.

O'Laughlin, Bridget. "Burning Cane: Sugar, Land, Work and Health in Southern Africa." Paper presented at the Conference "Land Divided: Land and South African Society in 2013 in Comparative Perspective", Cape Town, March 24–27, 2013.

Oya, Carlos. "Contract Farming in Sub-Saharan Africa: A Survey of Approaches, Debates and Issues." *Journal of Agrarian Change* 12, no. 1 (2012): 1–33.

Oya, Carlos. "Methodological Reflections on 'Land Grab' Databases and the 'Land Grab' Literature 'Rush'." *Journal of Peasant Studies* 40, no. 3 (2013): 503–520.

Peters, P. E. "Conflicts over Land and Threats to Customary Tenure in Africa." *African Affairs* 112, no. 449 (2013): 543–562.

Richardson, Ben. "Big Sugar in Southern Africa." *Journal of Peasant Studies* 37, no. 4, 609–629.

Richardson-Ngwenya, Pamela, and Ben Richardson. "Aid for Trade and African Agriculture: The Bittersweet Case of Swazi Sugar." *Review of African Political Economy* 41, no. 140 (2014): 201–215.

Rifkin, Jeremy. *Entropy: A New World View*. New York: Bantam Books, 1981.

Sauer, Sergio, and J. P. Pietrafesa. "Cana de açugar, financiamento publico e produçao de alimentos no Cerrado." *Revista de Geografia Agraria* 7, no. 14 (2012): 1–29.

Shivji, Issa. "South Africa's Second Primitive Accumulation." *CODESRIA Bulletin*, no. 3–4 (2005): 37–38.

Smalley, Rebeca, Emmanuel Sulle, and Lameck Malale. "The Role of the State and Foreign Capital in Agricultural Commercialization: The Case of Sugarcane out Growers in Kilombero District, Tanzania." Future-Agricultures Consortium, Working Paper 106. Brighton: University of Sussex.

Sprenger, Ellen. *Sugarcane Outgrowers and Kilombero Sugar Company in Tanzania*. Nijmegen: Third World Centre, 1989.

Sulle, Emmanuel. "An Hybrid Business Model: The Case of Sugarcane Producers in Tanzania." In *Alternative to Land Acquisitions: Agricultural Investment and Collaborative Business Models*, edited by Lorenzo Cotula and Rebeca Leonard, 71–80. London: IIED, 2010.

Sulle, Emmanuel, and Ruth Hall. *Reframing the New Alliance Agenda: A Critical Assessment Based on Insights from Tanzania*. Future Agriculture Consortium, Policy Brief 56. Brighton: University of Sussex.

Tibajuka, A. K., and L. A. Msambichaka. 1984. "The Role of Large-scale Farming in Tanzania". In *Readings of Economic Policies of Tanzania*, edited by L. A. Msambichaka and Sripati Chandrasekhar, 68–84. Economic Research Bureau, University of Dar es Salaam.

Weis, T. "The Accelerating Biophysical Contradictions of Industrial Capitalist Agriculture." *Journal of Agrarian Change* 10, no. 3 (2010): 315–341.

World Bank. *Agriculture for Development: World Development Report 2008*. Washington, DC: The World Bank, 2007.

World Bank. *Rising Global Interest in Farmland: Can It Yield Sustainable and Equitable Benefits?* Washington, DC: The World Bank, 2010.

Wuyts, Marc. "Accumulation, Industrialization and the Peasantry: A Reinterpretation of the Tanzania Experience." *Journal of Peasant Studies* 21, no. 2 (1994): 159–193.

Zoomers, Annelies. "Globalization and the Foreignization of Space: Seven Processes Driving the Current Global Land Grab." *The Journal of Peasant Studies* 37, no. 2 (2010): 429–447.

'Export or die': the rise of Brazil as an agribusiness powerhouse

Daniela Andrade ⓘ

ABSTRACT

This article explores the relationship between the rise of Brazil as an agribusiness powerhouse, the country's recent economic upswing and its subsequent crisis. Agribusiness is analysed in the context of the overall dynamics of production, trade and capital flows that have emerged since the neoliberal policy reforms of the 1990s. Statistical series on the country's Balance of Payments (BoP), macroeconomic and sector parameters show that the expansion of agribusiness is part and parcel of a policy-induced phenomenon of primary commodities export specialisation, which conjugates with BoP fragility, the reproduction of debt and external dependence – the core of the current crisis.

Introduction

In the course of the 2000s, the expansion of agribusiness production and exports has boosted economic growth in Brazil, contributing to its rise as an emerging economy and a major player in the global food system. Brazilian agribusiness has been predicated as strategic for economic and political power, including a place in global decision-making. Brazil has become a major supplier of a range of agro-commodities, a leader of the developing countries' coalition in agricultural negotiations at the World Trade Organisation (WTO), and a frontrunner of agribusiness expansion in Latin America, and more recently, in Sub-Saharan Africa. Important parameters justifying the country's membership of the BRICS (Brazil, Russia, India, China and South-Africa), such as the level of foreign reserves, inflow of foreign investments or GDP growth, have hinged upon the performance of its agribusiness sector. In 2007, when commodity prices peaked, most of the developing world suffered, but Brazil had its best economic performance in years, with 6.1% economic growth. Following the outbreak of the global financial crisis in 2008, the economy had a hiccup but continued to flourish – reaching a 7.5% growth rate in 2010 – while advanced economies were still in economic distress. However, even though the agricultural sector has kept breaking harvest and revenue records until today, Brazil plunged into the most severe economic crisis of the last 25 years in 2011, when growth fell to 3.9%, then to 1.9% in 2012, 0.1% in 2014 and −3.8% in 2015, thus technically entering into recession.[1] With cuts in credit, social spending, investments, wages and employment, the economy was in full-blown recession by 2016. How to make sense of that?

These events call into question not the agribusiness expansion, but its contextual meaning – not Brazil's growth as such, but its patterns of growth. The question is not about what went suddenly wrong in country's trajectory, but how events have been explained. This article explores the relationship between the empirical rise of Brazilian agribusiness and its fundamental historical and material sense (or essence), which is abstracted from its relations with the broader economy and its logic of reproduction and accumulation.

A brief historical overview shows the mutual development of agriculture with national capitalism until the transition to neoliberalism. The main aspects of this major economic reorganisation are explained in their historical unfolding, as they set the ground for the advancement of agro-commodities exports. Using statistical series from the country's Balance of Payments (BoP), macroeconomic and sector parameters, agribusiness expansion is analysed in the context of the overall transformations in the patterns of production, trade and capital flows, underpinned since the neoliberal policy reforms of the 1990s.

The analysis shows that the rise of Brazil as an agribusiness powerhouse is part and parcel of the economy-wide effects of financialisation, sponsored by state macroeconomic policies. While these policies have created opportunities for transnational financial – and often speculative – gains, they have also undermined production and exports, particularly in the industrial sector, inducing a process of primary commodities export specialisation. As it is discussed, reprimarisation has contributed to BoP fragility, the reproduction of debt and external dependence, which are at the core of the current crisis.

Agriculture and domestic capitalist development

Agriculture has marked the economic development of Brazil, although not always in the same way: the patterns of production have transformed, and so have the economic and social roles of agriculture. Until the Great Depression in 1930, agriculture and resource extraction were at the centre of domestic accumulation and economic development, and agro-extractive exports comprised the material basis of Brazil's relations with the rest of the world. After 1930, agriculture transformed along with the process of industrialisation and (in the 1990s) financialisation; both processes have redefined the dominant system of economic reproduction and accumulation.

When industrial production began to drive economic growth, the development of agriculture was subsumed to industrial expansion. Even if coffee remained the country's main export item for at least two more decades, the foreign exchange generated was a source of finance for imports of industrial equipment and machinery. Yet, that has allowed the plantation farms to continue existing, as well as the agrarian oligarchy, although they increasingly shared the political control of the state with the emerging industrial bourgeoisie.[2] The economic and political dominance of the latter became evident when the state placed the policy of 'Import Substitution Industrialisation' (ISI) at the heart of its national development project.

In the mid-1960s and 1970s, agriculture itself began to industrialise, incorporating industrial technology through a significant credit package promoted by the state.[3] Farms were integrated with upstream and downstream industry as a consumer of machinery and agro-inputs and supplier of raw material for processed consumer goods for the national and international market.[4] That was the origin of the Brazilian Agro-Industrial Complex, as progress in farming became linked to industrial capital and dynamics of accumulation.[5] The substantial and consistent growth of agricultural exports in this period shows that ISI and export-oriented agriculture were complementary strategies.[6] The Brazilian industry, once designed to serve the domestic market, did not generate foreign exchange necessary for its expansion, thus relying on the agro-export sector. Notably, Brazil became one of the most important 'New Industrial and Agricultural Countries' (NICs and NACs).[7]

Agro-exports, however, were an insufficient source of foreign exchange, exposing a structural flaw of ISI. The country increasingly resorted to foreign loans to acquire abroad crucial capital goods. By the 1970s, international creditors were essentially financing Brazil's 'economic miracle'.

Financial dependence – and the growth of external debt – became a problem only when Brazil's main creditor, the United States, endured two oil price shocks (in 1973 and 1979), followed by the stock market crash and recession. Interest rates in global capital markets skyrocketed, practically impeding access to international capital, besides provoking a dramatic increase in the cost of servicing the external debt. Indebtedness and debt service suddenly became inhibitors of growth.[8] In face of the greatest recession throughout the1980s, ISI was abandoned. The support for agro-exports, however, was maintained by the state[9] – this time, not to help to finance industry, but to service external debt.

The 1980s crisis and the changes it inflicted in the functioning of the economy reflected not only the structural limits of ISI, but also the fast-advancing process of financialisation of capitalism at the global scale – a process that has underpinned a 'worldwide shift towards neoliberalism'.[10] Neoliberalism encompassed a historic and systemic reorganisation of the material base for economic, social and political reproduction globally.[11] The control of financial capital over all spheres of production was a defining character of that reorganisation.[12] Before discussing how the transformations in agriculture were linked to neoliberalism, the next section explains the key aspects of neoliberalism itself and how it formed new patterns of growth.

Macroeconomic stability, consumption-led growth and foreign financing

In the transition from the 1980s to the 1990s, the state implemented successive policy and institutional reforms in an attempt to gain economic efficiency and recover previous economic dynamism.[13] The reforms had an underlying idea: the state should free the market from (state) regulation, and transfer (to the market) part of its functions and assets. That implied, among other things, privatisation of state-owned productive enterprises and services (including financial services), fiscal and labour market reforms, but most important, it included the liberalisation of trade, finance and capital flows. The control of debt and inflation were also central and led to the institutionalisation of contractionary fiscal and monetary policies.[14]

In 1994, a major economic plan, named the *Real*[15] Plan finally succeeded to contain inflation, promoting a 'virtuous circle of macroeconomic stability and consumption-led growth financed by foreign capital'.[16] Besides their role in taming inflation, combined effects of high interest rates, fixed exchange-rate at an overvalued rate and trade liberalisation were also highly appealing to consumers; imported goods were made affordable and available, also forcing an overall decline in local prices.[17] The initial success of the *Real* Plan helped its main architect – the then Minister of Finance, Fernando Henrique Cardoso (from the Social Democratic Party, PSDB) – to the Presidency of the country for two consecutive terms (1995–2003).

From 1993 to 1997, the volume of imports in Brazil skyrocketed from US$25.3 to US$59.7 billion, while exports increased at a much-reduced pace. Already in 1995, a trade deficit began to develop. In 1997, Brazil had a US$6.8 billion trade deficit, while in 1993 it had a US$13.3 billion surplus.[18] Behind the trade deficit, there was an abrupt process of deindustrialisation and increasing unemployment.[19]

At first, the trade deficit did not prevent imports or require a currency devaluation. Attracted by macroeconomic stability – and liberalised capital account – foreign investments returned to the country, financing the on-going consumption, as well as state expenses.

Keeping high interest rates, the state not only controlled inflation but was also able to regularly sell National Treasury bonds of the public debt in the national and international market, transforming debt into an asset to finance its expenses. The unprecedented increase in foreign portfolio investments reflected the interest of the international financial market in the high levels of financial return of the Brazilian Treasury bonds indexed to the interest and exchange rates. Yet, there was no magic trick: a new indebtedness cycle was inaugurated. The external debt – formed earlier through abundant external loans – was gradually being repaid, but substituted by an internal public debt, incurred by the sale of Treasury bonds in the national market. Yet, foreign investors were among creditors of the internal debt.

The main owners of the internal debt bonds were national investors, particularly public and private banks. Nonetheless, their investments were often coupled with external borrowing, thus also linked to a foreign creditor. With interest rates higher in Brazil than in the rest of the world, national banks and firms were stimulated to borrow abroad, and to invest not in production but in public debt bonds. As a consequence, the external private debt skyrocketed from less than US$10 billion in 1990 to US$116 billion in 1998.[20] However, once acquiring public debt bonds, national banks and firms perversely converted private external debt into public internal debt. Since 1994, the internal debt has escalated.[21]

The rapid increase of domestic assets owned by foreigners (including the public debt, state-owned enterprises and services) engendered an immediate rise of outflow of profit and dividends earned by foreigners. Income outflow was also enhanced by the interest paid on external private loans. Income repatriation, more than the trade of goods and services deficit, became the largest burden of the current account of the BoP – a burden that, in the 1980s, mostly corresponded to the interest paid on the public external debt.

In the timespan of five years, the current account deficit expanded from US$0.7 billion in 1993 to US$33.4 billion in 1998. Evidently, this translated into a structural and self-propelling vulnerability of the domestic economy, increasingly dependent on absorbing external savings to finance itself. The Brazilian external exposure was exacerbated in the context of great instability of international financial markets, affected by a sequence of currency and financial crises (Mexican in 1994, Asian in 1997 and Russian in 1998). In 1999, Brazil became the centre of a currency crisis of its own: foreign investors, fearing the government would fail to finance the BoP deficit and provoke an external default, promoted a massive asset sale (or a 'capital flight'), which led to the collapse of the domestic currency and depletion of foreign reserves. National banks and firms, fearing currency devaluation itself, anticipated the payment of their external debt, consuming foreign reserves of the Central Bank – which, in turn, resorted to interest rate increase to stimulate the return of foreign capital, yet promoting further recession and unemployment.

Erupting only five years after the start of the *Real* Plan, the crisis exposed the flaws of the new growth model, of which the state was the main agent. Yet, its core premises were maintained or deepened as 'solutions' to the crisis itself. President Cardoso's policy response consolidated the macroeconomic policy regime 'tripod':[22] (1) rigid monetary policy, tied to inflation targets and high interest rates; (2) fiscal policy attached to ambitious annual targets of the primary fiscal surplus, aiming to compensate the nominal public deficit and (3) a floating exchange rate regime, which allows the currency to fluctuate according to the market. This tripod, as will be seen below, has been maintained until the present.

Although the tripod policy regime intended to stabilise the public debt, the current account and prevent the return of inflation, it was structurally limited. As Mollo and Saad-Filho explain, currency depreciation favoured the stabilisation of the current account, but brought inflation back and increased the debt servicing. The debt was difficult to stabilise, as interest rates could not be significantly lowered, being a mechanism to control inflation and attract foreign capital, as well as avoid its outflow. High interest rates imposed a high cost of servicing the debt, besides constraining growth and investment.[23] That has limited fiscal revenue, leaving the state with little choice but to raise taxes and cut spending.[24] In brief, the country had fallen into a 'macroeconomic policy trap'.[25]

The policy trap creating BoP instability and dependence on foreign capital was, in fact, political. While premised upon the control of debt and inflation, 'technical' measures introduced by the *Real* Plan have in fact driven the process of financialisation of the Brazilian economy, including of the state's finances. That has inaugurated structural changes in the workings of the economy as a whole. The following section returns to the issue of agriculture and agribusiness, revealing how its role within the broader economy was re-defined in the early 2000s.

The expansion of agribusiness exports

Agribusiness for macroeconomic stabilisation (1999–2003)

With little margin for policy manoeuvre, re-adjusting the current account became a matter of either 'export or die'– as appealed President Cardoso in 2001 at the swearing in ceremony of the Minister of Development, Sérgio Amaral.[26] In that context, the agricultural export sector was re-launched as the country's best asset.[27] Until the mid-1990s, however, the sector was highly indebted, having been badly hit by inflation and a sequence of unsuccessful inflation-curbing plans that sent false signals to investors.[28] With the stabilisation of inflation, though, access to credit and new investments were stimulated. Also, in the harvest season of 1995/96, the rural debt was renegotiated and partly assumed by the state (which converted it into public debt bonds).[29] Furthermore, in September 1996, a large fiscal incentive for export was put into effect with the approval of a law (*Lei Kandir*) that exonerated primary and semi-manufactured products from trade tax ('ICMS').[30]

With the exchange rate devaluation in the early 2000s, the agricultural export sector was ready to take off. The country adopted an aggressive position in the negotiations at the World Trade Organisation (WTO) to increase access of Brazilian agro-exporters to international markets. In 2002, Brazil launched two landmark disputes (which it won in 2005) against US and EU subsidies.[31] Brazilian exports began to reach new commercial partners, particularly, China. Favoured by increasing Asian demand, agribusiness exports increased 50% from 1999 to 2003 – while agribusiness imports decreased 17% – thus generating a substantial surplus that began to counteract the total trade balance deficit (Figure 1).

Of course, trade expansion was coupled with progress in agriculture itself. Advancements in land and labour productivity, gains in scale of production and in total output resulted from state support on several fronts. Policies for agricultural modernisation adopted in the 1960s-70s – but dismantled in the early 1990s – were reintroduced. The National System of Rural Credit (NSRC) was perhaps the most important of them. Also, the incorporation of science and technology resulted in enormous gains in productivity – the main driver of the output increase, according to the Institute for Applied Economic Research (IPEA). Such achievement also reflected the efforts of the Brazilian Enterprise of Agricultural Research (Embrapa).[32]

Despite these positive results in agriculture, the economic context in 2002 was worsening. With a presidential election on the horizon generating further uncertainty, the domestic currency reached its lowest value, inflation was back to the levels of 1995 – and much higher than the target agreed with the IMF. The short-term nominal interest rate (*Selic* rate) was above 20% per annum,[33] foreign reserves were down to US$38 billion and the 'Brazil Risk' reached its historical high.[34] The multiple crises since 1999 cost the election for Cardoso's party and, in October 2002, Luiz Inácio Lula da Silva, from the Workers' Party (PT), was elected as President.

From the start, managing the immediate problems mentioned above, imposed an enormous pressure on President Lula's government. The 'need' to bring back macroeconomic stability, control the fiscal and external risks, regain market credibility and restore the

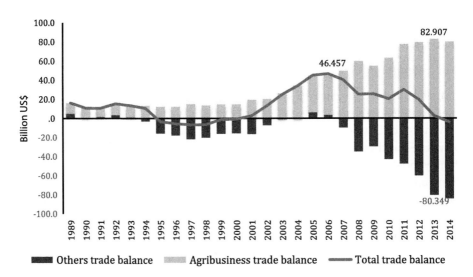

Figure 1. Agribusiness net export and 'all others' net export (1989–2014). Source: Ministry of Agriculture, Livestock and Supply (MAPA); Author's Elaboration.

Notes: The agribusiness trade balance estimated by the MAPA represents the total exports/ imports of all products of animal origin (including fishery and aquaculture), vegetal origin (including forest products and flowers) and the products of low-technology agro-industry (food, beverages, tobacco, oils, vegetable waxes, as well as furs, leather, fibres, natural fabrics), rubber, wood and cellulose.

confidence of foreign investors in the economy forced him to comply with the macroeco-nomic policy regime of his predecessor. Lula's acquiescence, in fact, was a political condition for power itself. Throughout all the Workers' Party administrations – lasting until September 2016 – the policy tripod has been upheld practically unchanged.

In 2003, the first year of his mandate, besides gradually soothing the tensions of the financial market, Lula harvested the results of the currency devaluation[35] and policy reforms initiated by Cardoso. The current account was back in surplus, leveraged by the 52% improve-ment in exports since 1999, while imports decreased only 2%. Net services and income remained practically unchanged, which means that agro-exports were largely responsible for improving the current account balance. At the end of 2004, Lula's second year in office, the trade surplus was larger than US$33 billion dollars – the seventh largest in the world.[36] With a substantial trade surplus-to-imports ratio the country began to generate 'a sizeable free cash flow for each dollar of additional exports, making it easier to earn the foreign currency it need[ed] to keep servicing the debt'[37] – besides building up its foreign reserves. The period of crisis was coming to an end, and the country was seemingly on the right path to take off.

The economic upturn

Agribusiness for growth and global power (2004–2008)

Between 2004 and 2008, average annual GDP growth rate was 5%, against 2% between 1999 and 2003. It is worth noting right away that, despite the improvement, the average growth rate in Brazil was still much lower than other emerging economies, the reason for which is commented below. The recovery of economic growth in this period was largely driven by the primary, or natural resource sectors, especially mining, oil and agriculture.

In Lula's administration, foreign trade gained major relevance. Lula himself made great efforts towards opening markets for Brazilian exports and was successful, as he encountered an international commodity market in expansion and prices on the rise – indeed, the begin-ning of the global 'commodities boom'. With exceptional global market prices for Brazilian exported commodities, agribusiness became more than a strategy for macroeconomic adjustment, but itself a driver of growth.

From 2004 to 2008, agribusiness exports generated an ever-increasing trade surplus, at an average of 19% increase per year, going from US$ 34.2 billion to approximately US$60.0 billion.[38] In 2010, the country was the world's biggest exporter of a series of agricultural products – coffee, sugar, orange juice, tobacco, ethanol, beef and poultry – and the sec-ond-biggest source of soy.[39] That was accompanied by record yields, year after year, pro-moted through the massive boost in the budget allocated to the NSRC, which reached US$38.4 billion of rural credit disbursed in the 2007/2008 harvest season, and US$82.8 billion in 2013/2014.[40]

In this period, food and agribusiness enterprises became some of the largest Brazilian transnational companies – in fact, the world's largest in several production segments.[41] That has been the case, for example, with companies involved in the internationalisation of the beef industry, such as Marfrig, JBS Friboi and Brazil Foods. Major public and private Brazilian firms operating in the natural resource-intensive sectors have also received long-term subsidised loans from the National Development Bank (BNDES) to consolidate their market position and expand operations abroad.[42]

Commodities export earnings enabled more public investments, credits, employment, tax collection and improved public budget, in a positive virtuous circle. That also favoured the accommodation – and expansion – of heterodox social policies of 'unquestionable – though provisional – success', delivering substantial gains in terms of employment, distribution and citizenship.[43] The increase in employment rates, real minimum wage, compensatory income distribution programmes and access to popular consumer credits boosted domestic consumption, the second pillar of the Brazilian growth model.

Both drivers of growth, primary exports and consumption, benefited and relied upon foreign investments and state policy support. Investors were attracted by the opportunities in the primary sector, as well as by the growing domestic market.

The World Investment Report 2009 showed that Brazilian agriculture received the third largest amount of FDI in the world in the period 2005–07, being only behind China and Malaysia.[44] In 2008, Brazil received half of the FDI inflow of the entire Latin America and Caribbean region, 34% of which was directed to the primary sector.[45] That is also indicative of the process of financialisation and internationalisation of Brazilian agribusiness at the farm and agro-industrial level.

The massive inflow of capital throughout this period forced the Central Bank to regularly buy hard currency in the exchange market to control the expansion of the monetary base and, thus its inflationary effect. That operation, called sterilisation, consisted of the purchase of foreign currency, not with domestic currency, but with government securities. That also explains why interest rates in Brazil were constantly high. For each dollar acquired, a debt of equal value in local currency (thus, multiplied by the exchange rate) was created. With such operation, Brazil increased its foreign reserves, which jumped from US$85.8 billion in December 2006 to US$180 billion in December 2007, reaching US$363.5 billion in December 2014.[46] Yet, that external asset was formed along with a corresponding internal debt, which implied a social fiscal cost, compromising the country's present and future income.[47]

After the global financial crisis in 2008, GDP collapsed, but the economy re-bounded in 2010, when Brazil reached a growth rate of 7.5%, its best performance. Having large foreign reserves at the time, the government was able to prevent a currency shock. In fact, it was able to react in the opposite direction compared to the 1999/2002 crises, adopting expansionary policy measures. In her first mandate (2011–2014), President Dilma Rousseff opened more room for growth, reducing the interest rate to the lowest level of the last two decades, introducing some capital controls, promoting selected sectors of the industry, among other interventions that made her administration the most heterodox of all PT's mandates – but only for a very short period.

The exceptional abundance of international liquidity also played a major role in Brazil's prompt economic recovery. In 2010, the country had accumulated 3.4% of the global stock of foreign investment, jumping from the 18th position in 2006 to the 7th as a destination of foreign investments – and the 1st position among the BRICS (retaken by China in 2011).[48] As various studies have observed,[49] the 2008 global financial meltdown further underpinned the entry of financial (and speculative) capital into agriculture, land and primary commodity production[50] – in a clear demonstration of the systemic integration of agribusiness with global circuits of financial capital. Brazil itself was also expanding agribusiness investments abroad. In 2009, for example, ProSavana was launched: an ambitious, and also controversial project to promote large-scale, export-oriented production of soybeans (but also corn and cotton) in Mozambique. ProSavana involved private agribusiness firms, complex global financing and diplomatic support from the Brazilian state in a trilateral cooperation agreement with Japan and Mozambique.

By the end of the decade, Brazil was not only thriving but also suggesting that neoliberalism, growth, global power and also equity, could be compatible. Yet, far from showing that its development dynamics were reason for optimism, the country's success (and shortly, its fall) showed precisely the contrary.[51]

From miracle to mirage

In 2014, GDP growth was zero, inflation was above Central Bank targets, the local currency was depreciating rapidly, unemployment was on the rise, the target of the primary fiscal surplus could not be met for the first time and the current account reached an unprecedented deficit. How to make sense of that?

Despite the persistent increase of net agribusiness-exports until the present day, the trade balance was in decline since 2006 (see Figure 2). It is also evident that after 2005, the (historical) deficit of services and income flows began to widen, particularly in the years of highest annual growth (2007–08, 2010–11). As expected, the current account balance was in a downward slope from 2008 onwards, as shown in Figure 3. This suggests that not only was the current account manifesting the burdens of the past, but also that these burdens were systemically related to the country's pattern of growth. Furthermore, it suggests that the relations previously observed between agribusiness trade performance, current account adjustment and recovery of economic growth were circumstantial; the continuous expansion of the agribusiness sector, however, seemed permanent and structural.

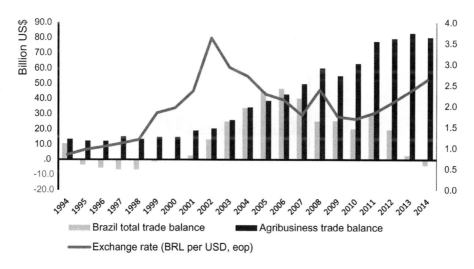

Figure 2. Brazil's overall and agribusiness trade balance (1994–2014). Source: MAPA.

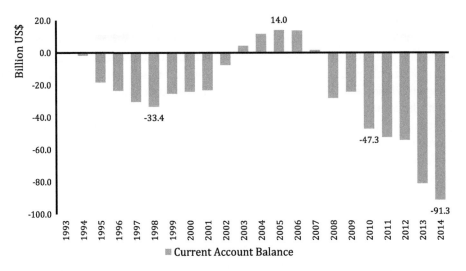

Figure 3. Current account balance: 1993–2014. Source: Brazilian Central Bank (Balance of Payments Series).

The pattern of growth, accumulation and trade

For the second time, Brazil is experiencing crisis after a period of accelerated growth. The fact that current account declines when growth accelerates reveals, first, the continuity, and second, the perverse character of the prevailing pattern of accumulation since 1990s. High interest rates and exchange rate appreciation have been the two main mechanisms undermining the overall transactions of goods, services and income with the world economy. Interest and exchange rates have also conditioned the forms and intensity of transnational financial gains.

State-sponsored high interest rates have intensified the inflow of foreign capital (Figure 4), which again explains the increase in income remittances (Figure 5) during the economic upturn.

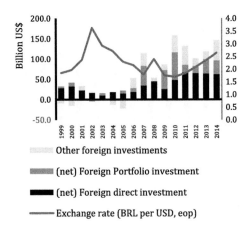

Figure 4. Net foreign investment by type and the exchange rate (1999–2014). Source: Brazilian Central Bank (BoP series) and IPEAdata (Exchange rate Series).

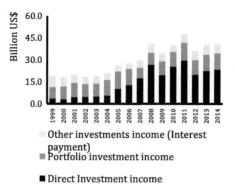

Other investments income (Interest payment)
Portfolio investment income

Direct Investment income

Figure 5. Net income outflow by type of foreign investment (1999–2014). Source: Brazilian Central Bank (BoP series) and IPEAdata (Exchange rate Series).

Foreign capital deriving from the primary commodities exports and foreign investments has flooded the domestic exchange market, provoking a progressive appreciation of the currency. Brazilian private banks and firms borrowing capital abroad at favourable rates – particularly since 2006 – also contributed to the massive inflow of foreign currency.[52] Brazil had 'one of the most appreciated currencies in the emerging world'.[53] However, differently from the years of the *Real* Plan –when overvalued currency resulted from a fixed exchange rate defined by the Central Bank – now currency appreciation was a systemic outcome of the growth model, anchored in foreign capital and markets. Yet, overvaluation itself is ultimately the result of a political choice: allowing the exchange rate to fluctuate according to market forces.

As mentioned before, the appreciation of the exchange rate increases the real return of foreign investments that are converted back to hard currency, thus stimulating both remittances and more foreign investments, in a self-indulging, manipulative scheme. From December 2008 to December 2009, a year of negative growth, the domestic currency appreciated more than 26% against the dollar. A foreign investor who bought domestic public debt bonds at the end of 2008 received, in one year, an average of 14% of interest (based on the Selic rate Dec 2008), plus the additional increase of 26% if earnings were converted back in dollars – that means, over 40% in real dollar gains.

In contrast, exchange rate appreciation constrained exports and hindered production. In the more sophisticated industrial segments – producing more technology and value-added products – the volume of imports increased more than its exports, thus, generating a bulky trade deficit (Figure 6). The opposite case is observed in the agribusiness and primary sectors in general – the producers of low-technology and low value-added products – where a robust surplus was generated (Figure 7).

As Carneiro explains, such a dynamic reflects the new industrial profile of the country, developed since the end of ISI and the beginning of neoliberal macroeconomic policies. The sudden exposure to international competition, overvalued exchange rate and privatisation in the early 1990s has led to the dismantling of certain industries, making production chains less integrated and more dependent on the import of production inputs.[54] Putting it differently, the domestic production of value-added and technology have been replaced by the consumption of imported goods – precisely the opposite of ISI. Despite having reached a significant level of industrial diversification in the 1980s, part of the Brazilian industry was gradually reduced to assemblers (of imported inputs) – or *maquilas*.[55] With the recovery of

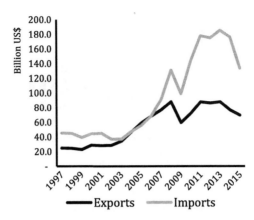

Figure 6. Import and exports from medium-low, medium-high and high technology industry (1997–2015). Source: Ministry of Industry, Foreign Trade and Services (MDIC).

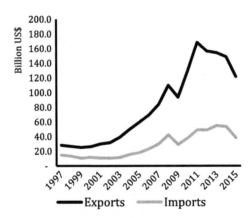

Figure 7. Import and exports of commodities and products of low-technology industry (1997–2015). Source: Ministry of Industry, Foreign Trade and Services (MDIC).

domestic consumption, accompanied by the currency appreciation, an industrial trade balance deficit began to show.

Contrariwise, the primary sector and low-technology manufacture exports were less sensitive to the exchange rate. In spite of the currency overvaluation, these export sectors are highly competitive. That is because they exploit cheap and abundant production factors (land and natural resources), an advantage that was magnified during the commodity price boom. Not only that, the primary sector had a low import coefficient, meaning that was easier to produce a surplus.

By the end of the decade, the composition of the country's foreign trade basket reveals a phenomenon of reprimarisation, or primary export specialisation.[56] That is, the decline of manufactured and the increase of primary products. Figure 8 illustrates these two parallel trends.

It must be clear that reprimarisation of exports was not only an exacerbated development of the primary sector as an effect of the global commodity boom or a 'China effect'; it was also the outcome of policy-induced constraints on production, diversification, competitiveness and export performance of the industrial sector. The next section further discusses that relation.

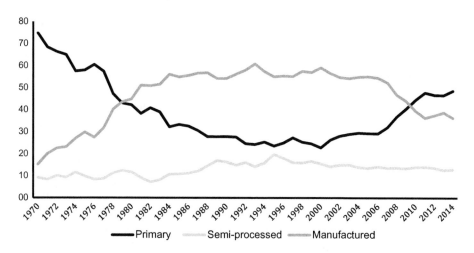

Figure 8. Brazilian exports: % primary, semi-processed and manufactured (1970–2014). Source: MDIC.

Reprimarisation: agribusiness for financial accumulation

Primary export specialisation, of which the agribusiness has been a spearhead, implied that earning foreign exchange became highly dependent on the primary sector (Gentil, 2014) – and in fact, on a hand full of commodities. In 2012, the export of only five commodities – iron ore, soybeans (and soy-related products), sugar, crude oil and meats – amounted to 42.5% of the value of all Brazilian exports. The soybean complex alone accounted for 14% of all Brazilian exports in 2014.[57]

Considering that the price of Brazil's main export commodities is defined in the stock market and commodity future markets, earning foreign exchange became more exposed to price volatility. That means that primary export specialisation has implied further external vulnerability. Furthermore, the fact that the total trade balance decreased during the economic upswing – when the commodity prices were soaring and the terms of trade were favourable[58] – suggests that primary export specialisation is structurally limited.

There are two reasons to argue so. First, because specialised, rather than broad-based export capacity is itself necessarily weaker. The more specialised the export basket, the more fragile the trade balance. Second, because – as discussed above – the greater the economic growth, the steeper is the decline of the industrial trade balance, making agro-commodity exports structurally ineffective to counteract the industrial trade deficit. Yet, primary exports are further stimulated because of that. The relentless expansion of primary exports – even when the price of soya and iron ore, Brazil's two major commodities, had collapsed (in 2014) – is indicative of the structural limitations to primary export specialisation.

Perversely, these exports reinforce the tendency for exchange rate appreciation that hinders the industrial exports. That is why intellectuals such as Bresser-Pereira have argued that Brazil presented, indeed, symptoms of the Dutch disease.[59] One key aspect is the regressive self-reinforcing dependence on export of commodities.

It is worth remarking that the large inflow of foreign investments, observed from 2006 onwards, failed to address the gaps in the industrial chains of production. Bresser-Pereira, discussed by Paulani,[60] argues that, contrary to orthodox views, the absorption of external savings in developing countries, being associated to cyclical exchange rate overvaluation, does not stimulate domestic investments, but consumption – thus reproducing external dependence, instead of the contrary.

Indeed, while until the 1990s the greatest part of FDI concentrated in manufacturing,[61] in the 2000s the focus has shifted to consumer-centred service sectors – particularly the services privatised in the previous decade[62] – and increased emphasis on the agro-extractive industry. Simultaneously, the type of FDI also changed, now reflecting mergers and acquisitions of national companies, foreign equity stakes, as well as intercompany loans, which substitute domestic sources of financing and do not necessarily increase gross fixed capital formation. Thus foreign investments might have actually reinforced a regressive productive structure.

Internally, macroeconomic policies have reduced the possibilities for reversing the dependency on foreign technology. As Anderson notes, specifically referring to Brazil: 'the highest long-term interest regime in the world' is 'manna for rentiers', but 'crippling for investors'.[63] High interest rates have increased the cost of credits and limited public and private investments, which explains why Brazilian growth was rather modest. Between 2005 and 2015, the total investment-to-GDP ratio (public and private) has varied between 16 to 21%, which is much below the average for emerging and developing economies.[64]

Brazil has also increasingly debilitated its capacity for domestic savings while anchoring its process of growth in the absorption of foreign savings.[65] Between 2003 and 2008, the government had an average primary fiscal balance of 3.4% of the GDP spent in interest on outstanding public debt, while the average spent on investments was only 2.0%.[66] National savings were used to pay interest on the internal debt and, consequently, were no longer available for financing productive investments. As Batista Jr. observes, 'fiscal constraints become, to a great extent, a by-product of the external vulnerability'.[67] Yet, that has imposed the need for an increasing tax load, with little counterpart to tax payers.

If primary exports are not strong enough to counteract the industrial trade deficit, they are also too weak to remunerate the stocks of foreign capital and balance the current account. Paradoxically, depleting the current account reproduces debt and the need to finance from external sources, both implying greater dependency on global capital liquidity and thus, further vulnerability.

For Delgado, the fact that the current account balance rapidly declined after a short period of surplus shows the weakness of specialisation in primary commodities as a solution to external dependence: it can only be a provisional fix to a structural imbalance of the Current account.[68] Yet, while primary export was a temporary solution to policy-induced external deficits, *reprimarisation* was a consequence of the dominant patterns of accumulation shaped by policy. Primary export specialisation therefore was not a solution to, but a product of, external dependence.

The limitation of agribusiness does not lie in the nature of the sector itself, but on its organic links with the dominant and financialised pattern of accumulation that constitutes and is reproduced through the very fabrics of agribusiness. As such, its expansion during the exceptional market circumstances in the 2000s did not, and could not, produce sustained growth. The windfall global commodity boom, therefore, was a missed opportunity to diversify, articulate and expand Brazil's productive structure, thus maximising the social gains from agriculture and related industry. So much so, that at the end of the cycle, the economy is in crisis, instead of more solid, stable or sovereign. Yet, the agribusiness, although weak and vulnerable as a driver of growth, seems to be reinforced as the material base for growth itself.

The current crisis and the political character of financialisation

The mounting deficit of the current account became a problem when the abundant global liquidity ended. With a lasting global recession, the inflow of FDI did not increase between 2011 and 2014 (see Figure 5), leading the country to rely on volatile and costly portfolio investment (also shown in Figure 5) to finance the public debt and the current account. This created further instability, which led to exchange rate devaluation, increasing the cost of external liabilities and of the imports that the industry was now dependent on. Even with little economic growth between 2011 and 2014, the value of imports increased resulting in a steep trade balance decline and growing BoP fragility.

In the face of that, Dilma Rousseff, who had just won her second election by a small margin in 2014, shifted back to the policies of the opposition. As *The Economist* wrote, the first task of the President's new team of Ministers was:

> […] restore credibility to economic policy. That means restating Brazil's commitment to its pre-2010 'tripod' – of independent monetary policy, fiscal responsibility and a floating exchange rate. It also means tightening the budget.[69]

The political consequences of substituting domestic by foreign savings were exposed: the state's strategic policies – chiefly, monetary policy – were now hostage of financiers, owners of the public debt and other financial assets. The main instruments of monetary policy, interest and exchange rates, are bargaining assets of financial investors. If their conditions are not met, investors can simply leave, therefore holding a major leverage power over the government to dictate economic policy. The more uncertainties and risks caused by inflation or current account deficit, the more the financial sector asks to lend the capital the economy depends on. Every month, investors in the internal debt market put the National Treasury 'on its knees to rollover tens of billions of *reais* in bonds'.[70]

Servicing the public debt has become the largest single expense of the Central Government annual budget (48.5% in 2010). Simultaneously, the systematic sale of debt securities became the major source of public financing (48% in the that same year).[71] According to the National Treasury, foreign investors (non-residents) owned 18.6% of the internal public debt security stock in 2014 – while national financial institutions, pension and investment funds held 67.2%.[72]

State-sponsored interest rates have functioned as mechanism of a massive public income transfer to private financial institutions (national and international). As Paulani notes, the forms of extraction through debt reproduction, debt servicing, income and dividends repatriation are much more efficient and intense than the extraction through the terms of trade, as in the time of the 'classic dependence',[73] or interest on external loans, as in the time of ISIs.[74]

With a full-blown recession, the government has resorted to draconian austerity measures, which are likely to exacerbate the difficulties in overcoming the faults (and the sources of inequality) of the country's structures for economic reproduction and accumulation. Indeed, at this moment, agribusiness continues to be stimulated as Brazil's salvation and best resource to promote stabilisation and output growth.

Conclusion

The prominence of agribusiness in the Brazilian economic upturn is not only a manifestation of the exceptional circumstances of the global commodity boom and excellent performance of the sector; it also reveals the effects of financialisation on patterns of production, trade and capital flows across the economy. Since the mid-1990s, state macroeconomic policies have undermined production and trade, particularly in the industrial sector, converting the country into a specialised primary commodities exporter. That meant becoming more dependent on agro-commodities export, but also on technology import and foreign capital inflow. State-sponsored interest and exchange rates have been key limits to output growth and export competitiveness, and simultaneously the fundamental mechanisms defining the rates of return on financial investments – which shows the pivotal role of finance in policy-making. The course of events described in this article shows that primary export specialisation is weak to offset the industrial trade deficit and remunerate the stocks of foreign capital; both have been perversely enhanced as a consequence of growth. That has translated in BoP fragility, reproduction of debt and external dependence – which together form the core of the crisis that erupted in 2014. That also shows that the crisis was not an anomaly in the country's development trajectory, but precisely a product of its very patterns of economic growth and accumulation in the past decades.

In brief, becoming a world agricultural powerhouse conceals an overall loss of economic power and political autonomy, as a consequence of the country's insertion in global circuits of financial capital accumulation. This justifies a critical approach to both agribusiness and the patterns of capitalist development in Brazil. 'Export or die' – this paraphrase of the country's independence slogan – was not a call for development or growth, as its herald intended to convey; as this article hopes to have shown, it was, quite literally, a condemnation to continue serving the imperatives of financial accumulation.

Disclosure statement

No potential conflict of interest was reported by the author.

Acknowledgements

The author would like to thank Ben Mckay, Max Spoor and the three anonymous reviewers for their feedback; and the many others who made this project possible. Any remaining errors are hers.

Notes

1. World Bank, GDP Growth (Annual %).
2. Albuquerque, "A formação da classe empresarial."
3. Leite, "State, Pattern of Development," 298.

4. Graziano, "A modernização dolorosa," 62.
5. Muller, "Agricultura e industrialização do campo."
6. Spoor, "Policy Regimes and Performance."
7. Friedmann, "The Political Economy of Food," 45.
8. Mollo, "O Desequilíbrio do Balanço."
9. Spoor, "Policy Regimes and Performance."
10. Saad-Filho, "The Political Economy," 224.
11. Saad-Filho, "Neoliberalismo: uma análise Marxista."
12. Ibid., 65–66.
13. Saad-Filho, "The Political Economy," 225.
14. Mollo and Saad-Filho, "Neoliberal Economic Policies," 101–103.
15. 'Real' refers to the domestic currency's name introduced by the Plan. Real ('reais' in the plural form) remains the official currency of Brazil.
16. Saad-Filho, "The Political Economy," 228.
17. Ibid., 226.
18. All data referring to the Brazilian Balance of Trade, as well as Services, Income and Investments come from the Brazilian Balance of Payments Series (based on IMF Manual 5, BPM-5) available at the Brazilian Central Bank website (https://www.bcb.gov.br).
19. Saad-Filho, "The Political Economy."
20. Auditoria Cidadã da Dívida, *ABC da Dívida*, 18.
21. Ávila, "Dívida interna," 6.
22. Morais and Saad-Filho, "Da economia política," 508.
23. Mollo and Saad-Filho, "Neoliberal Economic Policies," 108–109.
24. Ibid., 106.
25. Ibid., 107.
26. While phrase hints at the context of the time, it was widely reported as echoing the Brazilian historical cry of independence proclaimed in 1822: 'Independence or death'.
27. Delgado, "Especialização primária."
28. Gasques et al., "Desempenho e Crescimento."
29. Fuscaldi and Oliveira, "Crescimento da Agricultura Brasileira," 30.
30. Fuscaldi and Oliveira, "Crescimento da Agricultura Brasileira," 20 and Agência Senado, "Lei Kandir" available at https://www12.senado.leg.br/noticias/entenda-o-assunto/lei-kandir.
31. Hopewell, "New Protagonists in Global Economic," 609.
32. Gasques et al., "Desempenho e Crescimento."
33. IPEAdata.
34. IPEAdata, EMBI + Risco-Brasil. The Emerging Markets Bond Index-Brazil (EMBI + Br) is calculated by JP Morgan and measures the capacity of a country to honour its external debt securities.
35. Paulani, "Acumulação sistêmica," 243 and Boito Jr., "Estado e burguesia," 66.
36. Santos, "Brazil's Remarkable Journey."
37. Ibid.
38. MAPA, Brazilian trade balance and Agribusiness trade balance series: 1989–2014.
39. MAPA, *Agronegócio brasileiro em números*.
40. Annual Agricultural Harvest Plan (Plano Safra) available at the MAPA website (https://www.agricultura.gov.br), (Author's estimate).
41. Economist Intelligence Unit, "The Global Power of Brazilian."
42. Garcia, "A Internacionalização de Empresas Brasileiras."
43. Morais and Saad-Filho, "Da economia política," 507.
44. UNCTAD, "Transnational Corporations, Agricultural Production," 117.
45. Ibid., 64–66. In the manufacturing sector, which received 35% of investments, 80% accounted for the industry of semi-processed material. Ibid.
46. International Investment Position (IIP) Series, available at Brazilian Central Bank (https://www.bcb.gov.br).
47. Gentil and Araújo, "Dívida Pública e Passivo."
48. Ribeiro e Silva Filho, "Investimento Externo Direto," 33–34, based on UNCTADstat data.

49. Arezki et al., "What Drives the Global," 1 and Ghosh, "The Unnatural Coupling," 78.
50. Sauer and Leite, "Agrarian Structure, Foreign Investment" and Wilkinson, Reydon, and Di Sabbato, "Concentration and Foreign Ownership."
51. Amann and Baer, "Brazil as an Emerging Economy," 413.
52. Gaulard, "The 'Hot Money' Phenomenon," 370.
53. Amann and Baer, "Brazil as an Emerging Economy," 416.
54. Carneiro, "O Desenvolvimento Brasileiro Pós-crise."
55. Ibid.
56. Carneiro, "O Desenvolvimento Brasileiro Pós-crise", Delgado, "Especialização primária como limite"; Paulani, "Acumulação sistêmica, poupança externa" and Moreira and Sebag, "Um novo padrão exportador."
57. AGROstat, Agribusiness series per product: 1997–2015 (Author's estimate).
58. IPEAdata, Terms of exchange index (2006 = 100).
59. Paulani, "Acumulação Sistêmica" and Bresser-Pereira, "The Dutch Disease." "'Dutch disease', a term coined by this newspaper [The Economist] in 1977 to describe the impact of a North Sea gas bonanza on the economy of the Netherlands. This malady involves commodity exports driving up the value of the currency, making other parts of the economy less competitive, leading to a current-account deficit and even greater dependence on commodities'. The Economist, 'It's Only Natural'.
60. Paulani, "Acumulação sistêmica."
61. Hennings and Mesquita, "Capital Flows," 105.
62. Ibid.
63. Anderson, "Crisis in Brazil."
64. Brazilian Institute of Geography and Statistics (IBGE), Investment rate series: 1947–2014 (Author's estimate).
65. Paulani, "Acumulação sistêmica," 252.
66. Ministério da Fazenda, Secretaria de Política econômica.
67. Batista Jr., "Vulnerabilidade Externa," 178 (Author's translation).
68. Delgado, "Especialização primária."
69. The Economist, "Dilma Changes Course."
70. Ávila, "Dívida interna," 2.
71. Camara Legislativa Brasileira, "LDO-2010" (Author's estimate).
72. Ministério da Fazenda, "Dívida Pública Federal," 37.
73. The 'classic dependence' describes the exchange of primary products (from the periphery) for manufactured goods (from the centre). Evans, 'Dependent Development'.
74. Paulani, "Acumulação sistêmica."

ORCID

Daniela Andrade http://orcid.org/0000-0002-0766-5545

Bibliography

Albuquerque, Virgilius de. "A formação da classe empresarial brasileira." [The Formation of the Brazilian Business Class.] *Cadernos EBAPE.BR* 9, no. 2 (2011): 262–281.
Amann, Edmund, and Werner Baer. "Brazil as an Emerging Economy: A New Economic Miracle?" *Brazilian Journal of Political Economy* 32, no. 3 (128) (2012): 412–423.
Anderson, Perry. "Crisis in Brazil." *London Review of Books* 38, no. 8 (2016): 15–22. https://www.lrb.co.uk/v38/n08/perry-anderson/crisis-in-brazil.
Arezki, Rabah, Klaus Deininger, and Harris Selod. "What Drives the Global 'Land Rush'?" *International Bank for Reconstruction and Development* 29, no. 2 (2013): 207–233.
Auditoria Cidadã da Dívida, and Rede Jubileu Sul/Brasil. "ABC da Dívida: Sabe quanto você está pagando?" edited by Auditoria Cidadã da Dívida, 3rd ed., 48. Brasília: Auditoria Cidadã da Dívida/Rede Jubileu Sul-Brasil, 2008. http://www.auditoriacidada.org.br/wp-content/uploads/2012/08/ABC-da-Dívida-3-Edição.pdf.

Ávila, Rodrigo Vieira de. "'Dívida Interna': A nova face do endividamento externo." ['Internal Debt': The New Face of External Indebtedness.] Paper presented at the Primer Simposio Internacional sobre Deuda Pública, Auditoria Popular y Alternativas de Ahorro e Inversión para los Pueblos de América Latina, Caracas, September 22–24, 2006.

Boito Jr., Armando "Estado e burguesia no capitalismo neoliberal." [State and Bourgeoisie in Neoliberal Capitalism.] *Revista Sociologia Política* no. 28 (2007): 57–73.

Bresser-Pereira. "The Dutch Disease and its Neutralization." *Revista de Economia Política* 28, no. 1 (2008): 47–71.

Carneiro, Ricardo. "O Desenvolvimento Brasileiro Pós-Crise Financeira: Oportunidades e Riscos." [The Brazilian Development Post-financial Crisis: Opportunities and Risks.] *Observatório da Economia Global* 4 (2010): 1–35.

Delgado, Guilherme C. "Especialização primária como limite ao desenvolvimento." [Primary Specialisation as Limit to Development.] *Desenvolvimento em debate* 1, no. 2 (2010): 111–125.

Economist Intelligence Unit. "The Global Power of Brazilian Agribusiness : A Report from Economist Intelligence Unit." edited by Kieran Gartlan and Katherine Dorr Abreu, 18. London: The Economist, 2010.

Evans, Peter. *Dependent Development: The Alliance of Multinational, State, and Local Capital in Brazil.* Princeton, NJ: Princeton University Press, 1979.

Friedmann, Harriet. "The Political Economy of Food: A Global Crisis." *New Left Review* 197 (1993): 29–57.

Fuscaldi, Kelliane da C., and Andréa Christina Guirro de Oliveira. "Crescimento da Agricultura Brasileira, Período: 1996 a 2004." [Brazilian Agriculture Growth, Period: 1996–2004.] *Revista de Política Agrícola* 14, no. 3 (2005): 19–32.

Garcia, Ana E. Saggioro. "A Internacionalização de Empresas Brasileiras Durante o Governo Lula: Uma Análise Crítica da Relação Entre Capital e Estado no Brasil Contemporâneo." [The Internationalisation of Brazilian Companies During the Lula Administration: A Critical Analysis of the Relationship Between Capital and State in Contemporary Brazil.] Phd diss., *Pontifícia Universidade Católica do Rio de Janeiro*, 2012.

Gasques, José Garcia, Gervásio Castro de Rezende, Carlos Monteiro Villa Verde, Mario Sergio Salerno, Júnia Cristina P. R. da Conceição, and João Carlos de Souza Carvalho. "Desempenho e Crescimento do Agronegócio no Brasil." [Agribusiness Performance and Growth in Brazil.] Texto para Discussão N°1009, 39. Brasília: IPEA, 2004.

Gaulard, Mylène. "The 'Hot Money' Phenomenon in Brazil." *Brazilian Journal of Political Economy* 32, no. 3 (128) (2012): 367–388.

Gentil, Denise Lobato, and Victor Leonardo de Araújo. "Dívida Pública e Passivo Externo: Onde Está a Ameaça?" [Public Debt and External Liabilities: Where is the Threat?] In *Como Vai o Brasil?*, organised by Eduardo F. Bastian and André de Melo Modenesi Fabio Sá Earp, Imã Editorial, 2014. https://comovaiobrasil.pressbooks.com/chapter/cap5/.

Ghosh, J. "The Unnatural Coupling: Food and Global Finance." *Journal of Agrarian Change* 10, no. 1 (2010): 72–86.

Graziano, José da Silva. *A Modernização Dolorosa: Estrutura Agrária, Fronteira Agrícola e Trabalhadores Rurais no Brasil* [The Painful Modernisation: Agrarian Structure, Agricultural Frontier and Rural Workers in Brazil]. Rio de Janeiro: Zahar, 1982.

Hennings, Katherine, and Mário Mesquita. "Capital Flows to the Brazilian Economy: 2003–07." In *Financial Globalisation and Emerging Market Capital Flows*, 103–119. Basel: Bank for International Settlements, 2008. BIS Papers No44. http://www.bis.org/publ/bppdf/bispap44f.pdf.

Hopewell, Kristen. "New Protagonists in Global Economic Governance: The Rise of Brazilian Agribusiness at the WTO." *New Political Economy* 18, no. 4 (2011): 603–623.

Leite, Sérgio Pereira. "State, Pattern of Development and Agriculture: The Brazilian Case." *Estudos Sociedade e Agricultura* 2 (2006): 280–314.

Ministério da Fazenda. *Dívida Pública Federal: Relatório Anual 2014* [Federal Public Debt: Annual Report 2014], 59. Brasília: Secretaria do Tesouro Nacional, 2015.

MAPA (Ministry of Agriculture, Livestock and Food Supply). *Agronegócio brasileiro em números* [Brazilian Agribusiness in Numbers]. MAPA, 2010. https://www.agricultura.gov.br/arq_editor/file/Sala%20de%20Imprensa/Publicações/graficos_portugues_corrigido2.pdf.

Mollo, Maria de Lourdes Rollemberg. *O Desequilíbrio do Balanço de Pagamentos do Brasil 1966–1975: O Papel do Endividamento Externo* [The Disequilibrium of the Brazilian Balance of Payments 1966–1975: the Role of External Indebtedness]. Brasília: Editora Universidade de Brasília, 1977.

Morais, Lecio, and Alfredo Saad-Filho. "Da economia política à política econômica: o novo-desenvolvimentismo e o governo Lula." [From Political Economy to Economic Policy: New-developmentalism and Lula's Government.] *Revista de Economia Política* 31, no. 4 (2011): 507–527.

Moreira, Carlos Américo Leite, and Emanuel Sebag. "Um novo padrão exportador de especialização produtiva? Considerações sobre o caso brasileiro." [A New Export Pattern of Productive Specialisation? Considerations on the Brazilian Case.] Paper presented at *VI Jornada Internacional de Políticas Públicas: o desenvolvimento da crise capitalista e a atualização das lutas contra a exploração, a dominação e a humilhação*, São Luís do Maranhão, August 20–23, 2013.

Muller, Geraldo. "Agricultura e Industrialização do Campo no Brasil." [Agriculture and Industrialisation of the Countryside in Brazil.] *Revista de Economia Política* 2, no. 6 (1982): 47–79.

Paulani, Leda Maria. "Acumulação sistêmica, poupança externa e rentismo: observações sobre o caso brasileiro." [Systemic Accumulation, External Savings and Rentism: Observations on the Brazilian Case.] *Estudos Avançados* 27, no. 77 (2013): 237–261.

Ribeiro, Elton Jony Jesus, and Edison Benedito da Silva Filho. "Investimento Externo Direto no Brasil no Período 2003–2012: Aspectos Regionais e Setoriais." [Direct Foreign Investments in Brazil in the Period 2003–2012: Regional and Sectoral Aspects.] *Boletim de Economia e Política Internacional* 14 (2013): 29–46.

Saad-Filho, Alfredo. "Neoliberalismo: uma análise Marxista." [Neoliberalism: A Marxist Analysis.] *Marx e o Marxismo* 3, no. 4 (2015): 58–72.

Saad-Filho, Alfredo. "The Political Economy of Neoliberalism in Latin America." In *Neoliberalism: A Critical Reader*, edited by Alfredo Saad-Filho and Deborah Johnston, 222–229. London: Pluto Press, 2005.

Santos, Pablo Fonseca P. dos. "Brazil's Remarkable Journey." *Finance and Development: a quarterly magazine of the IMF* 42, no. 2 (2005): 429–430.

Sauer, Sérgio, and Sergio Pereira Leite. "Agrarian Structure, Foreign Investment in Land, and Land Prices in Brazil." *Journal of Peasant Studies* 39, no. 3–4 (2012): 873–898.

Spoor, Max. "Policy Regimes and Performance of the Agricultural Sector in Latin America and the Caribbean During the Last Three Decades." *Journal of Agrarian Change* 2, no. 3 (2002): 381–400.

The Economist. "Dilma Changes Course: The Appointment of a Capable Economic Team Is Good for Brazil but Signals Its President's Weakness." *The Economist*. Accessed November 27, 2014. https://www.economist.com/news/americas/21635056-appointment-capable-economic-team-good-brazil-signals-its-presidents

The Economist. "It's Only Natural: Commodities Alone Are Not Enough to Sustain Flourishing Economies." *The Economist*. Accessed September 9, 2010. https://www.economist.com/node/16964094

UNCTAD. "Transnational Corporations, Agricultural Production and Development." In *World Investment Report, 2009*. Geneva: UNCTAD-UN, 2009.

Wilkinson, John, Bastiaan Reydon, and Alberto Di Sabbato. "Concentration and Foreign Ownership of Land in Brazil in the Context of Global Land Grabbing." *Canadian Journal of Development Studies/ Revue canadienne d'études du développement* 33, no. 4 (2012): 417–438.

Utopian visions of contemporary rural-urban Russia

Alexander Mikhailovich Nikulin ⓘ and Irina Vladimirovna Trotsuk ⓘ

ABSTRACT

Rural Russia is undergoing changes in its agrarian economy and in its social and economic structure more generally in ways that differ greatly across the country's numerous regions. This is due to both internal transformations of the last decades of post-Soviet transition and external causes related to processes of globalisation. The most visible of these changes is the growing concentration of large-scale agribusiness landholdings. This concentration is transforming rural–urban linkages, intensifying rural–urban migration and leading to the disappearance of smallholders, family farmers and even entire rural settlements. This paper considers key aspects of contemporary reciprocity between rural and urban Russia through the analytical lens of the utopian models of rural development proposed by Russian economist and sociologist A.V. Chayanov in the early twentieth century. We argue that Chayanov's models of social development provide an optimal conceptual frame within which to understand the contemporary contradictions between town and village, industry and agriculture, the peasantry and the capitalist state.

Introduction

The specificity of the contemporary Russian agrarian path has been influenced mainly by two factors. On the one hand, it has been shaped by the historically tenacious conceptual visions of the necessary and desirable trajectories of social and economic development, some of which are presented in the works of prominent Russian social scientist A.V. Chayanov. On the other hand, it has been influenced by the enormous regional differentiation of the country with its diverse geographical features and historical traditions, and also by the leadership qualities of regional 'managers'. In other words, in Russia today there are no grounds to develop a conception of a divide between the Global North and Global South as the most significant dimension of inequality in power and wealth; there is no strong opposition to capitalism as a whole or to capitalist agricultural production in general. Rather, the situation in Russia presents a local-regional example of evolving polycentric rural and agricultural 'worlds' within the borders of a single country. As a result, contemporary rural Russia is a combination of large and small archipelagos of autarchic 'islands': agro-capitalist corporations, large and medium-scale capitalist farms, collective corporations, small family and peasant semi-subsistence farms, and a unique small rural-urban type of economy – the *dachas* [country houses used as secondary or holiday homes] of urban dwellers in rural areas.

The complex processes of agrarian change underway can be investigated systematically with the help of the conceptual framework of Chayanov's visions in combination with empirical regional case studies. This article considers the key aspects of contemporary rural–urban reciprocity in Russia through the analytical lens of the utopian models of rural development proposed by Chayanov for both Russia and the world almost a century ago – in the 1910–1920s. The concepts, images and forecasts of two of Chayanov's utopian publications – *Few Studies of the Isolated State* (1915–1923) and *My brother Alexey's Journey to the Land of Peasant Utopia* (1920) – are used to describe the realities of contemporary rural–urban Russia. In each utopia, Chayanov developed an original model of social development to find an optimal balance, and to resolve the contradictions, between the town and village, industry and agriculture, peasantry and the capitalist state, science and art. This article engages with questions concerning whether and to what extent Chayanov's dream of achieving harmonious social development has been realised in present-day Russia. Which of Chayanov's ideas proved shrewdly right and which ideas turned out to be rather naïve? Can we use Chayanov's utopian ideas for the analysis of contemporary social reality in both Russia and the world? The article seeks to provide some answers to these difficult questions.

To answer these questions, we start with a short overview of the key elements of Chayanov's utopias, his original forecasts of future scenarios for both agricultural development and general social processes. These elements include the triangle of the state, entrepreneurship and cooperative peasant relations. We then consider the phenomenon of (post) Soviet 'glocalization' – the preservation of domestic regional differences despite the general trend of globalisation – that was predicted by Chayanov in his concept of an 'isolated island-state'. We identify some indicators of capitalist and peasant economies to emphasise the variety of social and economic forms of differentiation in contemporary Russian society that are very similar to those typical for agriculture (and rural areas) a century ago and contribute to the reproduction of the autarchic character of some rural social strata. We present two cases to demonstrate the relevance of Chayanov's ideas for understanding contemporary Russian society: the 'neopopulist' Belgorod project of successful rural–urban development and mixed economic sustainability; and Moscow's transformation from a 'big village' into a 'mega-village' that resulted in the largest megalopolis of the country shaping a system of giant agroholdings determining the mode and trends of agricultural and rural development of the whole country.

Chayanov's utopian visions

Alexander V. Chayanov (1888–1937) is one of the most famous agrarian economists and rural sociologists in both the Russian and Western scientific world. He is famous not only for being an advocate of agrarianism and cooperatives or for publishing important works on agriculture, but also for his work for various government institutions after the October Revolution. Chayanov also promoted cooperative-based agrarian reform, with peasant households engaged in subsistence farming, as he was skeptical about the efficiency of large-scale farms. Predictably he was sharply criticised for his perception of Soviet agriculture and its development guidelines, and in 1930 he was arrested on fabricated accusations and sentenced to prison and then to exile. After his release in 1937, Chayanov was arrested again and shot dead.

One of the main and often underestimated features of Chayanov's versatile thinking was his ability to propose original forecasts of future scenarios for both agricultural development and general social processes under various possible political and economic conditions. He ended many of his academic articles and books with such predictions of the future as we see on the last page of his book *Basic Ideas and Forms of Agricultural Cooperation Organization* (1927) which underlines the importance of the peasant economy and the social, economic and even historical role of the peasantry in his theory and practical recommendations:

> In the critical moments … when all entrepreneurship methods will be powerless, when the economic crisis will sweep away our sophisticated enterprises, the only possible right way for our salvation, unknown and inaccessible to capitalist organizations, will be to shift the burden of the blow on the shoulders of … the peasant economy … its working resistance, and its con-scientiousness. And to prevent peasants from avoiding this burden, you need to make them feel, know, and get used to the idea that agricultural cooperation is truly their business! This is the only way to make cooperation a truly powerful social movement, and not just an enterprise!

This passage identifies virtually all the key concepts of his social theory: (a) the triangle of the state, entrepreneurship and cooperative peasant relations, which (b) amid social crises undermines the equilibrium, and explains the need for (c) the search for a utopia in which social and political decisions taken by leaders and elites are in harmony with the masses. His predictions aptly highlight some of the key problems of contemporary Russian society.

First, the state has often underestimated the role, potential and needs of the small farming and peasant economy in its contemporary form, in favour of big entrepreneurs or 'agrohol-dings'. Second, there is no social or economic equilibrium in Russian society; crises seem to have become an intrinsic part of our everyday life at all levels, but this does not eliminate the need to search for such equilibrium as an ideal state. For instance, one of the most acute problems of our time is the ecological balance of the industry that feeds the nation which at the same time is extremely detrimental to the environment and society at large.[1] Third, we live in a world with a widening gap between political, economic and social decision-makers and the masses, rendering Chayanov's idea of searching for a better balance very pertinent.[2] This is especially true in the Russian context. While there are not many open forms of protest against the state or capital, there are powerful peasant discourses that reflect their neglect, ignorance and violation of rural inhabitants and farmers' rights and aspirations.[3]

Scholars following in Chayanov's tradition tend to highlight his contribution to the study and development of the theory of agricultural enterprises and different optimal options. However, Chayanov worked with this idea of optimising situations – 'optima' – in the broadest sense of the word, by integrating virtually all of his agrarian-economic and socio-political studies under the intensifying dynamics of conflicts and crises at the beginning of the twentieth century. While he did not have access to reliable socio-economic statistics, which were quite incomplete in the past as they are in the present, and will likely be in the future. This is why Chayanov's thinking bravely forged ahead, with the construction of various models of alternative social realities as a basis from which to forecast possible trends and versions of social evolution, thereby entering the world of utopias.

Post-Soviet 'glocalization'

Here we introduce the concept of 'glocalization' to depict the character of contemporary Russian society which embodies both the trend towards globalisation and at the same time the preservation of Russian domestic regional differences.[4] This concept helps us to build on Chayanov's agrarian visions.

Chayanov's unique utopia appears in his collection of sketches on the economy of an isolated island-state, written in 1915–1922 and published in 1923. Chayanov developed a vision of an isolated state, named an 'island-state' to emphasise its extreme isolation. The aims of this abstract work were, first, to consider the correlation between agricultural and non-agricultural activities; and, second, to compare peasant and capitalist forms of economy in a series of abstract economic theorems. To achieve these aims, Chayanov based his work on the following theoretical assumptions: there is an isolated island-state with a city-market in the centre of it; abundant fertile land; only one food product *A* that satisfies all human needs in food; only one product of urban industry *T* that satisfies all other human needs; transport costs are equal to zero; means and instruments of production are made by the producers themselves; there is no private property; and the population of the isolated island-state grows extremely fast.[5]

Chayanov recognised the 'extreme simplification' of these abstractions. However, he applied the conditions proposed to question the changes in the intensity of agriculture and rural–urban interactions in this utopian country. With the help of an extensive gallery of tables and figures, Chayanov concludes that the peasant farming economy is more successful and sustainable than the urban economy, even if we introduce new conditions: transport costs, private property, capitalist enterprises, a larger territory and the annexation of another island to relocate the surplus population. Under these more complex conditions, Chayanov still shows the growth of peasant populations and the decline of the urban population and the capitalist economy in the utopian island-state.

The conclusions of his study are that the 'intensification of farming leads to agrarianisation and deindustrialization of the country. The peasant economy is more efficient than the capitalist one'.[6] However, after the 1917 Revolution, these assumptions came into conflict with the Soviet socialist reality. The capitalist economy was completely destroyed during the civil war of 1918–1921, and then the peasant economy was reduced to tiny subsidiary plots of 0.25 ha for collective farmers under the first Five-Year Plan in 1929–1933.

For almost half a century, the agrarian economy of the Soviet isolated island-state did not have either capitalist or peasant economies at all. This isolated country, by exporting its agrarian and political regime to a number of countries in Europe, Asia, Africa and Latin America contributed to the creation of an archipelago of isolated large and small 'island-states' within the so-called world socialist system, which also sought to manage without both capitalist and peasant economies. It was only in the 1990s that true capitalist and peasant economies again emerged in post-socialist agrarian Russia.

Indicators of capitalist vs. peasant economies and forms of differentiation

Present-day Russia has zones in which the capitalist economy is concentrated and others in which the peasant economy dominates. About a third of the Russian population (50 million) lives in big cities, a third (55 million) in small towns and nearly a third (40 million) in rural areas.[7] About 36 million families in Russia have private subsidiary plots and *dachas,* which are among the key features of a rural dweller, i.e. about a half of the Russian population to some extent can be considered to be at least part-time rural dwellers.[8]

Contemporary rural Russia is characterised by a combination of large and small archipelagos of autarchic islands: (1) about 700 agro-capitalist corporations, (2) about 20,000 large and medium market capitalist farms, (3) up to 1,000 collective corporations which are remnants of the former collective farms, and (4) about half a million small family and peasant semi-subsistence farms. The economies of the first and second types are concentrated mainly in the areas surrounding the big cities and in the fertile lands of southern Russia. The economies of the third and fourth types are typical for the hinterland and remote or infertile northern regions. However, there is also a unique small rural–urban type of economy: (5) *dachas* and personal subsidiary plots of rural-urban dwellers in rural areas – an economy which is widespread throughout Russia and represents one of its most important social-cultural features, which varies from country villas of rich city dwellers to rural sheds and huts of poor ones.[9] What problems do these people face? The main problems stem from differentiation in all its various forms – regional, economic and social. The artificially constructed (but never achieved) desire for a homogenous Soviet village[10] has sunk into the past and was replaced by uncontrolled market differentiation that stratifies and divides rural life in diverse ways.

The growing socio-economic differentiation between rich and poor rural regions, enterprises and households has a number of features.[11] First, the patterns of agrarian differentiation typical for agriculture a century ago are still obvious in Russia: market-based agriculture develops rapidly, especially around big cities and on fertile land.[12] In Russia, the 10 most developed agricultural regions surround the largest metropolitan agglomerations: Moscow and Saint Petersburg. Although they lack fertile land, these agglomerations are saturated with capital, highly qualified workforces, well-developed transport infrastructure and, most importantly, the existence of giant food markets which make the development of agriculture close to these metropolitan areas highly economically attractive. At the same time, neighboring regions close to Moscow and Saint Petersburg remain economically depressed and experience a chronic shortage of capital and a qualified workforce, as workers prefer to migrate to the cities. In the southern fertile regions, similar trends are observed: agriculture develops successfully around regional capitals, while in the hinterlands capital and skilled workers are scarce as higher wages pull workers to the cities.

All this has demographic effects in agrarian societies. Unlike the relatively overpopulated rural south, in 2012 three north-eastern federal districts (Far East Federal District, Northwest Federal District, and Central Federal District) showed a 15% reduction of the rural population compared to 1990.[13] Between the censuses of 1989 and 2002, nearly 10,800 villages disappeared, and on average 825 villages disappear annually. By 2002, in more than 34,000 Russian villages there were less than 10 residents. In 2010, almost 13% of Russian villages did not have any residents at all, while in more than two-thirds of Russia's regions the death rate exceeds the birth rate. According to the forecasts of the Federal State Statistics Service, the Russian rural population will decrease by five million by 2030. The rural population continues to age and the birth rate is in decline.[14]

Along with the growth of regional differentiation, there is increasing rural class differentiation in the Marxist sense. The privatisation of former collective and state farm property was not as scandalous and shocking as the privatisation of the extractive industries in favour of local elites. Even so, former collective farm chairmen and officials of local and regional agricultural administrations turned lands, buildings, facilities and machinery of former Soviet agricultural enterprises into their private property. In poor rural areas, local elites did not become rich for there was not much to privatise, unlike the situation in rich regions such as the central *Chernozemie* (Black Earth regions) and North Caucasus, in which the land and agricultural production now concentrated in private hands guarantees huge revenues to former *nomenklatura* (Soviet bureaucratic elites) that were named 'red landlords' in the 1990s.[15]

In the early 2000s, the largest financial and raw material-dependent companies rushed to the agribusiness sector, pursuing an aggressive policy of 'land grabbing'.[16] As a result, in the last 15 years we have witnessed the mushrooming of large agroholdings by large capitalist corporations such as Miratorg, Ostankino, Rus-Agro, Eco-Niva and Efko. These corporations have bought up entire local agricultural production systems, putting local rural elites under their economic control by bankrupting their enterprises or by paying them off. Today there are more than 700 registered agricultural holdings, ranging from ten to hundreds of thousands of hectares. Their headquarters are located in large metropolitan and regional centres. Agricultural holding companies continue to expand, especially in the fertile southern regions of Russia, where already in 2012 the top 30 agricultural holdings held more than 10 million hectares.[17] The 'red landlords'[18] of the 1990s associated with the Communist Party were attacked by the 'white oligarchs'[19] of the 2000s. The new rural power squabbles often make them ignore the urgent problems of the wider rural population. Certainly, in rural areas as a result of the post-Soviet redistribution of property there are some effective private large agricultural enterprises, working productively and profitably. Nevertheless, the gap between the few successful and many unsuccessful enterprises is increasing.

In addition to the growth of class differentiation, the Russian countryside clearly demonstrates variations arising from the agency of rural people. Among the many poor households and dilapidated agricultural enterprises, there are sometimes oases of cultural, highly productive agriculture in both peasant and corporate forms. For example, in the far north of Russia in the infertile lands of the Arkhangelsk region in the boreal forests there is an agricultural company, Stupino, with 35 employees and 700 head of cattle. It is a thriving enterprise which preserves some traditions of the former collective farm, is profitable and has the highest dairy-cattle milk yield in the region with an average of 8,000 litres per cow. Similarly, in the arid steppes of the South Siberian Kulunda there are large farms of 5,000–20,000 hectares, which are also profitable and dynamic. All of these enterprises are headed by talented managers combining market and collectivist incentives to work. These oases can function either in the form of a large family farm expanding its holdings by agglomerating those of poorer families, or as a wealthy traditional collective farm or post-Soviet joint-stock company surviving as viable agricultural enterprises. In the post-Soviet period, the will and talent of such families and village leaders sometimes manifest themselves, while for others collective apathy and feelings of the hopelessness of agrarian life grows.

In the 2010s, the above types of differentiation contributed to the reproduction of the autarchic character of some rural social strata. In the centre of the fragmented rural socio-economic structures, there is already a local microcosm of new rural Russian elites, whose annual family incomes exceed millions of dollars, while on the giant peripheral rural socio-economic areas of Russia we witness the reproduction of persistent poverty similar to most rural regions of the Third World, but aggravated by the specific Russian demographic crisis.

Chayanov's ideas as neopopulist roots of the Belgorod governor's project

The Belgorod region is located in the south-west of Russia, and is one of the smallest regions of the Russian Federation, with an area 27,000 square kilometres and a population of 1.5 million people. It has distinct economic and geographical advantages, for it possesses the world's largest iron ore deposits and agricultural lands located in the centre of the vast Russian-Ukrainian black soils. The urban share of the population is 70%, while 30% are rural, and the capital city of Belgorod has 350,000 inhabitants.

We contend that Belgorod governor's development project is rooted in the spirit of the neopopulist ideas of A.V. Chayanov's novel *My brother Alexey's Journey to the Land of Peasant Utopia*. These include the idea that the contradiction between urban and rural ways of life can be resolved with the help of the village and by prioritising the rural; a mixed economy can combine both capitalist and state economies provided that it is managed in the interests of cooperative and family-based economies; and active support for traditional culture requires careful consideration.

Belgorod has experienced an annual economic growth rate of 3%, which is exceptional even when compared to similar Russian and Ukrainian neighbouring regions with comparable natural resources. Even during the 2008–2009 crisis, when the Russian industry declined by 12%, the Belgorod region showed a 5% industrial growth rate – comparable with China's growth rate – and a 10% rate of agricultural growth. For Russia, the modernisation of the agricultural sector has always been and still is a great challenge. Yet, during the last decade, the Belgorod region experienced a pace of agricultural growth unreachable for other Russian regions, with pig and poultry production comparable and competitive with Western European and American production levels. Today about 15% of Russian pork and poultry is produced by this small region and, at the current rate of agricultural growth, this share is projected to rise to 20% in the coming few years.

In many ways, the modernisation of the Belgorod region is based on a sustainable and dynamic development of its agricultural sector and rural areas. In the early 2000s, the region actively attracted large investments to create big agricultural enterprises – agroholdings that proved to be among the best in Russia and successful enough to compete with other Russian and foreign companies. As Chayanov anticipated with the capitalist development of the countryside, present-day Russian agroholdings represent

> new ways in which capitalism penetrates agriculture. These ways convert the farmer into a labor force working with other people's means of production. They convert agriculture, despite the evident scattered and independent nature of the small commodity producers, into an economic system concentrated in a series of the largest undertakings and, through them, entering the sphere controlled by the most advanced forms of finance capitalism.[20]

However, in Belgorod these agroholdings are closely monitored by the regional authorities, who believe that the excessive reliance on huge agricultural corporations can be dangerous for other elements of rural life. Therefore, the Belgorod authorities also support the development of peasant farms and cooperatives of local communities.

Perhaps, the most impressive Belgorod regional programme, which is unique in Russia, is 'Family farms of *Belogorie*', an initiative aimed at social stabilization of rural areas in two ways: first, by providing farmers with inputs and technology necessary for agricultural production; and second, by making farm products competitive, while meeting the quality standards and ensuring availability to consumers. The programme clearly defines indicators for assessing its efficiency, such as the number of participants (25,000 people in 2015), revenues from the sale of farm products (USD$ 236 million in 2015), the development of rural cooperatives and rural social infrastructure. We visited some districts of the Belgorod region to conduct interviews with local residents – workers, managers and specialists in the agricultural sector – and found that these agrarian reforms in the region proved to be largely successful in promoting peasant farming and cooperatives. Success of these reforms was due to their general strategy, which combines the strict control of land planning and land use by regional authorities, the development of a mixed agrarian economy, and market interventions to establish fair pricing in the value chains between producers, processors and sellers.

Belgorod's mixed economy seeks to take advantage of both large- and small-scale agricultural production by adopting special development programmes and laying the foundations for the mutually beneficial coexistence of different economies. The rapid growth of production and labour productivity in powerful agroholdings increases rural unemployment. In this context, the special regional programmes for the development of family farms has enabled the absorption of surplus rural labour into family-farm based production in sectors in which the agroholdings are *not* involved – such as milk, small animals and birds (goats, geese) breeding, beekeeping, mushroom farming, rural tourism and crafts enterprises.

Though the Soviet symbiosis of large farm enterprises and smallholders has generally eroded since post-Soviet decollectivisation reforms, in Belgorod we find that this is not the case. Instead, symbiotic relations between these sectors are evolving into a sort of implicit corporate social responsibility model, in response to pressure from the regional government which has forced large farm enterprises to support smallholders and rural communities, even while, at the national level and elsewhere, the coalition between agroholdings and the state is pushing smallholders out of production. In the post-Soviet period, the national trend is that many of the declining large farm enterprises preserved the Soviet paternalistic logic in relation to households as well as with municipal administrations, maintaining their former functions in support of employees and smallholders. Their inability to achieve efficient economic performance and therefore to provide their workers with sufficient income, led to an informal agreement: resources for loyalty. The management of the successful large farm enterprises, on the contrary, tried to destroy that paternalistic symbiosis and to develop capitalist and contractual relations.

A sustainable mixed economy is impossible without the successful development of rural areas. This is why Belgorod regional authorities have implemented a wide range of social programmes to create a so-called 'social agricultural cluster', which includes in each locality a school, a kindergarten, medical, recreational, administrative and public institutions, a church, law enforcement agencies, a cemetery and a park. As a result, the Belgorod region is not only a successful leader of Russian agricultural production, but also a territory with stable demographic growth and vibrant rural areas. There are new development projects underway such as bio-gas production at livestock complexes, windmill installations, organic fertilizer production based on animal husbandry, and soil protection on the basis of these organic fertilizers, among others. At the same time, for the growth of a high-tech agricultural economy, the Belgorod region requires a corresponding level of local education and scientific research and development.

Belgorod region is an undisputed Russian leader not only in the agriculture, but also in almost all other important social and economic indicators. For instance, during the post-Soviet period, the formerly unknown provincial higher education institutions of Belgorod turned into important national scientific-educational centres (especially Belgorod State University, Belgorod State Technical University and Belgorod State Agricultural Academy). The regional authorities established a Council on Innovative Policies, adopted and supported a long-term programme on the 'Development of Nanotechnology Industry' by opening a business incubator, starting the construction of an industrial park, creating innovative industrial districts within the main regional economic clusters (agrifood, mining-metallurgy and construction), and by cooperating with the largest private companies in project funding and scientific research and development. In the economy, education and science, then, the Belgorod authorities have demonstrated skillful state dirigisme that has guaranteed them public support and stimulated the growth of a self-conscious and self-organised local population at the municipal level.

One of the basic prerequisites for the true self-organisation and local self-government is an adequate planning and housing policy oriented for the generations to come. Such a policy in the Belgorod region aims to create all necessary conditions for the population to build and reside primarily in low-rise, cottage-type houses. The Belgorod region has no equal in the Russian Federation in the pace of building private houses with standard smallholdings of 0.15 hectares. For the aims of humanisation of territorial-neighbour relations and building trust, the regional authorities adopted a programme to support family estates. Such a way of organising the rural living space aims, firstly, to overcome the Soviet legacy of excessive multi-storey, multi-family urbanisation, and secondly, to reconstruct and develop traditional neighbourhoods and neighbourly lifestyles.

From the state point of view, the so-called 'Belgorod project' represents the desire to teach the local bureaucracy about innovative thinking and project management. In the future, every Belgorod official will join one or more temporary groups developing different projects with the clear criteria to evaluate the work of each official within every project. For this purpose, the Belgorod authorities change and update programmes for training and retraining of administrative staff for promoting a project approach. It is too early to discuss the results of these measures; however, some changes in administrative thinking are already obvious. For instance, when we asked local and regional officials in different parts of Russia about the problems of their region, in general, the answer was as follows: 'What kind of problems? You'd better tell Moscow officials to give us some money and we will spend it to solve all our problems'. We were surprised to hear a completely different answer to this question at the meeting of the staff of the Belgorod Department of Agriculture:

> We still do not understand the mood and the needs of our population. Some of our economic and social programs are implemented and develop more successfully than the others. We would appreciate greatly if you, scientists, helped us to understand the situation and public opinion better.

It was here that we first discovered that Russian scientists and officials can speak the same language and discuss issues equally important and urgent for both groups, such as rural–urban labour migration and generational conflicts, among other things.

The Belgorod project actually aims to implement its own concept of the new economy with the following social-cultural features: extensive development of solidarity and cooperation within the cooperative movement; maintaining ideals of a healthy lifestyle including non-smoking; adopting special environmental programmes; ensuring free personal choice to work and to rest. In these and other ways, regional authorities support corporate, family and individual strategies of life. According to the governor E. Savchenko, 'the essence of the

Belgorod strategy of social and economic modernization is to help our active, cohesive, purposeful (i.e. solidarity) society to accelerate the advent of the new type of economy'. Since 2010, one can see on the billboards of Belgorod social advertising that draws on the call of the Russian religious philosopher Nikolay Fyodorov, which is considered a motto of a solidarity society: 'To live neither for ourselves or for others, but with all and for the sake of all'.

While one can hardly expect the imminent realisation of such a solidarity society in the Belgorod region, embryonic elements of this are in evidence. We would rather say that, in view of the economic history of the Belgorod region, we witness a moderated form of bourgeois New Economic Policy. Specifically, the expansion of the capitalist economy represented by large mining companies and agroholdings is quite successfully counterbalanced by the active regional policy in the state, municipal and co-operative sectors of the economy supported by a wide range of social programmes in the interests of rural families and community economies.

The utopia of peasant capital and rural–urban reality of mega-pop-polis[21]

In his next utopia, Chayanov introduced the directions of the peasant economy through urban-rural cooperation as the key problem of the future world. The novel *My brother Alexey's Journey to the Land of Peasant Utopia* is one of the most famous works of Chayanov, in which he presented his most important socio-economic and philosophical-aesthetic views.[22] It was written in the midst of the Civil War and the War Communism policy in revolutionary Russia. Chayanov, as if denying the horrors of the military-revolutionary chaos and bloody conflicts among fighting parties, imagines another Russia of the end of the twentieth century – one which is culturally rich, democratic, well-fed and comfortable. He envisages this within a changed global order, with the world split into five closed national economic systems: English-French, German, American-Australian, Japanese-Chinese and Russian: 'Each isolated system received different pieces of territory located in all possible climates and sufficient to complete the construction of national economic life. And in the future, while maintaining cultural communication, these begin to live very different political and economic types of life'.[23]

The economy of Chayanov's utopian Russia is a mixed market, for it combines state, cooperative, municipal and even capitalist economic forms. In the country of peasant utopia, these capitalist forms are carefully monitored and taxed, enabling incentives for individual entrepreneurship and national economic competition in general. The state has a monopoly on basic natural resources. The municipal sector is sufficiently independent and developed from both political-cultural and socio-economic points of view. However, at the core of this national economic system,

> as at the heart of ancient Russia, there is an individual peasant economy … Here a man is opposed to nature, here labor is in the creative connection with all the forces of universe and creates new forms of existence. Each worker here is a creator, each manifestation of his personality – an art of labor.[24]

That peasant economy, with its various forms of cooperation with all other types of economic and cultural modes of life, is considered the perfect social organisation in utopian Russia. In political terms, this country is a federation, in which the court, the state and some railway agencies are administered by the central authorities, while in other areas and levels of political organisation considerable diversity and self-management are allowed.

Regarding the ideology and internal organisation of the power elites of this peasant utopia, Chayanov stressed that in the twentieth century issues of cultural influence and development were no less, and perhaps even more, important for the elites than economic ones. That is why peasant leaders and ideologues in the previous decades of their rule sought to make a cultural revolution in the village in order to pull it out of the stagnation and simplification of traditional rural life. They were awakening the social energy of the masses by sending to the hinterland all elements of culture that were at their disposal: '... district theater and rural municipal theater, district museum with rural municipal branches, people's universities, sports of all kinds and forms, choral societies – everything up to the church and politics was thrown into the village to raise its culture'.[25]

Thus, the question is how accurately Chayanov predicted the possible rural–urban future of Russia and the world in his utopian novel. We must admit that Chayanov's belief in the future evolution of the political, economic, social and cultural diversity of the world in general was in part confirmed. On the one hand, his five isolated national economic systems can be considered a vestige of nationalist and even imperialist worldviews of the typical European intellectual of the first half of the twentieth century. On the other hand, this five-systems model can be a prototype of the modern multi-polar or 'polycentric' world consisting of various international economic and political blocs. Undoubtedly, Russia is by no means a self-governing peasant paradise with a mixed economy – rather it has become a bureaucratic authoritarian state with the predominance of large industrial collective-state farms. However, Chayanov noted the importance of the deliberate rural–urban *cultural* policy determined by the oligarchic leadership in the development of Russia. In this respect, Chayanov was right when he stressed the importance of oligarchism in the political system of Russia, which has been further strengthened in the post-Soviet period.

In the contemporary period, the Belgorod case shows how a cohesive oligarchy supportive of the ideal of cultural and economic symbiosis can achieve very impressive results. Nationally, the agrarian oligarchy plays an extremely important and controversial role in the development of Russian agriculture. On the one hand, agrarian oligarchs can concentrate substantial resources for the implementation of ambitious rural development projects. On the other hand, these vast resources of the oligarchy are not controlled by the state or society at large. The use of these resources is often accompanied by corruption scandals and accusations of the misuse of funds. Quite often the Russian countryside suffers the consequences of conflicts between the agrarian-oligarchic corporations over the redistribution of land and property in different regions, and between the capital and the provinces. Yet the Belgorod case shows how another agrarian pathway is possible.

Moscow: the transformation of the 'big village' into the 'mega-village'

The issue of relations between capital cities and the provinces – and the possibilities of rural–urban reciprocity – is extremely urgent for the contemporary world.[26] In contemporary Russia, Moscow seems to be the complete opposite of Chayanov's vision for Moscow, even though it is still known as 'a big village'. The metaphor 'Moscow is a big village' was revived spontaneously under the intensive processes of industrialisation and urbanisation in both Tsarist and Soviet Russia. Migrants from the countryside constantly come to Moscow bringing different values and traditions typical of the rural lifestyle of the peasantry. A huge number of these migrants have already become Muscovites and most become metropolitan residents. However, such a transition or even transformation from a villager to a city-dweller is far from being fast and simple, especially because more and more new villagers arrive in the capital from nearby provinces, joining recently settled city-dwellers. If we look at the historical changes in the population density of the area in a radius of 500 km around Moscow, we can observe that in the past hundred years Moscow absorbed almost all the rural population of central Russia, leading to inescapable and constant depopulation and economic depression across these rural regions.[27] Moscow also continues to attract millions of villagers living thousands of kilometres away, not only in the Russian Federation but also in the other former Soviet republics. Moscow has thus become a melting pot, turning different types of interregional and multinational provincial social and cultural norms into those typical of a megalopolis, largely based on of individuality.

For 150 years, the city of Moscow has been continuously expanding, as an ink blot does on wet paper, in all directions into the countryside, transforming former rural landscapes into chaotically mixed capital suburbs. The reason for such a long-term and ongoing expansion of the capital is Moscow's insatiable appetite for rural territorial absorption. In 2014 alone, 144,000 hectares of land were allocated for the development of the city of Moscow in the South-West area of the surrounding region.[28] This newly added area exceeds almost by a third the whole territory of Moscow before its administrative expansion. The Moscow region in the past decade has been developing intensively by undergoing an extremely fast type of urbanisation, which is turning Moscow from a big village into a mega-village. The question is why Moscow still stays a 'village' regardless of its formally urban history and the fact that most Muscovites and the Moscow authorities (together with the federal government) are so committed to the idea of Moscow and its suburbs as a super-modern mega-city devoid of any traces of rural life.

Nonetheless, the most advanced and innovative projects in the Moscow region are in agriculture. For instance, in terms of agricultural production, the Moscow region ranked 8th out of a total of 84 regions in the country.[29] The area under cultivation in the suburbs of Moscow declined more slowly than in the surrounding regions, and meat production, in contrast to its neighbours, even increased. As a result, by 2010 the Moscow Region produced more meat than the neighbouring Vladimir, Ryazan, Smolensk, and Tver Regions together.

This is rather a paradox: the largest megalopolis of the country that grabbed all the surrounding lands in the Moscow region mainly for housing construction and which strongly supports the symbiosis of bureaucracy and capitalism has created a system of giant agroholdings. This has implications for the mode and trends of agricultural and rural development, not only in the Moscow region but also across the whole country. Agroholdings have spread from the Moscow region up to the Siberian Federal district. Furthermore, the lands around Moscow are not too fertile and the intensive large-scale production of poultry, pork, beef and dairy products worsen the ecological situation in the densely populated region. But Moscow retains features of rurality. First, Moscow and its suburbs have abundant capital and labour resources, as well as the infrastructure for large-scale agricultural production on a national scale. Second, Moscow has also taken a major role in the trade and coordination of the old rural folk crafts, which are increasingly becoming urban activities due to the extinction and disappearance of the village. Third, authorities inventively use village symbols for the greater glorification of the Russian capital's greatness.

However, these are elements and remnants of the rural and village life rather than of the peasant economy. A few years ago, the Russian foundation Public Opinion conducted a poll to identify the interpretations and attitudes of Russian citizens to peasants.[30] Muscovites, urban and village dwellers and people living in rural areas of Russia were asked two questions: (1) Do peasants have any specific features that make them different from other citizens of Russia? (2) If they do have such features, what are they? Muscovites were the only group that considered peasants as having special traits (79% of respondents in Moscow) and, while recognising that most peasants are poor, also associated peasants with various positive features: hard working, modest, honest and cordial.

One of the key features of the Muscovites themselves is their restless desire to live in cottages in the countryside. In the suburbs of the Moscow Region alone, the number of rural settlements is 6,100 and there are nearly double this number (11,700) of gardening-only settlements. In the Moscow Region, these settlements without any official status form a kind of seasonal pseudo-town that radically transforms the 'official' settlement pattern. The peak of their formation happened in the 1980s and the first half of 1990s (respectively, 28 and 51%). The cottage settlements are the most visible sign of the changes taking place in the seasonal settlement network; and although their number is still small, it is growing rapidly. Despite the active development of cottage settlements, still the most widespread and typical in the Moscow suburban seasonal settlement network are dacha and gardening associations. In the mid-2000s in the Moscow Region, there were more than 1.3 million land plots in the gardening, vegetable-gardening and dacha associations, including 2.1 million households with private gardens.

During the 1990s crisis, Moscow families relied increasingly in production for their own households' consumption, growing potatoes, vegetables, fruits and berries on their subsidiary plots in the country. Today, such self-provisioning practices are not so important for Muscovites,[31] but the rural lifestyle in the form of country life at *dachas* remains a priority for Moscow families from both socio-economic and socio-cultural points of view. Quite often, the Muscovites contrive to purchase and keep two cottages in the country: one – the so-called nearby dacha – to spend the weekends, and another – a house in a far-away village – to spend summer vacations. The nearby dacha is usually located at a distance of 20–200 km from Moscow, while the far-away dacha can be situated 200–1200 km away. The summer cottages of Moscow and Saint Petersburg inhabitants have already formed a clear territorial belt-zone of country cottages between Russia's two major cities.[32] Quite often the summer enthusiasm of Muscovites has a positive economic effect on Russian villages, thanks to the city dwellers' *dachas*. Many rural depressed regions have managed to survive the depopulation and are changing for the better, at least during the summer holiday season.

However, it would be completely wrong to interpret the metaphor of Moscow as a village by only looking back to the conservative past of Russia. Certainly, Moscow has not yet overcome the challenges of its historical rural legacy, but it has already found itself in the centre of bright new contradictions as one of the biggest mega-cities of the world undergoing the transformations determined by processes of globalisation and its position as an emerging economy, and as one of the BRICS countries, in the global political economy. In order to successfully restructure old and new rural–urban forms, Moscow's future development will need to take into account both traditional Russian and international directions of development. Rapid transitions between rural and urban forms create new conditions of our everyday life, which can be conceived of as the land of 'transurbania', combining as it does both rural and urban elements. World mega-cities and mega-villages, such as Moscow, are essentially a kind of giant laboratory, which are conducting various experiments on the possibilities of symbiotic rural–urban coexistence in the 21st century.

Conclusion

Present-day Russia is an amazing composition of 'large' and 'small' forms of agricultural pro-duction and of different styles of rural–urban existence. Despite the expansion of giant agricultural enterprises or 'agroholdings', and the mega-urbanism epitomised by Moscow, these 'big' social and economic forms cannot exist without the 'small' ones. Though Russia's super-centralised state capitalism continues to exploit and control the 'small' forms – rural peasant households and communities – the authorities and businesses are forced to seek socio-economic integration, economic, political and cultural symbiosis of various autarkic rural–urban parts of the country. However, rural households and communities are not just passive elements of Russian and international globalisation; they do not confront it directly, but ideologically and culturally they often informally change the metropolitan state-capitalist structures in their own interests, or strive to achieve autarkic existence outside or within the state and the capitalist economy of Russia.

Chayanov provides a whole range of contextual frames that combine elements of peasant, class and cultural studies. We contend that Chayanov's legacy and his utopian ideas are relevant for explaining the current rural–urban reciprocity in Russia: '… Chayanov developed an analysis of peasant farm economics and household production units that is relevant wherever and whenever we find such forms'.[33] Teodor Shanin, considering the legacy of Chayanov, mentioned that 'rural society and rural problems are inexplicable any longer in their own terms and must be understood in terms of labor and capital flows which are broader than agriculture'.[34]

Chayanov's utopian views explored and contrasted the fundamental social, economic, cultural and political characteristics of human life to reconcile seeming oppositions of rural–urban, industry-agriculture, peasant-capitalist, state-public, and individual-social with solutions based on reciprocity and mutually beneficial coexistence necessary for the harmonisation of the world. The aim of his utopia was to propose a social and moral ideal; to provide and justify a new morality, a new ethic, a new and perfect future. However, the specific feature of Chayanov's utopias is the absence of any moral axiomatic premise so typical for utopianism in general – Chayanov did not like to make moral arguments. The utopian ethics of Chayanov were not immoral – rather, they were relativist, because he believed that the essence of evolution is just the increasing diversity of social life for the aim of peaceful coexistence.

This article shows some ways to apply Chayanov's ideas to the critical examination of contemporary Russian society. It is evident that the Russian state still underestimates the role, the potential and the needs of the small farming and peasant economy and openly favours big entrepreneurs or 'agroholdings'. Such an approach proved to be partly justified for the food security of the largest cities and has led to a paradox: the megalopolis of Moscow, together with the Moscow region, has created a system of giant agroholdings determining the mode and trends of agricultural and rural development for the whole country. However, quite an opposite approach proved to be successful in the Belgorod region, where the authorities' alternative approach to agrarian reform has traditional Russian roots, in the spirit of the neopopulist ideas of A.V. Chayanov and specifically his novel *My brother Alexey's Journey to the Land of Peasant Utopia*. The modernisation of the region is based on sustainable and dynamic development of its agricultural sector and rural areas by supporting both huge agricultural corporations under close monitoring by the regional authorities and other rural social-economic forms (peasant farms and cooperatives of local communities). Unlike many other parts of the country, this has created a mixed economy taking advantages of both large- and small-scale agricultural production by laying the foundations for mutually beneficial coexistence of different economies. We hope this article can contribute to reviving some of Chayanov's valuable insights as we continue the search for new ways to use the heuristic potential of Chayanov's utopia for the analysis of the contemporary rural–urban and centre–periphery relationship.

Disclosure statement

No potential conflict of interest was reported by the authors.

Notes

1. Harwood, *Europe's Green Revolution and Others Since*.
2. van der Ploeg, *Peasants and the Art of Farming*.
3. Visser et al., "'Quiet Food Sovereignty' as Food Sovereignty without a Movement?"
4. Travina, *Etnokulturnye i konfessionalnye konflikty v sovremennon mire*.
5. Chayanov, "Few Studies of the Isolated State," 79–88.
6. Kuznetsov, "Russian Agro-Economic Thought in the Thünen Perspective (1875–1925)," 403.
7. Russian Census // https://www.gks.ru/free_doc/new_site/perepis2010/croc/perepis_itogi1612.htm.

8. Nefedova and Travis, "Cities and Rural Areas: Status and Relationship in the Russian Space."
9. Uzun, "Classification of Russian Agricultural Producers."
10. Alexeev, *Mnogolikaya selskaya mestnost*.
11. Ioffe, Nefedova, and Zaslavski, "From Spatial Continuity to Fragmentation: The Case of Russian Farming."
12. Nefedova, "Major Trends for Changes in the Socioeconomic Space of Rural Russia."
13. *Russian Statistical Yearbook*, 2012, 79–80.
14. The rural birth rate in Russia is around 1.5, which is much below the level of reproduction of the population.
15. Rustamova, "Communist Party Found the 'red belt' in the Regions before the State Duma Elections."
16. Visser, Mamonova, and Spoor, "Oligarchs, Megafarms and Land Reserves."
17. Uzun, "Agroholdings of Russia."
18. 'Red landlords' refer to the former heads of collective (or Soviet) farms that survived in the post-Soviet period and managed to become powerful landlords under the slogans of supporting the former forms of economic and everyday cooperation, though in fact they became capitalist landowners.
19. 'White oligarchs' are capitalist landowners openly opposed the 'red landlords' and their socialist ideology.
20. Chayanov, *The Theory of Peasant Economy*, 202.
21. In Chayanov's utopia, there are no differences between the village and the city, for every type of settlement is a smaller or larger node of social ties In his utopia, Moscow is Russia's largest social and cultural hub with the permanent population of about 100,000 people, but more than 5 million people come daily to its hotels, theaters and museums, which enriches the cultural, educational and scientific life in both the city and in the countryside. Chayanov was an adherent of the cultural ideology of Russian populism as a strategy of 'enlightenment'. Thus, his utopian Moscow is a metropolis with a democratic folk culture following the highest standards of world and popular culture with the support of the ruling cultural and artistic oligarchy. Chayanov's utopian Moscow is a kind of art-pop capital and a mega-city relying on the synthesis of high and popular culture as the main branch of the utopian economy.
22. Chayanov, *My brother Alexey's Journey to the Land of Peasant Utopia*.
23. Ibid., 165, 166.
24. Ibid., 183.
25. Ibid., 198.
26. The new analytical approaches are presented in the book: *Metropolitan Ruralities* (2016).
27. 'In the last 40 years, the maximum depopulation of the rural areas was typical for territories around the Moscow region, especially to the north of it. Since 1965, thirteen regions of Central and North-Western Russia lost more than half of their rural population, mainly due to the migration to Moscow, partly – to migration to the capitals of these regions and Saint Petersburg': Nefedova, "Depopulation of Rural Areas and Agricultural Production," 341–356.
28. *The joint proposal of the Government of Moscow and the Government of the Moscow Region to change the boundaries of the capital of the Russian Federation – Moscow city.*
29. Nefyodova, *Ten Urgent Questions about Rural Russian*, 252, 253.
30. *Citizens Opinions on Agriculture* (2012).
31. Nefyodova, *Ten Urgent Questions about Rural Russia*, 234.
32. Ibid., 272.
33. Durrenberger, *Chayanov, Peasants, and Economic Anthropology*, 1.
34. Shanin, "Chayanov's Message," 19.

ORCID

Alexander Mikhailovich Nikulin http://orcid.org/0000-0001-7623-7985
Irina Vladimirovna Trotsuk http://orcid.org/0000-0002-2279-3588

Bibliography

Alexeev, Alexander. *Mnogolikaya selskaya mestnost* [Many-faced Countryside]. Moscow: Prosveschenie, 1990.

Chayanov, Alexander V. "Opyty izuchenija izolirovannogo gosudarstva" [Few Studies of the Isolated State.] *Ocherki po ekonomike selskogo hozjajstva* [Essays on Economy of Agriculture]. Moscow: Kooperativnoe izdatelstvo, 1923.

Chayanov, Alexander V. *Optimalnye razmery selskohozjajstvennyh predprijatij* [Optimal Sizes of Agricultural Enterprises]. Moscow: Novaya derevnya, 1928.

Chayanov, Alexander V. *Osnovnye idei i formy organizatsii selskohozjajstvennoj kooperatsii* [Basic Forms of Agricultural Cooperation Organization]. Moscow: Nauka, 1991.

Durrenberger, Paul E. *Chayanov, Peasants, and Economic Anthropology*. Orlando: Harcourt Brace, 1984.

Grazhdane o selskom hozjajstve [Citizens Opinions on Agriculture]. *Otechestvennye zapiski*, no. 6 (2012). http://www.strana-oz.ru/2012/6/grazhdane-o-selskom-hozyaystve

Harwood, Jonathan. *Europe's Green Revolution and Others Since: The Rise and Fall of Peasant-Friendly Plant Breeding*. Oxon: Routledge, 2012.

Hobsbawm, Eric J. *Age of Extremes: The Short Twentieth Century, 1914–1991*. Moscow: Izdatelstvo Nezavisimaja Gazeta, 2004.

Ioffe, Grigory, Tatyana Nefedova, and Ilya Zaslavski. "From Spatial Continuity to Fragmentation: The Case of Russian Farming." *Annals of Association of American Geography* 94, no. 4 (2004): 913–943.

Kuznetsov, Igor A. Rossijskaja agrarno-ekonomicheskaja mysl v thünenovskoj perspektive (1875–1925) [Russian Agro-economic Thought in the Thünen perspective (1875–1925)]. *Istorija mysli. Russkaja myslitelnaja traditsija* [History of Thought. Russian Intellectual Tradition]. Vyp. 6 / Pod red. I.P. Smirnova. Moscow, 2013.

Nefedova, Tatyana G. "Depopuljatsija sel'skoj mestnosti i agroproizvodstvo" [Depopulation of Rural Areas and Agricultural Production.] *Rossija i ee regiony v XX veke: territorija-rasselenie-migratsii*. O. Glezer. P. Polyana, eds. Moscow: OGI, 2005.

Nefedova, Tatyana G. "Major Trends for Changes in the Socioeconomic Space of Rural Russia." *Regional Research of Russia* 2, no. 1 (2012): 41–54.

Nefyodova, Tatyana G. *Desjat aktualnyh voprosov o selskoj Rossii. Otvety geografa* [Ten Urgent Questions about Rural Russian. Answers of a Geographer]. Moscow: Lenand, 2013.

Nefedova, Tatyana, and Andrey Travis. "Goroda i selskaya mestnost: sostoyanie i sootnoshenie v prostranstve Rossii" [Cities and Rural Areas: Status and Relationship in the Russian Space.] *Regionalnye issledovaniya*, no. 2 (2010): 42–56.

Nikonov, Alexander. *Spiral mnogovekovoy dramy: agrarnaya nauka i politika Rossii (XVIII-XX vv.)* [Spiral of the Centuries-Old Drama: Agricultural Science and Agrarian Policy of Russia (XVIII–XX Centuries)]. Moscow: Encyclopediya rossiyskih dereven, 1995.

Pilyasov, Alexander N. "Soobschestva severnoy periferii na etape industrialnoy transformatsii" [Communities of the Northern Periphery at the Industrial Transformation Stage]. *Sever: problemy periferiynyh territoriy*. Syktyvkar: Izd-vo Komi nauchnogo centra UrO RAN, 2007.

van der Ploeg, Jan D. *Peasants and the Art of Farming: A Chayanovian Manifesto*. Halifax: Fernwood Publishing, 2013.

Rustamova, Farida. "KPRF pered vyborami Gosdumy nashla v regionah 'krasnyj pojas'" [Communist Party Found the "red belt" in the Regions before the State Duma Elections]. *RBK*. January, 29, 2016.

Ruvil', Valentina S. *Rybnyj i ohotnichij promysly v ekonomicheskom razvitii pribrezhnyh territorij Severa i Dal'nego Vostoka* [Fishing and Hunting in the Economic Development of Coastal Areas of the North and the Far East]. Moscow, 2007.

Shanin, Teodor. "Chayanov's Message: Illuminations, Miscomprehensions, and the Contemporary 'development theory'." In A.V. Chayanov. *The Theory of Peasant Economy*, edited by D. Thorner, B. Kerblay, R. E. F. Smith, 1–6. Madison, WI: University of Wisconsin Press, 1986.

Sjöblom, S. M., K. W. Andersson, L. H. Granberg, P. Ehrström, and T. Marsden, eds. *Metropolitan Ruralities*. Cardiff: Emerald Group Publishing, 2016.

Surinov, A. E., ed. *Rossiiskiy statisticheskiy ezhegodnic* [Russian Statistical Yearbook]. Moscow: Rosstat, 2012.

Surinov, A. E., ed. *Rossiiskiy statisticheskiy ezhegodnic* [Russian Statistical Yearbook]. Moscow: Rosstat, 2013.

The Joint Proposal of the Government of Moscow and the Government of the Moscow Region to Change the Boundaries of the Capital of the Russian Federation – Moscow City. Press-release of the Moscow Government on July, 11, 2011.

von Thünen, Johann H. *Izolirovannoe gosudarstvo* [Isolated State]. Moscow: Ekonomicheskaja zhizn, 1926.

Travina, Elena M. *Etnokulturnye i konfessionalnye konflikty v sovremennon mire* [Ethno-Cultural and Confessional Conflicts in Contemporary World]. Saint Petersburg: Publishing House of Saint Petersburg University, 2007.

Uzun, Vasiliy Ya. "Klassifikacija sel'hozproizvoditelej Rossii" [Classification of Russian Agricultural Producers.] *Rossijskaja zemlja*. January, no. 1 (2010): 4–5.

Uzun, Vasiliy. "Agroholdingi Rossii: identifikatsija, klassifikatsija, rol', kontsentratsija zemlepol'zovanija" [Agroholdings of Russia: Identification, Classification, Role, and Land Concentration.] *Zemel'naja akkumuljatsija v nachale XXI veka: global'nye investory i lokal'nye soobschestva*. Moscow: "Delo", 2012.

Visser, Oane, Natalya Mamonova, and Max Spoor. "Oligarchs, Megafarms and Land Reserves: Understanding Land Grabbing in Russia." *Journal of Peasant Studies* 39, no. 3–4 (2012): 899–931.

Visser, Oane, Natalia Mamonova, Max Spoor, and Alexander Nikulin. "'Quiet Food Sovereignty' as Food Sovereignty without a Movement? Insights from Post-socialist Russia" *Globalizations* 12, no. 2 (2015): 513–528.

Wegren, Stephen, and Alexander Nikulin. "Agrarnye ambitsii Rossii i ee skromniy selskiy chelovecheskiy capital" [Agrarian Ambitions of Russia and Her Modest Rural Human Capital.] *Economicheskaya politika*, no. 3 (2014): 7–30.

Yakovets, Yury V. *Shkola russkogo tsyklizma: istoki, etapy razvitiya, perspektivy* [Russian Cyclism School: Origins, Stages of Development, and Prospects]. Moscow: MFK, 1998.

Growing South-South agribusiness connections: Brazil's policy coalitions reach Southern Africa

Carolina Milhorance

ABSTRACT

This paper focuses on the emergence of policy networks connecting diplomatic, technocratic, research and private actors from Brazil and southern Africa, which are contributing to the socialisation of Brazil's policy instruments and technical standards in the agribusiness sector. Technocratic dialogue within multilateral arenas, along with technical and economic cooperation, has stressed the significance of the Brazilian experience in the sector, encouraging the adoption of common standards, techniques and institutional frameworks on the basis of the country's experience. It argues that the consolidation of these networks helps reinforce Brazil's agribusiness internationally.

Introduction

The rise of a group of emerging economies such as Brazil, China and India during the 2000s has raised several questions about the implications of such a process for the production, circulation and consumption patterns of agricultural commodities. Brazil has become one of the most competitive agricultural producers in the world and a leading exporter of a large number of products such as soybeans, oranges and sugar. The country's agricultural modernisation experience has been internationally recognised,[1] and its state and business actors have positioned as important protagonists in global economic governance.[2] Increased economic relations with other economies such as China have reinforced a process of specialisation of Brazil's trade structure in primary goods.[3] Furthermore, its agribusiness sector has found new investment and trade expansion sites in Latin America[4] and Sub-Saharan Africa[5] – portrayed by Brazilian diplomats as 'mutual interests' to be operationalised through economic development instruments.[6] In this context, the international expansion of the country's agro-industrial sector has recently involved intensified relations with economies of the Global South.

This paper focuses on a particular aspect of these relations, namely the emergence of South–South networks of state and business actors sharing Brazil's policy instruments and technical standards for agribusiness development. It argues that the consolidation of these networks may help reinforce Brazil's agribusiness internationally, although this process may be influenced by the political dynamics of conflict and alliances both within and between these networks. Southern Africa is one of this country's preferred partners in agriculture.[7]

Drawing on case studies in this region, the empirical research relies on 18 months of field work and 280 semi-structured interviews with diplomats, policy-makers, business represent- atives, civil society organisations and farmers' associations conducted in Brazil, Malawi, Mozambique and South Africa in 2013, 2014 and 2015. The paper also uses documentary research conducted within ministerial and diplomatic archives in Brazil in 2013. For reasons of space, it focuses primarily on the dynamics from the Brazilian side; the concrete impacts of these dynamics in host countries are thus beyond the scope of this paper.

Starting from a theoretical discussion around policy networks, the following section describes three case studies in which Brazilian coalitions interact with southern African actors: (i) ethanol diplomacy and technocratic dialogue, (ii) development cooperation to facilitate investment; and (iii) subsidised credit for export of machinery. These shaped pat- terns of technology transfer, policy design and market development which contribute to increase Brazil's agribusiness sector's influence in commodities production and marketing. The paper combines an empirical basis with a theoretical approach intended to go beyond broad analysis of inter-governmental relations and to provide deeper information about political struggles and particular interest groups benefiting from the processes described.

Conceptual framework

Brazil has been increasingly involved in the formulation of international norms and devel- opment solutions, generally inspired by its own development experience.[8] Over the past decade, the country's position as an agricultural exporter of many raw materials and biofuels has earned recognition, and great progress has been made in implementing policies relevant to agricultural development. One common feature of the case studies analysed in this paper is the goal of promoting Brazilian agribusiness internationally by sharing some of the coun- try's public policy instruments. With respect to this, it is important to note that agribusiness has gained a central role within the state's strategy for international positioning since the 1990s, based on an 'export-oriented consensus' and close cooperation aimed at improving agricultural market conditions.[9] These ties to agribusiness have ensured domestic backing as well as technical expertise and organisational resources for trade negotiations and bilateral initiatives.[10] Thus, in addition to enhanced presidential diplomacy in the 2000s, Brazil's foreign action has involved a diverse range of state and non-state actors, organised via networks and keen to advance their interests.

Notions of policy networks and advocacy coalition have been used to highlight the power relations relating to actors' resources as well as to political and institutional contexts. Combining policy network and advocacy coalition frameworks has been a useful approach in explaining patterns of group formation and collective action in policy arenas.[11] Sabatier and Jenkins-Smith analyse public action as a result of conflicts between different belief systems brought on by multiple policy networks in which actors from diverse public and private institutions share basic ideas.[12] According to Stone, policy networks are always founded on some form of 'taken-for-granted' knowledge and expertise that are entrenched in their approach to economic, political and social issues.[13] A central assumption in the author's work is that the creators and distributors of policy knowledge – in the form of technical standards, scientific theories, policy analyses and evidence-based recommenda- tions – become central players in decision-making. The notion of 'network' used in this paper conceives power relations between actors.[14]

Drawing on policy networks and socialisation literature, I examine the emergence of distinct networks sharing Brazil's agribusiness promotion instruments. In International Relations studies, the notion of socialisation is subject to multiple interpretations, being used in the literatures of norm diffusion[15], transnational networks[16] and collective actors' relations.[17] Soulé-Kohndou analysed the socialisation process within multilateral groups of emerging economies such as the IBSA Forum (India, Brazil and South Africa).[18] According to the author, socialisation may be understood as an assimilation of individuals to social groups. In the IBSA case, it would imply learning processes based on interaction between actors in the various informal and formal meetings that form trans-governmental networks. It would also imply the internalisation of norms, values and cognitive structures and practical knowledge which contribute to adjust actors' behaviour.

From an economic sociology perspective, the notion of socialisation goes beyond a mechanical or egalitarian view of learning as the mere transfer of knowledge from one organisation to another. According to Favre, it constitutes rather a vector of social discipline that is part of a collective learning of norms.[19] Learning is thus a social mechanism of concentration of authority so it has both a hierarchical and cohesive dimensions. In doing so, the control of arenas of socialisation and interaction mechanisms implies the control of the dissemination of norms and standards which results in the endorsement of relevant knowledge and mutual adjustments within networks. Moreover, Peck and Theodore reminded us that policy instruments reveal their character as 'relational' constructions; they do not simply travel, intact, from sites of invention to sites of emulation, like silver bullets.[20] Instead, through their very movement, they (re)make connections between these sites and actors.

These studies are employed to argue that emerging policy networks including Brazil's state and agribusiness actors interact with southern African actors in the socialisation of policy instruments and technical standards identified with the Brazilian development experience. The process of socialisation provides southern African actors with additional financial, technical and political resources with which to instigate reforms in the field of agricultural development, while also contributing to the adjustment of cognitive structures and behaviours of related actors in accordance with Brazil's agribusiness sector interests.

Diplomatic and technocratic dialogue to develop a global ethanol market

According to Brazilian diplomacy, the absence of a well-organised international ethanol market constrains this sector's development in Brazil.[21] In addition to their interest in accessing major markets in the United States and Europe, representatives of this sector consider the organisation of a global market to be positive, as this would contribute to diversification of producer countries, reducing investment risks.[22] In this context, one approach to building such a market relies on sharing Brazil's 'acquired experience' in the domestic development of the sector. Multilateral arenas such as the IBSA Forum seem to be privileged spaces in which to socialise the country's policy instruments and technical standards. Furthermore, technical dialogues with private and public institutions in the African countries have also been identified as a means of promoting the perspectives of Brazilian actors.

The so-called 'ethanol diplomacy' driven by the former President Lula da Silva (2003–2010) has been effective in promoting international awareness of ethanol production. Wilkinson describes how Brazil presented itself, at the start of the 2000s, as a model of clean energy sources, given the importance of hydroelectric and renewable biomass in its energy matrix.[23]

The co-generation of bioelectricity was also projected to further encourage this sector's contribution to renewable energy, in a context of increased visibility of climate change challenges. In the following years, sharp increases in oil prices and the launch of flex fuel cars in 2003 helped expand the domestic market. The United States, the European Union and Japan began providing export markets for ethanol. In this context, presidential diplomacy led by Lula da Silva was the driving force behind the promotion of ethanol – both as a policy for adoption at international fora and as a global market to be developed.

Interviews with representatives of the ethanol industry[24] reveal that a concerted effort between the Ministry of Foreign Affairs (MRE), the Ministry of Foreign Trade (MDIC), the Ministry of Agriculture, Livestock and Supply (MAPA) and the Brazilian Sugarcane Industry Association (Unica) was fruitful. This active coalition of public and private actors was expected to both encourage other countries to invest in biofuel, and consolidate a global market for Brazilian products, machinery and services. At the global level, Brazil's diplomacy has advocated the adoption of common standards at international biofuels meetings. The country's bureaucrats have promoted the adoption of ethanol in Latin America and Africa, providing expertise in building legal and institutional frameworks as well as in technology transfer.

In 2010, an important agreement was signed between Brazil and the European Union for the development of bioenergy in African countries – Mozambique in particular.[25] According to Unica's executive director:

> Mozambique exhibits a great deal of potential for agricultural expansion, particularly when it comes to tropical crops, including sugarcane. The country's geographic location gives it a clear advantage as a privileged route to ship biofuels to Asia and Europe, with three suitable ports along the coast. This is an additional comparative advantage that increases its potential as an ethanol exporter.[26]

For the Brazilian private sector, this was thus an opportunity to gain privileged access to European and Asian markets.[27] A similar agreement was signed with the United States, aimed at sharing technology in order to enhance ethanol production in Latin America and the Caribbean countries, the purpose of which was, according to Hollander, to enlarge the ethanol market at the hemispheric scale and to develop ethanol production in other countries via equipment sales.[28] This agreement led to the promotion of common standards and norms to enable the development of a global market, as well as to the achievement of joint feasibility studies for sugarcane in several countries in the African continent.[29]

These initiatives attracted strong criticism from international NGOs which contributed to linking the biofuel industry to food price volatility. Brazilian 'biofuel diplomacy' reacted by defending sugarcane ethanol, involving organisations such as the private Institute for International Trade Negotiations (Icone) and the public Brazilian Agricultural Research Corporation (Embrapa).[30] This public-private coalition succeeded in getting Brazil's sugarcane ethanol classified by the United States Environmental Protection Agency as an 'advanced fuel', stressing that it was not produced from primary food crops and that it would comply with agro-ecological zoning.[31]

However, during Rousseff's administration (2011–2016), ethanol diplomacy was downgraded from the president to ministry-level technocrats. According to Brazilian officials, this was a change in diplomatic profile rather than a retraction of the country's biofuel offensive: 'President Lula used biofuels as a flag. The subject used to appear in every official pronouncement, raising the sector's profile'.[32] Furthermore, the outlook for the development of an international biofuel market lost traction as the European Union moved to a lower blending mandate, and oil prices declined in the 2010s.[33] Other countries also revised their targets as food security concerns undermined the legitimacy of first-generation food crops as feedstock.[34]

Despite the reduced presidential emphasis in ethanol diplomacy, Brazilian state and business actors retained their expert status in the ethanol sector internationally. It is noteworthy that Brazilian companies in the private sector (and even Unica) have been visited and consulted several times by delegations composed of public and private African actors.[35] Therefore, in addition to their existing arenas of ethanol promotion, these technocratic experts, diplomats, research institutions and business associations formed coalitions independent of president decisions that found new arenas in the Global South. These include such multilateral spaces as the IBSA Forum and other technical delegations and projects in southern African countries in which these policy coalitions were able to socialise technical standards identified with the Brazilian experience in the sector.

First, at the IBSA Forum, a number of technical meetings bringing together bureaucrats and private companies helped weave social links that were independent of government decisions. Several diplomatic letters consulted in the MRE archives confirm that harmonisation of technical standards would represent a critical step in building a global ethanol market.[36] In this regard, a more in-depth dialogue on matters such as the automotive industry, bioelectricity co-generation, integrated distillery plantation plants, the Brazilian public bidding system for biodiesel, and the 'social label'[37] have been discussed at several IBSA meetings. Technical dialogue has also taken place at the IBSA Energy Working Group, with Brazilian experts often taking part. An agreement was signed in 2008 to establish an IBSA task force for encouraging technology transfer, common legal frameworks, technical cooperation, trade and innovation in the ethanol sector. Many workshops have been organised by Brazilian counterparts on sector-related issues.[38] As a result of these meetings, a deeper relationship has been built with IBSA technocrats – South Africans in particular – having shown their intention to benefit from Brazilian experience in the development of the sector, as confirmed by Brazilian officials in this country.[39]

In addition to the harmonisation of technical specifications within this multilateral group, Brazilian diplomatic documents highlighted other major strategies, namely experience-sharing of policy and institutional frameworks aimed at fostering development of the sector in other countries. For instance, Brazil has relied on the Global Bioenergy Partnership (GBEP) as a partner for the promotion of bioenergy capacity building and training in Latin America, Africa and Asia, through short courses and events such as Bioenergy Week (2013 in Brazil, 2014 in Mozambique and 2015 in Indonesia). A GBEP Task Force has been developing a set of 24 voluntary sustainability indicators for bioenergy since 2008.[40] This initiative has sought to build and socialise consensus across a broad range of national governments and international institutions, including such elements as addressing the 'food x fuel' conflict in ethanol production and enhancing the international image of Brazilian ethanol.

Second, as claimed by Patriota and Pierri, the riots that erupted in many African countries in 2007/2008 were linked not only to rising food prices, but also to higher costs of public transport as a result of a hike in oil prices.[41] Lower energy foreign dependence was also seen as a strategic goal in the region, hence their interest in acquiring Brazilian biofuel production technology. Moreover, according to the same authors, the transfer of Brazil's biofuel technology to African countries would also generate demand for equipment linked to its ethanol-specific processing and manufacturing industries. This technology exchange also contributes to align producer-countries in terms of production techniques and standards taking into account the Brazilian frameworks and experience. Brazilian diplomats confirmed that experience-sharing with these countries represents an additional means of establishing a global ethanol market. They also explained that 'from a political point of view, besides the feasibility studies, it would be interesting to have a concrete case of investment to showcase the potential benefits of our model'.[42]

In this respect, the National Economic and Social Development Bank (BNDES) of Brazil and other private companies such as the mining corporation Vale and Getulio Vargas Foundation (FGV) contributed to funding and conducting biofuel feasibility studies in African countries and prospecting potential economic agreements. Senegal, Zambia and Mozambique, having benefited from the elaboration of feasibility studies, were identified as the most promising countries for the development of biofuels.[43] In Mozambique, for instance, these studies were developed under a joint Brazil–European Union initiative, though later funded by Vale. A previous study was conducted by the World Bank in 2008, and in 2009, the country approved a national biofuel plan, subsequently starting experimental projects. Furthermore, the 'Latin America, Caribbean and Africa Sustainable Bioenergy' Programme (Lacaf/GSB) – a global initiative funded by the São Paulo Research Foundation and involving research networks in various countries – has promoted workshops and technical visits to evaluate prospects for ethanol production in Mozambique and South Africa, based on the Brazilian (sugarcane-based) model. As announced by Lacaf's organisers, 'we want a group of friendly countries participating in this global ethanol market. (…) Mozambican and South African researchers will come to Brazil and short delegations will interact with the ministries to formulate a solid strategy'.[44]

In addition, BNDES established a hub office in Johannesburg, South Africa, and signed agreements with the African Development Bank (AfDB) and the New Partnership for Africa's Development (NEPAD) to explore bioenergy collaboration on the African continent. The bank's representatives in Johannesburg explained that

> Brazil is exporting its model to several countries and BNDES is interested in this process. It has funded several biofuel feasibility studies. There are Brazilian companies exporting Brazilian machines. There is business going on! (…) The bank's role as a hub is to collect strategic information by establishing technical, financial and institutional relations.[45]

However, despite this apparent business optimism regarding ethanol in southern Africa, concrete actions, according to Brazilian diplomats, have been scarce due to Brazilian companies' poor knowledge of the African investments environment and aggravated by the lack of a favourable policy framework in these countries.[46] Representatives from the ethanol sector concluded that

> Africa, and particularly Mozambique, is an interesting site for production. (…) they have favourable climate, soil, availability of labour, privileged tariff status and proximity to consumer markets. However, they lack qualified labour, infrastructure and an adequate regulatory framework. (…) This kind of investment has a potential in terms of regional development because the integrated plan of production and distillery could bring industry and services to the rural areas. There is also the potential of promoting bioelectricity. In brief, there is a great potential but it is important to first create the legal framework to foster a regional market.[47]

Third, in the face of these institutional constraints on promotion of the ethanol industry, several countries in southern Africa such as South Africa, Mozambique, Zimbabwe and Zambia adopted or revised their policy frameworks. All these countries received support from Brazilian private or public institutions. Brazilian diplomats believe, for instance, that the revision of South Africa's Biofuels Industrial strategy was largely inspired by Brazilian laws.[48] The country has also looked up to Brazil for investments in this sector. A joint South African-Brazilian venture, SilvaPen Group, benefited from Brazil's expertise and equipment, and was consulted by the South African Government during the formulation of the country's biofuel strategy.[49] Drawing on statements provided by the Ethanol Producers Association of southern Africa[50], Zimbabwean private actors have also recently followed the Brazilian distilleries model. The Green Fuel company established, in 2011, an ethanol plant whose design and machines were imported from Brazil and installed under the supervision of Brazilian experts.[51]

However, in addition to difficulties arising from the lack of policy frameworks, private investments have also faced major funding constraints. These needs were taken into account in the design of other agribusiness development initiatives involving Brazilian actors, as it will be discussed in the next section. Other challenges include society's critical attitude towards these initiatives. In Mozambique, for instance, biofuels are currently viewed with some suspicion, as the country's experience in promoting *jatropha* in the southern province of Gaza led to the failure of several projects and renewed patterns of land concentration in the region.[52] In South Africa, the main biofuel-related concern is the need to irrigate the biofuel crops that have been adopted. South Africa is a water-stressed country with agriculture consuming about 60% of the available resource for irrigation.[53]

To sum up, a public-private coalition (including representatives of the Brazilian diplomacy, foreign trade institutions, research establishments and the private ethanol sector) has emerged, with the aim of promoting the country's ethanol sector internationally. This coalition has increasingly participated in socialising southern African technocrats with regard to the technical standards and regulatory set-ups identified with the Brazilian experience. Despite weaker presidential support for this agenda during Rousseff's administration, several arenas of exchange have remained active: (i) technical meetings within multilateral forums such as IBSA and the GBEP; (ii) feasibility studies conducted by Brazilian organisations; and (iii) delegations by public and private actors aiming to enhance learning about Brazil's ethanol policy and technical instruments. Though engagement through 'ethanol diplomacy' and foreign direct investment may not have matched expectations, recent years have seen some renewed efforts to stimulate the promotion of a global ethanol market. New South–South policy networks are helping reinforce the presence of Brazil's ethanol sector in southern Africa, consolidating their viewpoints in the production of the norms and building a nascent market.

Development cooperation to promote investments

Despite the fact that Brazil's investments are normally restricted to the industrial stage of international agribusiness chains, its public-private strategies have recently been characterised by more direct investment in farming. This renewed interest is consistent with the global rise of foreign investment in farmland following the 2007–2008 world food crisis.[54] These land deals have also been promoted in a context in which the G8/G20 have responded to the food crisis by renewing its focus on agricultural investment as a mechanism for development and poverty reduction – through the Alliance for Food Security and Nutrition and the World Bank's Global Food Security Fund.[55] Sub-Saharan Africa and a portion of South-East

Asia are the zones most affected by these investments, drawing particularly on leasing mechanisms and long-term concessions allocated by host country governments.[56] These investments are often marked by strong regionalism, so Brazil's presence is stronger in Latin America.[57] Yet rising demand for agricultural commodities from Asian markets, combined with Brazil's state support to agribusiness, have helped consolidate the sector's presence in other regions such as southern Africa.

However, according to Borras and Franco, many of the reported land transactions remain mere paper allocations, while others are more speculative in nature.[58] As demonstrated by Anseeuw et al., a great deal of agricultural investment approved worldwide fails to be implemented due to factors such as (i) underestimation of technical and management difficulties; (ii) the lack of necessary attributes, given high transaction costs and (iii) the speculative positioning of investors aiming to secure property.[59] For instance, recent studies have shown that farmland project failure rates are very high in Mozambique in both negotiation and implementation processes.[60] Many projects are not economically viable, once the pricing system, cost of capital, settlement and transaction costs, and technical and managerial difficulties are taken into account.

Brazil's foreign investments in farmland have also faced major challenges, including lack of funding, poor knowledge of markets and national institutional/legal frameworks, and increasingly challenging local politics and civil society struggles. Few pioneer investors have managed to settle on the African continent. An example is the Pinesso Agroindustrial Company, which has investments in cotton, maize, sorghum, beans and sunflower cultures in Sudan, as well as in the soy culture of Northern Mozambique.[61] Diverse financial strategies have been observed within this scenario of high failure rates and a varied set of challenges to farmland investments. One of these is the establishment of joint ventures in partnership with companies more familiar with the local institutional, political and agricultural particularities. For instance, South African commercial farmers became service providers for other foreign investors seeking to become established in Mozambique[62] and Brazilian investors have reported their interest in benefiting from expertise gained through joint ventures.[63] In addition, Brazil is deploying technical cooperation that is based on strong institutional and financial arrangements and on the socialisation of the country's own policy instruments and technologies to succeed in international agri-food investments.

In this context, a second coalition, comprising Brazilian governmental, private and research institutions, has promoted technical cooperation aimed at developing agricultural research capacity and economic development in Mozambique and Malawi. Mozambique is Brazil's leading partner in terms of technical cooperation in Africa, and an important destination in the internationalisation of Brazilian companies.[64] More recently, Malawi established relations with Brazil, in the context of Lula's rapprochement with Africa. The Brazilian Embassy in Malawi was inaugurated in June 2013, and bilateral relations focus on exploring potential in the biofuel sector, the development of agricultural research, rural development policy experience-sharing and the private investments made by Vale.[65] The company is rehabilitating the railway that connects mining investments in Tete province, Mozambique, to the Nacala port on the Indian Ocean, travelling through Malawian territory. The former Malawian Minister of Foreign Affairs, Ephraim Chiume, has also mentioned the country's interest in being included in ongoing cooperation projects in Mozambique such as ProSavana, a trilateral Japan–Brazil–Mozambique initiative aimed at developing commercial agriculture in the Nacala Corridor, northern Mozambique.[66]

ProSavana is the biggest cooperation programme in the Brazilian Cooperation Agency's (ABC) entire portfolio.[67] It was initially inspired by Prodecer, a commodity-export oriented agricultural development programme supported by Japan and implemented in the Cerrado region of Brazil, since the 1970s.[68] The key goals of ProSavana were increasing agricultural productivity and establishing agroindustrial production chains. It is worth noting that, according to diplomatic documents,[69] the Japanese government had expressed its interest in funding a trilateral project with Brazil in Mozambique as long ago as the early 2000s. In addition to ProSavana, Japan funds other major agricultural initiatives in the country, also in the Nacala corridor. This strategy is consistent with a change observed in Japanese cooperation policy towards giving greater priority to private interest.[70] Other studies also highlight this government's interest in increasing global agricultural production, which is understandable given the country's dependence on international food markets.[71]

On the Brazilian side, the diplomatic channel thus joins forces with public financial support for the establishment of the private sector. Efforts have been consolidated in order to attract investment to the Nacala Corridor, including business delegations, public-private seminars, technical reports and strategic meetings. In November 2010 a business delegation organised by the National Confederation of Agriculture and Livestock (CNA) of Brazil, with the support of ABC, brought Brazilian agribusiness investors to Mozambique to work with the ProSavana team. Leading the delegation, Senator Katia Abreu, former CNA president, invited the Mozambican Ministry of Agriculture to visit Brazil and suggested that the CNA's technical branch, SENAR, become directly involved in ProSavana. As a result of this visit, the seminar 'Agribusiness in Mozambique: Brazil-Japan International Cooperation and Investments Opportunities' was held in São Paulo in April 2011, with the aim of publicising potential for investments in the Nacala Corridor for Brazil's private sector.[72]

These business delegation and cooperation mechanisms were designed to overcome investors' lack of familiarity with the rural and political reality in Mozambique, as well as their reluctance due to the high costs of these projects. One of the programme's former coordinators confirmed that the funding aspect of the programme was crucial to overcoming the 'insecurity of the investment environment',[73] and he explained at the same occasion that 'in the initial conception of ProSavana, technology was planned to come first, then rural extension and finally the private sector'. Indeed, the connection between bilateral cooperation and the 'potential to leverage opportunities for Brazilian companies in the sector of agribusiness' has been identified by both governmental and private actors as an important component ever since the early stages of the programme, back in 2003, as recorded in diplomatic archives.[74] Other diplomatic documents confirm Mozambican public interest in Brazilian soy production expertise via technology transfer and joint ventures, given the crop's priority status in the country.[75]

ProSavana therefore includes a comprehensive scheme to attract investment to Mozambique: infrastructure development, research into the adaptation of agricultural varieties, financial mechanisms, and legal/institutional security. These incentives were mainly inspired by the Brazilian experience in developing agribusiness and were expected to overcome the problems of unfamiliarity and high costs experienced by Brazilian and other foreign investors on the African continent, especially the Japanese. Interviews also confirm that Mozambique's proximity to Asian markets has represented a major encouragement to the internationalisation of Brazil's productive component to southern Africa.[76]

Other similar (though smaller-scale) initiatives were intended to develop technical cooperation to support the cotton sector in Malawi and Mozambique. This went through a prospecting phase even prior to the establishment of the Brazilian Embassy in Malawi.[77] According to official documentation, the project is based on two major events: (i) the Cotton Initiative, concretised in a coalition against subsidies being granted by developed countries to their own cotton sectors, and brought forward at the World Trade Organisation in 2003, and (ii) the settlement of this dispute in favour of the Brazilian complainants, requiring that the US make compensation payments to the Brazilian government institutions and cotton farmers.[78] In this context, the Brazilian Cotton Institute (IBA) was created to receive the US$ 147.3 million temporary compensation paid annually by the United States. The Institute and MRE jointly signed in 2011 an agreement committing 10% of this income to finance international cooperation projects in the cotton sector including the test, capacity building and transfer of Brazilian technologies to the African countries that traditionally grow this crop.[79]

The objective of the project was to help increase the competitiveness of the cotton sector in Mozambique and Malawi by strengthening technological, institutional and human resources, as well as technical assistance capacities. It includes (i) test and dissemination of technologies developed by Embrapa (regarding production systems, seed qualities, crop management, pest management); (ii) capacity-building among researchers, extension professionals, local experts and farmers' leaders; (iii) improvement of facilities at certain research units. Brazilian companies and agribusiness associations showed particular interest in being integrated to the project. The IBA's director described it thus: '[The] Brazilian private sector was interested in this initiative, for instance, Pinesso, CNA and the Brazilian Cotton Growers Association (Abrapa), but they were not directly involved. They were very interested in investing in Africa'.[80]

The patterns observed here are, then, similar to those of other initiatives described in this paper: policy coalitions involving diplomatic, research and private actors interacting through initiatives aimed at socialising the institutional and technical instruments of Brazilian experience in agribusiness development. These coalitions are characterised by belief systems promoting instruments of agricultural investments and productivist modernisation founded on Brazil's agribusiness expertise. As claimed by Stone,[81] the creators and distributors of policy knowledge in the form of technical standards and evidence-based recommendations become central players in decision-making. This socialisation process is part of a collective learning of norms developed by Brazilian actors.

However, ProSavana has been subjected to strong criticism by a network that includes Brazilian and Mozambican NGOs and social movements, as well as Japanese[82] and other international organisations such as Oxfam – which contributed to delaying implementation of the programme. Alarmist articles produced by national and international media sought to draw the public's attention to the risk of 'land grabbing'.[83] The Nacala Fund, originally conceptualised as a private equity fund based in Luxembourg, has been reformulated due to fundraising failures, lack of strategic alignment among partner countries, inefficient institutional communication and pressure from civil society.[84] Brazil's technical cooperation, which was designed to increase agricultural productivity, did not exclusively target large-scale agribusiness companies; it also included promotion of narratives for smallholder agriculture, as discussed in the next section.

Subsidised credit to foster agricultural machinery exports

In addition to policy dialogue and technical cooperation described above, the loans provided by the More Food International (MFI) Programme were expected to boost agricultural machinery exports. This programme, launched under Lula da Silva's leadership, was meant to provide concessional credits to certain African countries willing to buy Brazilian agricultural machines suitable for family farming. Inspired by a public programme initiated in Brazil as a Ministry of Agrarian Development (MDA) response to the 2007/2008 food price crisis, it bore the same name and operated through similar instruments.[85] It aimed to strengthen the productive capacity of smallholder farmers in African countries by combining preferential credit (2% interest rates, a 10-year term and 3-year grace period) for the import of a wide variety of agricultural equipment and machinery geared towards small- and medium-scale farming (with discount of up to 17.5%).[86] Furthermore, it intended to provide technical assistance in the design of rural extension policies for family farming. Its implementation was mainly provided by MDA, in collaboration with the Foreign Trade Chamber in the MDIC.

In concrete terms, it also furnished the industrial sector, gathered under the Brazilian Machinery Builders' Association (Abimaq), with steadily increasing demand. The synergy generated by family farmers' access to the programme and the consequent demand for agricultural machinery aimed to operationalise a 'countercyclical industrial policy' in a context of global financial crisis.[87] In the words of the sector's representative:

> Abimaq's traditional market is Latin America (...), but there is an ongoing expansion towards the African continent. The Moore Food Programme represented an opportunity to such an expansion. (...) Besides, partnerships with the MRE and Apex [the Brazilian Trade Investment Promotion Agency] contributed to organize business delegations and participation in international fairs. (...) Finally, the companies face important funding constraints which have been in part overcome thanks to collaboration with the BNDES.[88]

This kind of initiative is in line with the government's developmental plans. According to the programme's coordinators at the MDIC, 'the fact that it constitutes an official cooperation initiative implemented by public institutions and based on sovereign financial guarantees presupposes more security to the creditors'.[89] It has also led to the creation of a working group – GTEX Africa – aimed at strengthening economic relations with African countries. As informed by a representative of this group 'public resources deployed on exports to Africa have the potential to generate income, jobs and promote technology transfer. These mechanisms support the Brazilian economy. Input providers of these companies are also Brazilian'.[90]

Similarly, Cabral et al. argue that this programme is not regarded as a conventional export operation; rather, it is portrayed as an example of Brazil's 'responsible approach' to business and African development.[91] Indeed, this initiative relied on South-South cooperation principles, particularly the idea of the 'mutual interests' of economic development between southern partners. Some staff responsible for the programme in the MDA recognise that it represents a transition in Brazil's cooperation paradigm, as its previous commitment to separating cooperation from commercial interest (and, arguably, from conditionalities) has been shelved.[92]

In southern Africa, Mozambique and Zimbabwe are priority partners for this initiative, which was well received by African delegations.[93] However, several scholars have questioned the extent to which rural extension and technologies favourable to smallholder farmers have been effectively transferred to Africa, since technical cooperation and machinery exports have actually concentrated on relatively sophisticated items with limited applicability for the small- and medium-scale farmers who were the supposed beneficiaries of this program.[94]

Despite the programme's emphasis on the promotion of the family farming sector in its Brazilian version, it has been adopted in Mozambique through its mechanisation component. Fostered in Brazil as a policy instrument of production support for family farmers, which has been criticised by academics and civil society for its exaggerated emphasis on a modernising perspective,[95] it has been adopted in Mozambique as a result of this very component. Cabral et al. argue that despite differences, both the MFI and ProSavana relied on agricultural modernisation to increase production.[96] The complementary objectives of the MFI, of building 'an emancipatory system of technical assistance and food security oriented towards family farming'[97] was considered a mere accessory by the Mozambican government.[98] Other studies conducted in Zimbabwe showed similar results, as the country's farmers and technical staff saw the programme as having been established to provide affordable farm machinery, missing both the extension component and the exchange of public policy experiences on family farming.[99]

Policy instruments inspired by the Brazilian experience have been reframed by national actors in line with their own political preferences and perspectives. Brazilian actors interacting with government and private organisations in African countries were more efficient in sharing their perspectives in agricultural mechanisation than a state-led strategy of promoting family farming production. This reaffirms the claim that policy instruments are 'relational' constructions that do not 'travel' intact.[100] Furthermore, although these are not detailed in this paper, it is worth noting that there are other initiatives promoting distinct rural development instruments in Brazil and in the host countries. These include civil society criticisms against the internationalisation of Brazil's agribusiness as well as the Purchase from Africans for Africa Programme (PAA Africa), which intends to secure food markets for family farmers by government procurement of school meals in five African countries. According to Sabatier and Jenkins-Smith, public action may be analysed as a result of conflicts between different belief systems brought on by multiple policy coalitions.[101]

Conclusion

The international expansion of Brazil's agro-industrial sector has recently involved enhanced relations with countries from the Global South, which have benefited from its connection with state institutions as well as from a gradual recognition of its 'agribusiness experts'. This paper focused on the emergence of policy networks connecting diplomatic, technocratic, research and private actors from Brazil and southern Africa that contributed to the socialisation of Brazil's policy instruments and technical standards. Technocratic dialogue within multilateral arenas, as well as economic and technical cooperation, have emphasised the significance of the Brazilian experience in this sector, favouring the adoption of common standards, techniques and institutional frameworks based on the country's experience. This socialisation process provides southern African actors with additional financial, technical and political resources to undertake reforms in the field of agricultural development, and also contributes to a collective internalisation of norms capable of reinforcing Brazil's agribusiness in the medium to long term, as these form the foundations upon which investments and commodity trade are built.

This influence in the dissemination of commodity production and marketing standards demonstrates increased capacity in establishing international norms. According to a Brazilian diplomat, this process builds the country's political capital: 'we show how to do, but in the Brazilian way. This is not only technology, there is a philosophy behind'.[102] However, more than an analysis of the increasing legitimacy of Brazilian models, this paper has sought to set out the emergence of distinct South–South networks benefiting particular interest groups in their international expansion as well as the intra-sectoral struggles. Furthermore, it is noteworthy that these technical and institutional set-ups constitute 'relational' constructions that are subject to transformation and selection by the 'recipient' actors. Policy instruments travelling the Atlantic have been reframed by national actors in line with their own political preferences, and Brazilian instruments have been criticised by actors promoting other rural development perspectives. This shows how the country's agribusiness prospects of productivist modernisation and market liberalisation is reinforcing its international presence – yet these do not necessarily work into the domestic fabric of all societies; these transnational development solution 'fronts' are in a state of constant confrontation and renewal.

Disclosure statement

No potential conflict of interest was reported by the author.

Funding

This work was supported by the The BRICS Initiative for Critical Agrarian Studies (BICAS).

Notes

1. Milhorance, "Brazil's Cooperation with Sub-Saharan Africa."
2. Hopewell, "New Protagonists in Global."
3. Vadell et al., "The International Implications."
4. Oliveira, "The Geopolitics of Brazilian Soybeans."
5. Amanor, "Expanding Agri-business."
6. Cabral et al., "Brazil's Agricultural Politics."
7. Gabas and Goulet, "Chinese and Brazilian Agricultural Cooperation."
8. See note 1.
9. Søndergaard, "Public-private Re-alignments."
10. See note 2.
11. Weible and Sabatier, "Comparing Policy Networks."
12. Sabatier and Jenkins-Smith, *Policy Change and Learning*.
13. Stone, *Knowledge Actors and Transnational*.
14. Marsh and Smith, "Understanding Policy Networks"; and Sabatier and Jenkins-Smith, *Policy Change and Learning*.
15. Finnemore and Sikkink, "International Norm Dynamics."
16. Keck and Sikkink, *Activists beyond Borders*.
17. Alderson, "Making Sense of State Socialization."

18. 'Les 'clubs' de puissances 'émergentes'.
19. Favre, *Des rencontres dans la mondialisation*.
20. Peck and Theodore, *Fast Policy*.
21. Kloss, *Transformação Do Etanol*.
22. Interview, Unica's Executive Director, July/2013, São Paulo.
23. Wilkinson, *Brazil, Biofuels and Bio-Diplomacy*.
24. Interview, Unica's Director, July/2013, São Paulo.
25. Council of the European Union, *IV European Union-Brazil*.
26. UNICA, "Brazil-EU-Africa Agreement."
27. Seibert, "Brazil in Africa."
28. Hollander, "Power Is Sweet."
29. Wilkinson, *Brazil, Biofuels and Bio-Diplomacy*.
30. Ibid.
31. The term 'advanced biofuels' is defined in Section 201 of the Energy Independence and Security Act of 2007 and includes mature technologies and those that reduce lifecycle of greenhouse gas emissions by 50%. This category includes biofuels produced from non-corn feedstocks.
32. Interview, diplomat, head of the Renewable Energy Division in MRE, July/2013, Brasilia.
33. See note 29.
34. USDA-FAS, *Brazil: Biofuel Annual*.
35. Unica, "Produtos Da Cana Podem Contribuir"; Unica, "Comitiva Africana Destaca"; and Unica, "África vê No Brasil". Interview, Unica's Executive Director, July/2013, São Paulo.
36. MRE, "IBAS. Energia"; and Brazilian Embassy in Pretoria/MRE, "Energia. IBAS. África do Sul."
37. This label corresponds to a certification mechanism granted by Brazilian government to biodiesel producers that comply with a number of criteria considered important to promote social inclusion of family farmers. Producers obtaining the label receive fiscal and commercial incentives, besides specific lines of public funding.
38. Brazilian Embassy in Pretoria/MRE, "Energia. IBAS. África do Sul."
39. Interview, Brazil's agricultural attaché in South Africa, Johannesburg, March/2013 and March/2014.
40. GBEP and FAO, *The Global Bioenergy Partnership*.
41. Patriota and Pierri, "Brazil's Cooperation for Agriculture."
42. Interview, Head of Energy Division in MRE, July/2013, Brasilia.
43. Ibid.
44. Speech by one of the organizers during the 'Bioenergy in Africa Workshop', Maputo, April/2014.
45. Interview, Director of BNDES Africa , March/2014, Johannesburg.
46. Interview, Head of Energy Division in MRE, July/2013, Brasilia.
47. Interview, Unica's Director, July/2013, São Paulo.
48. Interview, diplomat in charge of bilateral cooperation with South Africa, March/2013, Pretoria.
49. Silvapen Group, *Tecnologia Brasileira Em Solo* Fértil'; Interview, SilvaPen Director, March/2014, Johannesburg.
50. Interview, EPASA President, March/2014, Johannesburg.
51. Green Fuel, "Our Vision."
52. Franco et al., "Global Land Grabbing and Trajectories of Agrarian Change"; and Boche, *Contrôle Du Foncier, Agricultures*.
53. Pradhan and Mbohwa, "Development of Biofuels in South Africa."
54. FAO *Trends and Impacts of Foreign*.
55. Margulis and Porter, *Governing the Global Land Grab*.
56. Boche, *Contrôle du foncier, agricultures*.
57. Hall, "Land Grabbing in Southern Africa."
58. Borras and Franco, "From Threat to Opportunity-Problems."
59. Anseeuw et al., *Transnational Land Deals*.
60. Boche, *Contrôle du foncier, agricultures*.
61. Pinesso, *Terras Africanas Com Lavouras*.
62. Anseeuw et al., *Towards New Production Models*.

63. Interview, FGV ProSavana representative, Mozambique, March/2013.
64. Chichava et al., "Brazil and China in Mozambican Agriculture."
65. Interview, Brazilian Ambassador, April/2014, Lilongwe.
66. MRE, "Encontro com o Ministro."
67. Nogueira and Ollinaho, "From Rhetoric to Practice."
68. FGV Projetos, *Nacala Corridor Fund*.
69. Brazilian Embassy in Maputo, "CTPD. Cooperação com o Japão para."
70. Kondo, "Improving Japanese ODA."
71. Funada-Classen, *Fukushima, ProSAVANA and Ruth*; and Okada, *Role of Japan in Offshore*.
72. MRE to Brazilian Embassy in Maputo, "Missão empresarial da CNA."
73. Interview, Embrapa International representative, July/2013, Brasilia.
74. Brazilian Embassy in Maputo, "CTPD. Brasil-Moçambique. EMBRAPA-MADER." 1.
75. Brazilian Embassy in Maputo, "Assinatura do Protocolo de Entendimento MADER."
76. Interview, Embrapa International representative, July/2013, Brasilia; Interview, Brazilian investor, July/2013, Brasilia.
77. See note 66.
78. ABC, *Program of Technical Support*.
79. 'Protocol of Intentions between the Ministry of External Relations and the Brazilian Cotton Institute for Technical Cooperation on the Cotton Sector', 10 October 2011, Ministry of External Relations, Brasilia.
80. Interview, July/2013, Brasilia.
81. See note 14.
82. "Japanese Civil Society Statement."
83. GRAIN et al., "Brazilian Megaproject in Mozambique ."
84. Fase, *Fundo Nacala*.
85. Zanella and Milhorance, "Cerrado Meets Savannah."
86. See note 41.
87. Ibid.
88. Interview, Abimaq international relations representative, July/2013, São Paulo.
89. Interview, MDIC director, June/2013, Brasilia.
90. Ibid.
91. See note 6.
92. See note 86.
93. See note 6.
94. Ibid.
95. IBASE, *Relatório Pronaf*.
96. See note 6.
97. Interview, MDA International Relations Director, June/2013, Brasilia.
98. See note 85.
99. Mukwereza, "Zimbabwe-Brazil Cooperation."
100. See note 20.
101. Sabatier and Jenkins-Smith, *Policy Change and Learning*.
102. Interview, Councilor diplomat, July/2013, Brasilia.

References

ABC. *Program of Technical Support to the Development of the Cotton Sector in Africa: Mozambique/Malawi Component*. South-South technical cooperation projects. Brasilia: ABC, October 2013.

Alderson, Kai. "Making Sense of State Socialization." *Review of International Studies* 27, no. 3 (2001): 415–433.

Amanor, Kojo Sebastian. "Expanding Agri-business: China and Brazil in Ghanaian Agriculture." *IDS Bulletin* 44, no. 4 (2013): 80–90.

Anseeuw, Ward, Mathieu Boche, Thomas Breu, Giger Markus, Jann Lay, Peter Messerli, and Kerstin Nolte. *Transnational Land Deals for Agriculture in Global South: Analytical Report Based on the Land Matrix Database*. Bern: CDE/CIRAD/GIGA, 2012.

Anseeuw, Ward, Antoine Ducastel, and Mathieu Boche. "Towards New Production Models, Increased Concentration and the Export of the South African Model." In *South Africa's Agrarian Question*, edited by Hubert Cochet, Ward Anseeuw and Sandrine Freguin-Gresh. Cape Town: HSRC Press, 2016.

Boche, Mathieu. *Contrôle du foncier, agricultures d'entreprise et restructurations agraires: une perspective critique des investissements fonciers à grande échelle: Le cas de la partie centrale du Mozambique* [Land control, corporate agriculture and agrarian restructuring: A critical perspective of large-scale land investment: The case of central Mozambique]. Doctorat., Université Paris XI Sud, 2015.

Borras, Saturnino, and Jennifer Franco. "From Threat to Opportunity-problems with the Idea of a Code of Conduct for Land-grabbing." *Yale Hum. Rts. & Dev. LJ* 13 (2010): 507–523.

Brazilian Embassy in Maputo. Brasil-Moçambique.Agricultura. "Assinatura do Protocolo de Entendimento entre o Instituto de Desenvolvimento Industrial de Minas Gerais e o MADER." [Signing of the memorandum of understanding between the Industrial Development Institute of Minas Gerais and MADER.] Internal Official Letter. Maputo: MRE. December 18, 2003.

Brazilian Embassy in Maputo. "CTPD. Brasil-Moçambique. EMBRAPA-MADER. Projeto na área de Agricultura. Assinatura de Memorando de Entendimento [TCDC. Brazil-Mozambique. EMBRAPA-MADER. Project in the area of agriculture. Signing of memorandum of understanding]." Official Internal Letter MRE. January 13, 2003.

Brazilian Embassy in Maputo/MRE. "CTPD. Cooperação com o Japão para projetos em Moçambique. Visita de funcionários da Cooperação Japonesa em Maputo." [TCDC. Cooperation with Japan in Mozambique. Visit of officials of the Japanese cooperation in Maputo.] Official Internal Letter. Maputo: MRE. January 13, 2003.

Brazilian Embassy in Pretoria/MRE. "Energia. IBAS. África do Sul. Workshop sobre Padrões e Especificações Técnicas para Biocombustíveis. Relato [Energy. IBAS. Workshop on technical standards and specifications for biofuels. Report]." Internal Official Letter. Pretoria: MRE. December 6, 2010.

Cabral, Lídia, Arilson Favareto, Langton Mukwereza, and Kojo Amanor. "Brazil's Agricultural Politics in Africa: More Food International and the Disputed Meanings of "Family Farming"." *World Development* 81 (2016): 47–60.

Chichava S., J. Duran, L. Cabral, A. Shankland, L. Buckley, T. Lixia, and Z. Yue. "Brazil and China in Mozambican Agriculture: Emerging Insights from the Field." *IDS Bulletin* 44, no. 4 (2013): 101–115.

Council of the European Union. *IV European Union-Brazil Summit Joint Statement*. Brasilia: Presse, 2010. https://www.consilium.europa.eu/uedocs/cms_data/docs/pressdata/en/er/115812.pdf.

FAO. *Trends and Impacts of Foreign Investment in Developing Country Agriculture: Evidence from Case Studies*. Rome: Food and Agriculture Organization, 2012.

Fase. *Fundo Nacala: estrutura original e desdobramentos* [Nacala fund: Original structure and developments]. Rio de Janeiro: FASE - Solidariedade e Educação, 2014.

Favre, Guillaume. *Des rencontres dans la mondialisation: réseaux et apprentissage dans un salon de distribution de programme de télévision en Afrique sub-saharienne* [Globalization encounters: Networking and learning in a television program distribution fair in sub-Saharan Africa]. Thèse de doctorat., Université Paris Dauphine, 2014.

FGV Projetos. *Nacala Corridor Fund*. Information Memorandum. OECD Forum. São Paulo: FGV Projetos. May, 2014. http://www.oecd.org/forum/issues/NACALA%20CORRIDOR%20FUND-FGV%20Projetos.pdf.

Finnemore, Martha, and Kathryn Sikkink. "International Norm Dynamics and Political Change." *International Organization* 52, no. 4 (1998): 887–917.

Funada-Classen, Sayaka. *Fukushima, ProSAVANA and Ruth First: Examining Natalia Fingermann's "Myths behind ProSAVANA*. Working Paper. Observador Rural. Maputo: Observatorio do Meio Rural de Moçambique, 2013.

Gabas, Jean-Jacques, and Frédéric Goulet. "Chinese and Brazilian Agricultural Cooperation in Africa: Innovation in Principles and Practices." *Afrique Contemporaine* 243, no. 3 (2013): 111–131.

GBEP, and FAO. *The Global Bioenergy Partnership Sustainability Indicators for Bioenergy*. Rome: FAO, Climate, Energy and Tenure Division, 2011.

GRAIN, UNAC, and via Campesina Africa. "Brazilian Megaproject in Mozambique Set to Displace Millions of Peasants." *GRAIN*. November 29, 2012. http://Www.Grain.Org/Article/Entries/4626-Brazilian-Megaproject-in-Mozambique-Set-to-Displace-Millions-of-Peasants.

Green Fuel. "Our Vision|Green Fuel." 2015. http://www.greenfuel.co.zw/our-vision/.

Hall, Ruth. "Land Grabbing in Southern Africa: The Many Faces of the Investor Rush." *Review of African Political Economy* 38, no. 128 (2011): 193–214.

Hollander, Gail. "Power is Sweet: Sugarcane in the Global Ethanol Assemblage." *The Journal of Peasant Studies* 37, no. 4 (2010): 699–721.

Hopewell, Kristen. "New Protagonists in Global Economic Governance: Brazilian Agribusiness at the WTO." *New Political Economy* 18, no. 4 (2013): 603–623.

IBASE. *Relatório Pronaf: Resultados Da Etapa Paraná* [Pronaf report: Results from the Paraná stage]. Rio de Janeiro: Instituto Brasileiro de Analises Sociais et Econômicas (Ibase)/ Ministério do Desenvolvimento Agrario (MDA), 2006.

"Japanese Civil Society Statement on ProSAVANA: Call for an Immediate Suspension and Fundamental Review." *Farmlandgrab*. September 30, 2013. http://farmlandgrab.org/post/view/22777.

Keck, Margaret E, and Kathryn Sikkink. *Activists beyond Borders: Advocacy Networks in International Politics*. Ithaca: Cornell University Press, 1998.

Kloss, Emerson. *Transformação Do Etanol Em Commodity: Perspectivas Para Uma Ação Diplomatica Brasileira* [Ethanol transformation in commodity: Perspectives for a Brazilian diplomatic action]. Brasília: Fundação Alexandre Gusmão, 2012.

Kondo, Yasuo. "Improving Japanese ODA Based on Scientific Research: Cases of Pesticide Assistance and ProSAVANA in Mozambique - beyond KAIZEN." International Conference Presented at the Exchange of Experiences on the Role of Scientific Research in the Advocacy of Public Policies, Maputo, August 6, 2014. http://farmlandgrab.org/post/view/23838-improving-japanese-oda-based-on-scientific-research-cases-of-pesticide-assistance-and-prosavana-in-mozambique-beyond-kaizen.

Margulis, Matias E., and Tony Porter. *Governing the Global Land Grab: Multipolarity, Ideas and Complexity in Transnational Governance* SSRN Scholarly Paper. Rochester: Social Science Research Network, 2013.

Marsh, David, and Martin Smith. "Understanding Policy Networks: Towards a Dialectical Approach." *Political Studies* 48, no. 1 (2000): 4–21.

Milhorance, C. "Brazil's Cooperation with Sub-Saharan Africa in the Rural Sector: The International Circulation of Instruments of Public Policy." *Latin American Perspectives* 41, no. 5 (2014): 75–93.

MRE. Letter to the Brazilian Embassy in Maputo. "Brasil - Moçambique. Missão empresarial da Confederação Nacional de Agricultura. Seguimento de atividades." [Brazil - Mozambique. Business mission of the national confederation of agriculture. Follow-up activities.]" Brasilia: MRE. January 28, 2011.

MRE. "Encontro com o Ministro de Negócios Estrangeiros do Malaui. Entrega de cópias figuradas. Relato [Meeting with the minister of foreign affairs of Malawi. Report]." Official Internal Letter. Lilongwe: MRE. July 4, 2013.

MRE. "IBAS. Energia. VII Reunião do GT de Energia (Pretória, 12/10/11). Relato." [IBAS. Energy. VII meeting of the energy WG (Pretoria, 10/12/11). Report.] Official Internal Letter. Pretoria, November 4, 2011.

Mukwereza, Langton. "Zimbabwe-Brazil Cooperation through the More Food Africa Programme." Working Paper. China and Brazil in Africa Agriculture (CBAA) Project. Sussex: IDS, March 2015.

Nogueira, Isabela, and Ossi Ollinaho. "From Rhetoric to Practice in South-South Development Cooperation: A Case Study of Brazilian Interventions in the Nacala Corridor Development Program1." 2013. http://www.unige.ch/ses/socioeco/institut/postdoc/Nogueira/NOGUEIRA_OLLINAHO_WorkingPaper_NACALA_CORRIDOR.pdf.

Okada, Kana. *Role of Japan in Offshore Agricultural Investment: Case of ProSAVANA Project in Mozambique*. International Institute of Social Studies: Master of Arts in Development Studies, 2014.

Oliveira, Gustavo de L. T. "The Geopolitics of Brazilian Soybeans." *The Journal of Peasant Studies* 43, no. 2 (2016): 348–372.

Patriota, Thomas, and Francesco Pierri. "Brazil's Cooperation for Agriculture Development and Food Security in Africa: Assessing the Technology, Finance, and Knowledge Platforms." In *Agricultural Development and Food Security in Africa: The Impact of Chinese, Indian and Brazilian Investments*, edited by F Cheru and R Modi, 125–144. London: Zed Books, 2013.

Peck, Jamie, and Nik Theodore. *Fast Policy: Experimental Statecraft at the Thresholds of Neoliberalism.* Minneapolis: University Of Minnesota Press, 2015.

Pinesso. *Terras Africanas Com Lavouras Brasileiras. Grupo Pinesso Ja Produz Soja, Milho, Feijão e Algodão* [African lands with Brazilian crops. Grupo Pinesso produces soy, maize, beans and cotton]. Boletim Informativo do Grupo Pinesso. Semear. Campo Grande: Grupo Pinesso October, 2011.

Pradhan, Anup, and Charles Mbohwa. "Development of Biofuels in South Africa: Challenges and Opportunities." *Renewable and Sustainable Energy Reviews* 39 (2014): 1089–1100.

Sabatier, Paul A., and Hank C. Jenkins-Smith, eds. *Policy Change and Learning: An Advocacy Coalition Approach.* Theoretical Lenses on Public Policy. Boulder: Westview Press, 1993.

Seibert, Gerhard. "Brazil in Africa: Ambitions and Achievements of an Emerging Regional Power in the Political and Economic Sector." 2011. https://repositorio.iscte-iul.pt/handle/10071/6328.

Silvapen Group. *Tecnologia Brasileira Em Solo Fértil* [Brazilian technology in fertile soil]. Silvapen Group - Renewable Energy Solutions, 2014. http://silvapengroup.com.br/.

Søndergaard, Niels. "Public-private Re-alignments: The Role of Structural Economic Transformations in Spurring the Joint International Engagement of Agribusiness and the Brazilian State." *Política & Sociedade* 15, no. 32 (2015): 204–290.

Soulé-Kohndou, Folashadé A. *Les "clubs" de puissances "émergentes": fonctions objectives et usages stratégiques: le cas du forum de dialogue IBAS (Inde-Brésil-Afrique du Sud)* ["Clubs" of emerging powers: Objective functions and strategic uses: The case of the dialogue forum IBAS (India-Brazil-South Africa)]. Thèse de doctorat., Institut d'Etudes Politiques de Paris, 2014.

Stone, Diane. *Knowledge Actors and Transnational Governance: The Private-public Policy Nexus in the Global Agora.* London: Palgrave Macmillan, 2013.

Unica. *África vê No Brasil Oportunidade de Parceria Para a Produção de Etanol* [Africa sees in Brazil opportunity for partnership for the production of ethanol]. União Da Indústria de Cana-de-Açúcar. August 15, 2008. http://www.unica.com.br/noticia/35416218/-por-centoC3-por-cento81frica-ve-no-brasil-oportunidade-de-parceria-para-a-producao-de-etanol/.

Unica. *Brazil-EU-Africa Agreement Encourages``commoditization" of Biofuels.* Brazilian Sugarcane Industry Association. July 29, 2010. http://www.unica.com.br/news/38990375920330267015/unica-por-cento3A-brazil-eu-africa-agreement-encourages-por-cento60-por-cento60commoditization-por-centoC2-por-centoB4-por-centoC2-por-centoB4-of-biofuels/.

Unica. *Comitiva Africana Destaca Profissionalismo E Tecnologia Em Setor Sucroenergético Brasileiro* [African committee highlights professionalism and technology in Brazilian sucroenergy sector]. União Da Indústria de Cana-de-Açúcar. May 4, 2010. http://www.unica.com.br/noticia/41956566920341709819/comitiva-africana-destaca-profissionalismo-e-tecnologia-em-setor-sucroenergetico-brasileiro/.

Unica. *Produtos Da Cana Podem Contribuir Para Avanços Econômicos Na Africa* [Sugarcane products can contribute to economic advances in Africa]. União Da Indústria de Cana-de-Açúcar. March 6, 2014. http://www.unica.com.br/na-midia/27781786920328579439/produtos-da-cana-podem-contribuir-para-avancos-economicos-na-por-centoC3-por-cento81frica/.

USDA-FAS. *Brazil: Biofuel Annual: Annual Report 2013.* Required Report - public distribution. GAIN Report. Washington, DC: Global Agricultural Information Network/U.S. Departement of Agriculture, 2013. http://gain.fas.usda.gov/Recent%20GAIN%20Publications/Biofuels%20Annual_Sao%20Paulo%20ATO_Brazil_9-12-2013.pdf.

Vadell, Javier, Leonardo Ramos, and Pedro Neves. "The International Implications of the Chinese Model of Development in the Global South: Asian Consensus as a Network Power." *Revista Brasileira de Política Internacional* 57, no. spe (2014): 91–107.

Weible, Christopher M., and Paul A. Sabatier. "Comparing Policy Networks: Marine Protected Areas in California." *Policy Studies Journal* 33, no. 2 (2005): 181–201.

Wilkinson, John. *Brazil, Biofuels and Bio-diplomacy with a Specific Focus on Africa and Mozambique.* Report prepared for ActionAid within the Framework of the Project: Impact of Biofuel on Food, Farmers and the Environment. Rio de Janeiro: ActionAid, August 2014.

Zanella, Matheus A., and Carolina Milhorance. "Cerrado Meets Savannah, Family Farmers Meet Peasants: The Political Economy of Brazil's Agricultural Cooperation with Mozambique." *Food Policy* 58 (2016): 70–81.

South African supermarket expansion in sub-Saharan Africa

Melodie Campbell

ABSTRACT

Supermarket expansion in the developing countries of the world has been conventionally led by 'first tier' transnational corporations (TNCs) based in the United States and Europe. The case of sub-Saharan Africa (SSA) presents an instance where supermarket expansion has been primarily propelled by 'second tier' TNCs, South African-based supermarket chains. In order to identify patterns and trends of South African supermarket expansion into SSA and the contribution thereof to creating dynamic shifts in the region's agro-food systems, explorative research was undertaken based on grey literature sourced from company annual reports, sector databases and newspaper articles. Emerging patterns and trends of South African supermarket expansion reflect sub-regional variations within SSA and the integral role of modern import-based procurement systems in rolling out supermarket expansion across the region. Resistance to the imports driven model of South African supermarket expansion reflect a common trend among host markets within the SSA. The import-based expansion strategy of South African supermarkets in the region suggests emulation of the international neo-liberal model of food retailing and development, more generally. South African supermarket expansion is further problematised, given South Africa's BRICs status, as 'supermarketisation' appears to facilitate the stronghold of TNCs in the region.

Introduction

For formal food retail transnational corporations (TNCs) keen to expand beyond saturated domestic markets, the dearth of formal food retailing in emerging countries across the globe continue to present 'untapped markets' for supermarket expansion, as is evident by the ongoing 'supermarket revolution.'[1] As part of advancing the supermarket revolution, modern procurement systems which facilitate highly consolidated value chains, have served to tip the power of consumer goods distribution in the favour of TNCs and leverage their ability to determine the character of and actors within supply chains. Operating from this position of power, appears to allow food retail TNCs to further circumvent the 'challenges' of sourcing FFV from small-scale farmers in domestic host markets and hence, contribute to the exclusion of actors in the traditional channels of domestic supply chains.[2]

From the 1990s, supermarket expansion has been primarily propelled by the first tier TNCs from the 'global north' (i.e. international US based and European retailers), as in the case of Latin America and East/South-east Asia.[3] Brazil presents a case of a BRICS country (i.e. Brazil, Russia, India, China and South Africa), where by the late 2000s the market leaders in formal food retail were all foreign owned. Similarly, exogenous forces from the 'global north' have contributed significantly to supermarket expansion within the BRICS countries of Russia, India and China.[4] South Africa presents a case where supermarket expansion has been primarily driven endogenously, by domestic food retailers within the country, (due to the economic and political sanctions during the apartheid regime).[5]

The emerging economies of sub-Saharan Africa (SSA) have come under the spotlight more recently, as 'lucrative markets' for retail expansion, given the growing middle-class consumer segment and rate of urbanisation, both which are regarded as drivers of the demand for supermarket expansion.[6] However, in the context of SSA, it is also small-scale farmers who tend to be the pre-dominant agricultural producers who supply the traditional informal domestic markets. While, examples of the successful integration of small-scale farmers into South African supermarket(s) value chains in Southern Africa exist, they appear to be the exception rather than the norm.[7] Ortmann and King further highlight that 31 peer-reviewed articles were published on the subject of how small-scale farmers in SSA can participate in supermarkets supply chains in the South African journal *Agrekon* between 2000 and 2009.[8] Despite much research on the subject, exclusion from supermarket value chains (or exploitation) appears to remain the fate of small-scale farmers.

Reardon and Gulati suggest that two basic sources of conflict arise between supermarkets on one hand and the traditional retailers and supermarket suppliers on the other.[9] Firstly, it is the inequality of power, which is based on supermarkets' greater concentration and scale as well as access to technologies and commercial practices because of that scale. Secondly, the practices and strategies through which supermarkets wield their power, magnify their initial advantages through pricing, quality, location, payment and contracting. The introduction of formal food retail and the modern procurement systems which accompany it, appears to not be without implications for the actors (e.g. small-scale farmers) in predominant informal or traditional agro-food systems operating within the food retail markets of emerging countries of SSA.

Furthermore, supermarket expansion and its concomitants play out within an ever-increasing globalised agro-food system which is situated in what McMichael refers to as the global corporate regime.[10] A further assertion regarding the concept of the food regime is that it is not about food per se but about the relations within which food is produced and through which capitalism is produced and reproduced.[11] In addition, transnational supermarket chains and businesses involved in various sectors of the agro-food system, as part of the 'Big Food' movement, have become powerful developers (of land and intellectual property etc.) as well as speculators invested in large-scale acquisitions of agricultural land in developing countries – (re)shaping societies' relationship to land, farming and food globally.[12]

Paying attention to the tensions arising between supermarkets and actors within, as well as outside of the traditional channels of domestic supply chains, potentially provide signifiers to determine how in the SSA context, South African supermarket expansion strategies are contributing to creating dynamic shifts in the power relations of agents in the region's food retail sector and agro-food systems. Transformation in the food retail market of SSA countries by South African-based supermarkets (i.e. TNCs within the region) furthermore, shifts the focus to South Africa as a BRICS country and the role it is playing as a regional power in the SSA region. Piper highlights the debate pertaining to whether BRICS are effectively serving as sub-imperialists by better integrating the regions into global neo-liberal capitalism.[13] In the case of South Africa, its role as a clear economic leader of Africa beyond Southern Africa is often disputed given the growing leadership role of middle-income countries (MICs) such as Nigeria, Kenya and Zambia within their respective sub-regions. The role of other BRICS countries (e.g. China) are also regarded as heavyweights, in terms of driving Africa's economic and developmental future.[14] Of particular interest here, is how supermarket expansion by South African-based supermarkets, which represents emulation of a western model of supermarket expansion evident in the abovementioned developing regions, is similarly contributing to creating dynamic shifts in the power relations of agents in the food retail sector and agro-food systems within the emerging countries of SSA.

To locate the exploratory investigation into South African food retailers' expansion across SSA within a globalised food system, this paper will start with a brief overview of the current scholarship on the supermarket revolution. Supermarket expansion in the SSA context will then be discussed in terms of the emerging patterns and trends identified.

Supermarket revolution

The phenomenon of the 'supermarket revolution' as conceptualised by Reardon, Timmer, Barrett and Berdegue' posit that rampant supermarket expansion evident across emerging countries and regions has introduced modern procurement systems and associated safety and quality standards, thereby creating requirements which serve to exclude small-scale farmers from supermarkets supply or value chains.[15] Retail transformation has also been associated with supermarket diffusion over space, consumer segments and product categories.[16] Emerging trends of 'supermarket diffusion' include the progressive spread of supermarkets along a continuum, starting with the richest and largest consumer market (e.g. urban higher income consumers), format diversification to facilitate differentiation in spatial and consumer segments (e.g. neighbourhood and 'no-frills' discount or wholesale stores) and the progressive spread of product categories from processed foods (e.g. mass produced highly processed 'cheap food') to increasing proportions of fresh produce. In order for food retailers to expand their sale of fresh produce, modern procurement systems are introduced which have implications for food production and distribution in developing countries.

The concept of 'Big Food' has also emerged, which defines the large transnational corporations (TNCs) and national commercial entities within the food and beverage industry (e.g. food and beverage manufacturing companies, fast food outlets and retailers) that through a corporatised food system wield market dominance.[17] The supermarket revolution has been implicated as contributing to the transformation of retail food environments within emerging economies through its increasingly influential role as 'gate-keeper' for Big Food infiltration into developing world markets.[18]

Locating the implications of the supermarket revolution through the lens of food regimes and its embeddedness in the current food regime requires paying attention to mechanism and/or relations operating in the supermarket revolution which appear to facilitate a variant of 'accumulation through dispossession'.[19] Wrigley and Lowe provide evidence of the embeddedness of the supermarket revolution in the current corporate food regime.[20] For example, the facilitative role of structural adjustment programmes such as the liberalisation of market access (e.g. deregulation) and the subsequent deluge of foreign direct investment (FDI) which 'changed the existing "rules of the game"' in terms of the acceleration of supermarket diffusion trends within the BRICS countries and in the SSA context, by a BRICS country.[21] In terms of supermarket expansion, the import of practices and organisational innovations (e.g. supply chain/distribution-logistic systems reorganisation, enhanced customer service and the introduction of quality assurance standards and regulations) has diversified the product offering, store formats and reach of TNCs in emerging economies. Cumulatively, the above-mentioned factors contribute to the accumulation of power in the hands of TNCs. Having gained the upper hand, TNCs are able to squeeze established informal retail channels, which is here regarded as a form of dispossession for small-scale farmers and informal retailers in the host countries of SSA.[22]

Supermarket expansion in SSA: South African food retailers as drivers

According to Wrigley and Lowe the retail transformation associated with the supermarket revolution has been driven from both demand and supply-side forces.[23] Key demand-side factors include, rising incomes associated with a growing middle class and urbanisation. Currently, sub-Saharan Africa is one of the fastest urbanising regions in the world.[24] Yet, the distinguishing feature of the region's urbanisation is its informality, with the largest share of urban populations living in slums.[25] The food retail landscape within the countries of the sub-Saharan African region, has retained its 'informal' character, with kiosks, small independent stores and wet markets remaining prevalent.[26] According to AT Kearney, an estimated 90% of commerce in Africa occurs through informal means, even among the growing middle-class.[27] Yet, the increasing clamour of supermarket expansion (i.e. formal food retail) in the SSA region, is captured as part of an on-going process of retail transformation in the emerging markets of the developing world.[28] Subsequent published works echo that the internationalisation of retail activity in SSA has plunged the continent into a retail revolution with ever more supermarkets emerging on the African landscape.[29]

In the SSA context, the supermarket revolution has been driven by the 'Big 4' South African food retailers – Shoprite, Pick n Pay, Woolworths and Spar, globally regarded as 'second tier' regional TNCs.[30] Here, the focus will be on supermarket expansion by Shoprite and Pick n Pay, as the major South African food retailers driving formal food retail expansion into the SSA. Shoprite, the front runner in SSA's supermarket revolution, opened its first store outside South Africa in 1995. Shoprite's Integrated Report for 2015 reported a total of 226 multi-store formats (e.g. Shoprite, Checkers, uSave and OK Franchise) within 12 countries of the SSA region, outside of South Africa and excluding operations in Mauritius and Madagascar.[31] Comparatively, Pick n Pay currently has 116 retail operations (e.g. Pick n Pay, Boxer and as part of TM Supermarkets) within 6 countries outside of South Africa.[32]

Walmart's 2011 acquisition of the South African retailer Massmart has through its Game stores food retail division also recently extended first tier TNCs reach into the wave of the supermarket revolution happening within the emerging economies of SSA. Game currently operates 13 stores within nine countries of the SSA region outside of South Africa.[33] More recently, the French-based first tier TNC, Carrefour, is also gearing up to enter the region with two franchised stores set to open in the Kenyan capital of Nairobi.[34]

Notwithstanding, informal retail channels in emerging economies have also shown resilience to market domination of retail TNCs. This is especially the case, for the retailing of fresh produce where 'wetmarkets' have a significant market share.[35] In the SSA context, Wegerif provides evidence of the resilience of informal retail channels with regards to the supply of and egg buying patterns in the city of Dar es Salaam, Tanzania.[36] The case study revealed multiple and differently connected actors who have choices and hence make for more adaptable and replicable modes of food provisioning. Similarly, Battersby highlights that integral role of informal food retail channels and alternate food sourcing (e.g. sharing and borrowing of food) for the urban poor in South Africa, where supermarkets are common place in the retail food environment.[37]

Sub-regional variations

The seminal work of Weatherspoon and Reardon suggest that the general pattern of the supermarket revolution in the sub-Saharan African region could be described as 'predictable', having started in the richer countries within the region (e.g. South Africa, Kenya) with expansion into smaller and/or poorer countries primarily through FDI. A similar trajectory of supermarket diffusion has been observed in Latin America and East/Southeast Asia, with reference to Brazil, Russia, India and China (i.e. BRICS countries).[38] However, the cumulative acceleration from the early 2000s was noted as less predictable and surprising. In terms of the development of supermarkets in SSA, outside of South Africa, East Africa was identified as the most advanced sub-region due to the presence of domestic supermarket chains. With the exception of Nigeria, the probability of supermarket expansion in Western and Central Africa making much headway soon after 2003, was projected as less likely given it is much poorer than Eastern and Southern Africa, is plagued with political instability and has much lower rates of urbanisation.[39]

From 2003 onwards, there has been a sharp acceleration and extension of the geographical spread of South African supermarkets in SSA further north, progressing into Western and Central Africa. While, Weatherspoon and Reardon were correct about the acceleration and extension of South African supermarket expansion in the region, the geographical spread has been less predictable, with sub-regional variations in the diffusion of supermarkets within emerging markets.[40] Variation in the geographical spread of Shoprite and Pick n Pay supermarkets are noteworthy. The Southern African market represents the most established market for South African supermarket expansion where both retailers have a strong presence. Shoprite has a total of 169 multi-format stores and Pick n Pay currently operates 116 multi-format stores. Outside of Southern Africa, it is Shoprite that has the largest market share. Currently, in West Africa (Nigeria and Ghana), Shoprite has a presence with 22 multi-format stores. In the Central African market (Angola and the DRC), Shoprite has 30 multi-format stores. Until 2015, Shoprite had two supermarkets in the East African market but has since exited the food retail market of East Africa.[41]

The acceleration of supermarket expansion within countries across the Southern African region post 2003 appears significant, given the context of the region's predominantly rural population (estimated to comprise 63% of the total population).[42] However, a closer look at variations in the overall size and the urban to rural share of the population within the countries of the sub-regions of Southern Africa provides insight into the geographical spread of South African supermarket expansion. Although rural populations are predominant in the sub-regions, the urban to rural share ranges from 25:75% in East African markets (Kenya, Tanzania, Uganda and Rwanda) to a 49:51% share in West African markets (Nigeria, Ghana and Gabon). Proportionately, the urban to rural share of the West African markets equates to approximately 104 million to 108 million compared to 38 million to 114 million in the East African markets, which suggests a significant difference in the urban share of these populous sub-regions.[43] In terms of the posited implications of supermarket expansion, the variations in the urban to rural share could suggest very different trajectories within the sub-regions of the greater Southern African region.

Southern Africa: treading a 'predictable' path of supermarket expansion

Supermarket expansion by South African TNCs in the Southern African sub-region dates back to the early 1990s.[44] On-going investment into this established food retail market by South African supermarket retailers (Shoprite, Pick n Pay, Woolworths and Spar) to expand operations, the market entry of latecomers such as Fruit & Veg City and more recently first tier TNCs like Walmart through its acquisition of South African retailer Massmart, suggest a predictable path of transformation of the sub-regions food retail sector, as was observed in Latin America and East/South-east Asia.[45]

The transition of formal food retail into the existing Southern Africa markets is not without episodes of resistance and tension. In Zambia, local farmers in the rural town of Chipata threatened to burn down the local Shoprite as it was competing directly with their estab-lished market. To appease local farmers, a collaborative initiative was implemented whereby the farmers would supply Shoprite with five designated vegetables.[46] In 2003, strikes by Zambia's Shoprite employees against unfair labour practices were documented.[47] Similarly, Shoprite and Pick n Pay (which has a 49% share in Zimbabwe's TM Supermarkets) were both implicated in unfair labour practices with strikes by employees demanding salary increases in Zimbabwean stores (IPS News, 22 November 2010). Shoprite's exit from the Zimbabwean market in 2013, comes a year before the Zimbabwean government imposed new import restrictions measures (e.g. higher taxes and import tariffs) as a protectionist measure for the local market (IOL News, 3 October 2014). Recently, tensions appear to be rising between the Zambian Government and South African supermarkets due to the importation of food prod-ucts. In 2015, it was reported that Zambia was importing frozen foods (pies and pre-packaged samosas) to the tune of $1 million, with the majority coming from South Africa into South African supermarkets – namely, Shoprite, Pick n Pay and Spar. The question raised by the Zambian Government relates to why frozen food (e.g. pies) and produce grown locally cannot be sourced from local suppliers and farmers, who produce or grow similar products for the local market (Lusaka Times, 20 May 2015). In addition, there have been reports that the Zambian Bureau of Standards raided Shoprite and Spar supermarkets to confiscate illegally imported products. Shoprite came into the spotlight of the illegal imports scandal, when it was found that the retailer was importing ultra-pasteurised milk from Poland via South Africa, thereby ignoring 'rules of origin' which enable preferential trade agreements between South Africa and the countries within the South African Development Community (SADC) (Lusaka Times, 7 October 2015 & Zambia Daily Nation, 5 December 2015).

In the midst of tensions regarding the importation of food products, the established food retail markets of the Southern African sub-region have been a site for investment and col-laboration by Big Food corporations. Zambia, in particular, has been touted as Africa's next breadbasket, as it has gained attention as a desirable destination of international investors (*Mail&Guardian*, 1 October 2010). For example, in 2013, RCL Foods – a leading South African food producer – acquired a 49% shareholding of Zam Chick, which manages and operates the broiler business of Zambeef, a major player in the in Zambian agri-business market. Zambeef, in turn, has an established relationship with Shoprite as it operates the South African retailer's in-house butcheries in Zambia, Nigeria and Ghana.[48]

The importation of food products and capital from South Africa appear to be contributing to tensions and new power alliances arising in the agro-food systems within the Southern Africa sub-region. The resistance towards South African supermarket expansion from actors (e.g. the state, farmers and employees) in the agro-food system of host markets, raises questions about the implications of South African supermarket expansion for local economies as it advances neo-liberal capitalism across the region.[49] Furthermore, the emerging power alliances between supermarket retailers and Big Food corporations from South Africa, the global north and in the Zambian agri-business market highlight the influential role of private sector actors in restructuring agro-food systems within and across the emerging economies of SSA as well as their accumulation of power (e.g. Shoprite expansion and product offering in Nigeria facilitated by alliances with the Zambian agri-business, Zambeef).

East Africa: market failure and the path of domestic emulation

The trajectory of South African supermarket expansion into East Africa has been plagued with market failure, characterised by Shoprite's mass exodus out of this sub-region. However, the absence of South African TNCs does not suggest an embargo on the supermarket revolution. As Weatherspoon and Reardon have posited more than a decade ago, East Africa is the most advanced sub-region in terms of the presence of domestic supermarket retailers and why supermarket expansion is driven by the domestic East African retailer chains – Nakumatt, Uchumi and Tuskys.[50]

Shoprite has sold its stores in both Tanzania and Uganda to the East African retailer Nakumatt, in 2014 and 2015, respectively. According to *The East African* (14 June 2014), analysts are divided over reasons for Shoprite's exit from East Africa. Some suggest it is due to the failure of the retailer's business model, which primarily positioned itself as a vendor for South African manufacturers, while others highlight the aggressive emergence of domestic retail competition. Meanwhile, Mr Whitey Basson (CEO: Shoprite) has been emphatic that Shoprite just could not compete with the informal trade in the East African market and stated that the west coast of Africa is much more profitable for the retailer (*Saturday Monitor, 28 July 2015*).

> We just couldn't compete with the informal trade. It is just a waste of time for us to expand in a market where we can't get the optimum size for having enough stores to make a meaningful contribution for us. The west coast is so much more profitable for us. *Saturday Monitor* (28 July 2015)

The stakes remain high for domestic retail chains market domination in this sub-region, with the market entry of first tier TNC Walmart through its Massmart operations and the European-based retailer Carrefour's market entry into Kenya *(Business Daily*, 4 August 2015). Choppies, Botswana's largest food retail chain, presents a Southern African retailer that has also entered the East African market with the acquisition of 10 supermarkets in Kenya and its plans to move into the Tanzanian food retail arena in 2016. However, Carrefour's market entry has been rife with contention pertaining to the terms and conditions of contractual agreements (*BDlive,* 25 September 2015; *Business Daily Africa,* 4 August 2015).

An aggressive bid for domination and further supermarket diffusion of the East African food retail markets appears to be mounting from domestic, intra-regionally and global actors. Shoprite's failure to make inroads into the East African market demonstrates the fallacy of an easy or inevitable route for foreign-based TNCs domination of modern food retail sectors in emerging economies.[51] In addition, resilient informal retail channels have also been cited as facilitating a form of implicit resistance.[52] In cases where domestic retailers have retained market domination amidst a supermarket revolution driven by foreign-based TNCs, it is asserted that domination is due to successful emulation of the organisationally innovations and best practices of the latter (Humphrey, 2007).[53] The East African case of supermarket expansion provides a case of the role of domestic retail market domination from within a MIC, that is able to challenge powerful corporations emanating from South Africa (as a BRICS country), expansion by Choppies from Botswana (a MIC) and Carrefour from the global north. A crucial question, would be whether emulation paves the way to the replication of implications for local food production and distribution practices, linked to retail transformation, with its 'neo-liberal capitalist' tenet.

West Africa: the focus of aggressive expansion strategies by Shoprite and more recently Walmart

West Africa represents a rapidly evolving retail landscape. The Nigerian market is currently the fastest growing economy on the continent and a destination of much South African FDI.[54] In terms of regional leadership by BRICS, South Africa's role as a clear economic leader of Africa beyond southern Africa is disputed.[55] However, the South African supermarket, Shoprite is heavily invested in growing its West African market. According to *Bloomberg* (*2 August 2013*), Shoprite intends to focus on growing its African market along the west coast, particularly Nigeria and Angola as well as improve economies of scale. Shoprite is the dominant South African food retailer in the sub-region with 16Shoprite supermarkets in Nigeria and six multi-format stores (Shoprite and Usave) in Ghana currently. The building of a distribution centre in Nigeria provides further evidence of Shoprite's growing investment in West Africa. In addition, Resilient Africa has recently been established as a joint venture between Shoprite, Resilient Property Income Fund and Standard Bank. Through this joint venture, shopping malls will be developed throughout the metropolitan areas of Nigeria, with Shoprite as the anchor tenant. Four malls (Delta mall in Effurun, Benin City mall, Asaba mall and Owerri mall) are currently in the process of development.[56] The question raised with regards to Shoprite's investment in a highly-consolidated distribution centre in Nigeria, relates to whether its import-based procurement system will circumvent the 'challenges' of sourcing FFV from small-scale farmers and hence, contribute to the exclusion of actors in domestic supply chains.[57] Small-scale farmers produce more than 90% of Nigeria's food and supply the traditional distribution channels involved in the food retail market.[58]

In a bid to overtake Shoprite, WalMart/Massmart's food retail division is launching a pilot project in Nigeria. As part of the pilot phase, this retailer plans to open 10 small-format stores in Lagos over the next two years. Thereafter, a more aggressive roll-out is planned. According to the *BDlive (2 March 2014)*, WalMart/Massmart's strategy is geared towards taking business away from spaza shops (i.e. informal retailers) as opposed to formal retailers, given the predominantly informal food market in Nigeria. While, Walmart has been in talks with the Nigerian government, which welcomes the retailer's introduction into the domestic retail sector, informal traders and civil society have voiced concerns about cheap labour and competition for informal retail. With foreign TNCs growing investment in Nigeria's food retail sector, the case of supermarket expansion in West Africa appears to explicitly illustrate a variant of the pursuit of accumulation through dispossession, through joint ventures, investment in a highly-consolidated distribution centre to facilitate import-based procurement and aggressive expansion plans geared towards attracting the predominant price-sensitive lower-income consumer base.

Central Africa: the high risk high cost retail landscape

The central African market includes a profile of war-torn countries associated with political instability.[59] The Angolan market, which is the newest market for South African supermarket expansion, is booming although it is rated as one of the most difficult countries in which to do business (ease of doing business ranking – 179 out of 189 countries).[60] South African FDI which has been directed into food retail operations in both Angola and the Democratic Republic of Congo (DRC) is predominantly from Shoprite.[61] Shoprite opened its first store in Angola in 2003 and entered the Democratic Republic of Congo (DRC) in 2012, where it currently operates one Shoprite supermarket.[62]

Currently, the number of Shoprite stores in Angola (29 stores) has overtaken that of Zambia (26 stores) which is one of Shoprite's most long-standing markets (first store opened in 1995), highlighting the acceleration of supermarket expansion from the mid-2000s.[63] The acceleration of supermarkets in Angola is further reflected by the fact that it has replaced Zambia as Shoprite's biggest revenue contributor outside South Africa (*Financial Mail*, 25 February 2016). Angola currently has 17 Shoprite supermarkets and 12 Usave stores (Shoprite's 'no-frill' small format stores) in contrast to 25 Shoprite supermarkets and one Usave store in Zambia as well as it fast food outlet. The distribution of multi-store formats in relation to the two countries, has demonstrated Shoprite's flexible approach to supermarket expansion not only between countries but also within countries.[64] It could be argued that the Angolan food retail market displays vulnerability in that it is heavily reliant on food imports, importing more than half of its food with some estimates putting the figure as high as 90%, which could be perceived as a form of inherent dispossession.[65] In addition, the low penetration of TNCs into the food retail market have played favourably into Shoprite's accelerated expansion of supermarkets in the country.[66] However, food imports facilitated by a foreign TNC, which is focused on churning out 'cheap food' from elsewhere (through global sourcing), appears to perpetuate relations of dependency for Angolan consumers and the country, as a whole.

Procurement

Infiltrating the pre-dominant informal food retail markets of emerging economies in SSA is an important aspect of supermarket expansion for foreign based supermarkets/TNCs. To do so requires maximising economies of scale to enable cost reduction of products in order to penetrate the predominantly price-sensitive lower-income consumer base, while raising produce quality to hold onto and deepen the middle-class market. Modernising procurement systems has proven critical to the process of ensuring this inverse relationship (i.e. low costs, high quality), as it facilitates efficiency gains, economies of scale and the reduction of co-ordination costs. In addition, advancements in information and communications technology (ICT) have further accelerated the modernisation of procurement system. Cumulatively, a supermarket's procurement system therefore determines, *ceteris paribus*, the cost of products and the economies of scale to provide competitively priced food products.[67]

Globally, supermarkets consolidated procurement systems have also served to tip the power of consumer goods distribution in the favour of TNCs, which has leveraged their ability to determine the character of and actors within their highly-consolidated supply chains.[68] Freshmark, the Shoprite-owned FFV procurement division, presents as example of the critical role of retailer owned modern supermarket procurement systems in enabling the accelerated supermarket expansion, currently happening in the riskier retail terrains of West and Central Africa. South African supermarkets position of power in the South African home market, appears to have allowed South African food retailers to further circumvent the 'challenges' of sourcing FFV from small-scale farmers in domestic host markets, in their quest to achieve the necessary economies of scale to infiltrate the emerging markets throughout SSA. In addition, Shoprite has commented that the continued weakening of the rand against the US dollar and certain African currencies make imports from South Africa more affordable (*AFKInsider,* 26 March 2014).

A procurement system which is hinged on sourcing produce primarily from the South African home market, appears to remain integral to South African supermarket's expansion into SSA. For example, in the East African markets, it has been reported that the Tanzanian government has repeatedly cautioned the South African TNC of flooding its market with South African products.[69] Shoprite responded by exiting the East African market, which suggests that in countries where it cannot operate from an import-based procurement system it chooses to opt s out. In addition, a 2011 study noted that 50% of Shoprite's inventory in Namibia and 99% of the fresh fruit and vegetables sold in its Angolan stores were imported from South Africa. Similarly, Pick n Pay sources 70% of its produce from South Africa.[70] Surveys conducted in Botswana, Namibia and Zambia in 2004, 2005 and 2007 to ascertain the impact of supermarkets on participants in the supply chain indicated that over 80% of all processed food products were imported from South Africa. That said, the procurement of FFV, followed a combination of procurement systems.[71]

Various sources suggest that, while South African food retailers operating in African countries may have established local procurement networks to source FFV, in host countries it does not necessarily imply the inclusion of small-scale farmers, since imports from South Africa continue to be an important contributor in their current FFV procurement systems. For example, Pick n Pay undertook to source 50% of its fruit and vegetables for the Zambian store from local producers. However, the retailer stated that local procurement of FFV has since increased to between 60 and 70% (*Fastmoving,* 27 March 2013). On the other hand, Fruit & Veg City acknowledges that it is likely to continue to export substantial quantities of produce from South Africa to its various stores on the continent. However, the retailer die state that it is eager to buy from local farmers to counter high export costs (*African Trader,* 31 August 2013).

Wrigley and Lowe highlight two important issues related to food retail TNCs linking their emerging market operations to their global/regional procurement networks, as is evidenced by intra-regional procurement networks such as Shoprite's Freshmark.[72] The first relates to the extent to which food retail TNCs use their global procurement capabilities and purchasing scale as (i) a competitive advantage against emerging market local retailers, while (ii) inflating imports into the emerging markets they have entered. Similarly, Reardon et al. question whether food retail TNCs essentially act as highly efficient 'Trojan horses' of imported goods dreaded by governments in many developing countries.[73] Shoprite's exit from the East African market, tensions between the Zambian Government and South African supermarkets due to the importation of food products and Zimbabwe's new import restrictions as mentioned earlier, appear to suggest so.

An interesting turn of events also occurred in 2012, when Africa superseded Europe as a leading export destination of South African agricultural products for the first time (*Financial Mail,* 10 October 2013). It is posited here, that South African TNCs predominant import-based procurement system driving the supermarket revolution underway in SSA, can be implicated as contributing to this rerouting of South African's fresh produce export markets.[74] Available export data of South African fresh fruit and vegetables (FFV) provides a source of information to establish the trade flows of various FFV between South Africa and African countries, particularly in West and Central Africa, in which South African food retailers operate.[75]

However, the publicly available data does not always provide the full story of the intra-regional procurement systems which enable supermarket expansion, especially in the established food retail markets of Southern African countries. This seeming anomaly could possibly be due to the fact that road-based freight is not always reflected in the FFV exports data.[76] Yet, given the geographical proximity, road based freight is often the most effective mode of transporting South African produce into the rest of Southern Africa. South African exports into Southern Africa are further facilitated by the Free Trade Agreement (i.e. no import tariffs and duties applicable on imports from South Africa) within twelve of the fifteen member states of the SADC with the exception of Angola, DRC and Seychelles.[77] However, on-going investment into retail operations in the Southern African countries by South African supermarket retailers (Shoprite, Pick n Pay, Woolworths, Spar and more recently Fruit & Veg City) who admittedly import fresh produce from South Africa, suggest well established intra-regional procurement systems.

South African supermarkets ability to infiltrate host countries fresh produce markets by means of highly consolidated import-based procurement system, as in the case of Shoprite's Freshmark division probably holds the greatest implications for the agro-food systems of host markets of SSA. Reardon and Gulati suggest that gaining control of fresh produce markets is a much slower and longer process due to procurement challenges, price, cultural habits and the resilience of informal or traditional retail channels (such as wet markets).[78] However, the acceleration of supermarket expansion in Central Africa has been regarded as surprising based on Weatherspoon and Reardon's projections.[79] While, domination by South African supermarkets is not inevitable, the rapid rise of supermarkets across the region potentially highlight the agility of TNCs to further exploit the vulnerabilities and weaknesses of traditional and informal supply chains.[80]

Conclusion

As it stands, the supermarket revolution continues to March on across SSA and has gained particular traction in the West and Central African countries of Nigeria and Angola, with its combined urban population of approximately 98 million potential consumers.[81] While the 'formalisation' of food retail by means of supermarket expansion has shown sub-regional variation, the deluge of FDI by South African supermarkets into the SSA food retail market and its modus operandi – the 'modern' import-based procurement system – appears to be exporting new relations of food distribution and provisioning into the traditional informal food retail markets of SSA. It is argued here that it is these relations or mechanism of capitalist production operating within corporate food retail which facilitate a variant of 'accumulation through dispossession', by means of the consolidated web of powerful alliances between actors within the BRICS (e.g. South Africa), MICs such as Kenya and Nigeria and from the 'global north' who have a vested interest in monopolising the agro-food system.

From the emerging patterns and trends observed 'accumulation through dispossession' may not be immediately evident or explicit, in terms of the exclusion of small-scale farmers. However, in a world with an estimated seven billion food consumers and one-and-a-half billion producers, approximately only 500 companies control 70% of food choice by means of supply chains which churn out food produce en masse.[82] The supermarket revolution rolling over the emerging markets of SSA thus position TNCs, both regional African retailers and the international retailers entering the market, as powerful 'gate-keepers' for establishing powerful alliance among the corporatised few by means of highly consolidated import-based procurement systems, which facilitate new patterns in the movement of capital and produce sans the responsibility for the externalities thereof on host economies. For example, South African supermarket expansion into West and Central Africa and the simultaneous rerouting of various South African fresh produce exports from European to African markets.[83] In the SADC countries, free trade agreements have similarly reinforced import-based procurement systems. In addition, transnational supermarket chains and businesses involved in various sectors of the agro-food system as part of the 'Big Food' movement, have become powerful developers (of land and intellectual property etc.) as well as speculators invested in large-scale acquisitions of agricultural land in developing countries – (re)shaping societies' relationship to land, farming and food globally.[84]

The centrality of Shoprite's import-based procurement systems, which enable economies of scales, is particularly evident in the provision of 'cheap food' through its accelerated roll-out of its 'no-frill' Usave stores in Angola (which is a country heavily dependent on food imports), to reach the predominant price-sensitive lower-income consumer base. Competition for the lower-income consumer base is rife, also bearing in mind that populous West African markets have the largest share of urban populations living in slums.[85] As mentioned previously, WalMart/Massmart's strategy is geared towards taking business away from the predominantly informal food market in Nigeria.[86] As modern import-based procurement systems enable TNCs to roll out 'cheap food' across SSA through formal food channels to rival produce offering of traditional informal channels, it appears to highlight a conflict of interest between and among the growing urban poor populations (e.g. lower-income consumers, wage workers, informal traders) and rural poor (e.g. small-scale farmers) which may be compounded by the supermarket revolution. Fair asserts that peasant [rural] populations and urban slum populations do not have the same class interests. Peasants desire land redistribution, rural infrastructure, and stable, high food prices. While, the urban poor want industrial employment, urban infrastructure, and low living costs (including food).[87]

With regards to the poor, it is proposed that the supermarket revolution has the potential to create a relation of dependency on the one hand (e.g. by flooding the urban market with 'cheap food' through global sourcing which enable greater economies of scale), while contributing to dispossession on the other (e.g. consolidating the ownership and use of agricultural land in the rural areas for improved production to increase economies of scale, monopolising food retail supply chains). While, the investment in agricultural land and agri-business in the SSA region is not explored here, land grabs in the countryside and joint ventures in agro-processing notwithstanding shopping mall developments in the urban centres are ever-increasing within the region.[88] As such, South African supermarket expansion seems bound to traverse the urban and rural landscape of host and home countries given the powerful web of alliances emerging across the region within the agro-food system.[89]

As for South Africa's role as a regional leader, the case of South African supermarket expansion into SSA appears to represent emulation of a western model of food retail and more broadly speaking – of a development trajectory which is problematised, given the predominant informal character of retail in SSA. Similarly, South Africa's leading role in driving supermarket expansion in the region is also problematised, given its BRICs status, as supermarket expansion appears to facilitate, if not extend, the increasing stronghold of large TNCs in shaping food retail and to a greater extent agro-food systems. In the case of the SSA region, it would appear supermarket expansion has opened the gate for 'Big Food' infiltration.

Disclosure statement

No potential conflict of interest was reported by the author.

Notes

1. Weatherspoon and Reardon, "The Rise of Supermarkets in Africa."
2. Wrigley and Lowe, "The Globalisation of Trade in Retail Services."
3. Weatherspoon and Reardon, "The Rise of Supermarkets in Africa."
4. Reardon and Gulati, *The Supermarket revolution in Developing Countries.*
5. Weatherspoon and Reardon, "The Rise of Supermarkets in Africa."
6. AT Kearney, 2014.
7. Reardon and Gulati, *The Supermarket revolution in Developing.*
8. Miller et al., "South African Corporations and Post-Apartheid Expansion"; Louw et al., "Dynamics of the Restructuring Fresh Produce Food Markets"; and Emongor and Kirsten, "The Impact of South African Supermarkets on Agricultural Production in the SADC."
9. Ortmann and King, "Research on Agri-food Supply Chains."
10. Reardon and Gulati, *The Supermarket revolution in Developing.*
11. McMichael, "A Food Regime Genealogy."
12. Ibid.
13. Forster and Escudero, *City Regions as Landscapes for People.*

14. Piper, "The BRICS Phenomenon."
15. Reardon et al., "The Rise of Supermarkets in Africa."
16. Ibid.
17. Igumbor et al., "Big 'Food', the Consumer Food Environment."
18. Ibid and Oxfam.
19. Harvey, 2003 as cited in McMichael, "Historicizing Food Sovereignty."
20. Wrigley and Lowe, "The Globalisation of Trade in Retail Services."
21. Reardon and Gulati, *The Supermarket revolution in Developing Countries*; Piper, "The BRICS Phenomenon."
22. Wrigley and Lowe, "The Globalisation of Trade in Retail Services."
23. Wrigley and Lowe, "Introduction: Transnational Retail."
24. United Nations, 2014.
25. African Development Bank, "The Middle of the Pyramid."
26. Emongor, "The Impact of South African Supermarkets"; Crush and Frayne, "Supermarket Expansion and the Informal Food."
27. AT Kearney, 2014.
28. Weatherspoon and Reardon, "The Rise of Supermarkets in Africa."
29. Emongor and Kirsten, "The Impact of South African Supermarkets on Agricultural Production in the SADC"; Louw et al., "Dynamics of the Restructuring Fresh Produce Food Markets"; Crush and Frayne, "Supermarket Expansion and the Informal Food"; Miller, "Spaces of Resistance"; Miller et al., "South African Corporations and Post-Apartheid Expansion"; Dakora and Bytheway, "Entry Mode Issues in the Internationalisation"; Okeahalam and Wood, "Financing Internationalisation."
30. Weatherspoon and Reardon, "The Rise of Supermarkets in Africa."
31. Shoprite Holdings Limited, Geographical Spread.
32. Pick n Pay Investor Relations, Corporate Profile.
33. Massmart, 2015.
34. Maritz, "Good News for African Farmers."
35. Humphrey, "The Supermarket Revolution in Developing Countries."
36. Wegerif, "Exploring Sustainable Urban Food Provisioning."
37. Battersby, "The State of Urban Food Insecurity in Cape Town"; "Beyond the Food Desert."
38. Weatherspoon and Reardon, "The Rise of Supermarkets in Africa."
39. Ibid.
40. Ibid.
41. Shoprite and Pick n Pay website.
42. African Development Bank, "The Middle of the Pyramid"; World Bank, 2015; Forster and Escudero, *City Regions as Landscapes for People.*
43. United Nations 2014.
44. Shoprite and Pick n Pay website.
45. Shoprite website.
46. Miller et al., "South African Corporations and Post-Apartheid Expansion."
47. Miller, "Spaces of Resistance."
48. Zambeef Products PLC, 2014.
49. Piper, "The BRICS Phenomenon."
50. Weatherspoon and Reardon, "The Rise of Supermarkets in Africa."
51. Wrigley and Lowe, "The Globalisation of Trade in Retail Services."
52. Wegerif, "Exploring Sustainable Urban Food Provisioning."
53. Humphrey, "The Supermarket Revolution in Developing Countries."
54. Wesgro, Country Sector: Africa – Food and Beverages.
55. Piper, "The BRICS Phenomenon."
56. Resilient Africa, Resilient Africa Real Estate.
57. Wrigley and Lowe, "The Globalisation of Trade in Retail Services."
58. Mgbenka, Mbah and Ezeano, 2015.
59. AT Kearney, 2014.
60. Wesgro, Country Sector: Africa – Food and Beverages; AT Kearney, 2014.

61. Wesgro, Country Sector: Africa – Food and Beverages.
62. Shoprite Holding Limited, 2015.
63. Reardon et al., "The Rise of Supermarkets in Africa."
64. Okeahalam and Wood, "Financing Internationalisation."
65. USDA, "Angola: Agricultural Economic Fact Sheet."
66. Shoprite Holding Limited, 2015.
67. Reardon et al., "Links between Supermarkets and Food Prices."
68. Ibid.
69. Resilient Africa, Resilient Africa Real Estate.
70. Weatherspoon and Reardon, "The Rise of Supermarkets in Africa"; Wangalwa, "Nakumatt Opens Former Shoprite Store in Tanzania."
71. Crush and Frayne, "Supermarket Expansion and the Informal Food."
72. Wrigley and Lowe, "The Globalisation of Trade in Retail Services."
73. Reardon et al., "Links between Supermarkets and Food Prices."
74. Fresh Fruit Portal, SA's Growing Apple Export Opportunities.
75. PPCEB, 2013; DAFF, 2012 & 2013.
76. Nleya, "Routes to Market."
77. SACU, 2016.
78. Reardon and Gulati, The Supermarket revolution in Developing Countries.
79. Weatherspoon and Reardon, "The Rise of Supermarkets in Africa."
80. Wrigley and Lowe, "The Globalisation of Trade in Retail Services"; Reardon et al., "The Rise of Supermarkets in Africa."
81. United Nations, 2014.
82. Oxfam.
83. Fresh Fruit Portal, SA's Growing Apple Export Opportunities.
84. Forster and Escudero, City Regions as Landscapes for People.
85. African Development Bank, "The Middle of the Pyramid."
86. Massmart, 2015.
87. Fair, "The Peasantary with Modern Capitalism."
88. Forster and Escudero, City Regions as Landscapes for People; Resilient Africa, Resilient Africa Real Estate.
89. Ibid.

Bibliography

African Development Bank. "The Middle of the Pyramid: Dynamics of the Middle Class in Africa." 2011. www.afdb.org.

Banda, I. 2010. "Consumers May Be Happy But Workers Aren't." Inter Press Service News Agency, November, 22 (Online). Accessed April 9, 2016. http://www.ipsnews.net/2010/11/economy-zimbabwe-consumers-may-be-happy-but-workers-arenrsquot/

Battersby, J. "The State of Urban Food Insecurity in Cape Town." Urban Food Security Series, no. 11. Kingston, Cape Town: Queen's University, AFSUN, 2011.

Battersby, J. "Beyond the Food Desert: Finding Ways to Speak about Urban Food Security in South Africa." Geografiska Annaler Series B: Human Geography 94, no. 2 (2012): 141–159.

Clark, J. 2010. "Is Zambia Africa's next breadbasket?" Mail & Guardian, October 1. Accessed April 10, 2016. http://mg.co.za/article/2010-10-01-is-zambia-africas-next-breadbasket

Crush, J., and B. Frayne. "Supermarket Expansion and the Informal Food Economy in Southern African Cities: Implications for Urban Food Security." Journal of Southern African Studies 37, no. 4 (2011): 781–807.

Department of Agriculture Forestry and Fisheries. Abstract of Agricultural Statistics 2013. 2013.

Department of Agriculture Forestry and Fisheries. A Profile of the South African Onion Market Value Chain 2012. 2012a.

Department of Agriculture Forestry and Fisheries. A Profile of the South African Potato Market Value Chain 2012. 2012b.

Department of Agriculture Forestry and Fisheries. Trends in the Agricultural Sector 2013. 2014.

Department of Agriculture Forestry and Fisheries (Online). http://www.daff.gov.za/docs/statsinfo/ Trends13.pdf.

Dakora, E. A. N., and A. J. Bytheway. "Entry Mode Issues in the Internationalisation of South African Retailing." *Mediterranean Journal of Social Sciences* 5, no. 4 (2014): 194–205.

Emongor, R. "The Impact of South African Supermarkets on Agricultural and Industrial Development in the Southern African Development Community." PhD thesis, University of Pretoria, 2008.

Emongor, R., and J. Kirsten. "The Impact of South African Supermarkets on Agricultural Production in the SADC: A Case Study in Zambia, Namibia and Botswana." *Agrekon* 48, no. 1 (2009): 60–84.

Fair, E. "The Peasantary with Modern Capitalism: Power, Position, and Class." The Global Labour University, 2011. www.global-labour-university.org/fileadmin/GLU...2011/.../Ely_Fair.pdf.

Forster, T., and A. G. Escudero. *City Regions as Landscapes for People, Food and Nature.* Washington, DC: Landscapes for People, Food and Nature Initiative, 2014.

Fresh Fruit Portal. SA's Growing Apple Export Opportunities in Africa. Fresh Fruit Portal (Online). Accessed April 9, 2016. http://www.farmingportal.co.za/index.php/farming-interest/item/1068-sa%E2%80%99s-growing-apple-export-opportunities-in-africa

Humphrey, J. "The Supermarket Revolution in Developing Countries: Tidal Wave or Tough Competitive Struggle?" *Journal of Economic Geography* 7 (2007): 433–450.

Igumbor, E., D. Sanders, T. Puoane, L. Tsolekile, C. Schwarz, C. Purdy, R. Swart, S. Durao, and C. Hawkes. "'Big Food', The Consumer Food Environment, Health, and the Policy Response in South Africa." *PLoS Med* 9, no. 7 (2012): e1001253. doi:10.1371/journal.pmed.1001253.

Kisembo, D., and M. K. Muhumuza. 2015. "The Shoprite Exit was Evident But Just Delayed." *Saturday Monitor*, July 28. http://www.monitor.co.ug/Business/Prosper/The-Shoprite-exit-was-evident-but-just-delayed/-/688616/2810688/-/o58tgoz/-/index.html.

Khisa, I. 2014. "Shoprite Exits Tanzania, in Talks to Sell Out in Kampala Too." *The East African*, June 14. Accessed April 9, 2016. http://www.theeastafrican.co.ke/business/Shoprite-exits-Tanzania–in-talks-to-sell-out-in-Kampala-too-/-/2560/2348238/-/rl6lbtz/-/index.html

Louw, A., D. Chikazunga, C. Haankuku, and L. Ndanga. "Dynamics of the Restructuring Fresh Produce Food Markets in the Southern African Region." Conference Paper, Beijing, 2009.

Lusaka Times. 2015. "Why is Zambia Spending $1 Million Importing South African Frozen Foods – Sampa." *Lusaka Times*, May 20. Accessed April 8, 2016. https://www.lusakatimes.com/2015/05/20/why-is-zambia-spending-1million-importing-south-africas-frozen-foods-sampa/

Lusaka Times. 2015. "State Agents Raid Shoprite and Spar to Confiscate Illegally Imported Products." *Lusaka Times*, October 7. Accessed April 8, 2016. https://www.lusakatimes.com/2015/10/07/states-agents-raid-shoprite-and-spar-to-confiscate-illegally-imported-products/

Mantshantsha, S. 2016. "Shoprite Holdings: Nigerian Attraction." *Financial Mail*, February 26. Accessed April 8, 2016. www.financialmail.co.za

Maritz, J. 2013. "Good News for African Farmers." *African Trader*, August 31. http://www.africantrader.co/?p=693

McMichael, M. "Historicizing Food Sovereignty: A Food Regime Perspective. Food Sovereignty: A Critical Dialogue." International Conference, Yale University, New Haven, CT, September 14–15, 2013.

McMichael, P. "A Food Regime Genealogy." *The Journal of Peasant Studies* 36 no. 1 (2009): 139–169.

Miller, D. "Spaces of Resistance: African Workers at Shoprite in Maputo and Lusaka." *Africa Development* 3, no. 1 (2006): 27–49.

Miller, D., R. Saunders, and O. Oloyede. "South African Corporations and Post-apartheid Expansion in Africa – Creating a New Regional Space." *African Sociological Review* 12, no. 1 (2008): 1–19.

Mutegi, M., and S. Ciuri. 2015. "Carrefour Sparks Supplier Unease with Sh1.4m Fee." *Business Daily*, August 4. Accessed April 6, 2016. http://www.businessdailyafrica.com/Corporate-News/Carrefour-sparks-supplier-unease-with-Sh1-4 m-fee/-/539550/2818592/-/item/1/-/2xwibiz/-/index.html

Nleya, L. 2014. "Routes to Market: Enhancing Competition in Regional Road Freight." *Centre for Competition, Regulation and Economic Development*, August 13. http://www.competition.org.za/review/2014/8/13/routes-to-market-enhancing-competition-in-regional-road-freight

Okeahalam, C., and S. M. Wood. "Financing Internationalisation: A Case Study of an African Retail Transnational Corporation." *Journal of Economic Geography* 9 (2009): 511–537.

Ortmann, G. F., and R. P. King. "Research on Agri-food Supply Chains in Southern Africa Involving Small-scale Farmers: Current Status and Future Possibilities." *Agrekon* 49, no. 4 (2010): 397–417.

Peters, F. 2015. "Choppies Pursues Targets in Spite of Opening Delays." *BDlive*, September 23. Accessed April 9, 2016. http://www.bdlive.co.za/business/retail/2015/09/23/choppies-pursues-targets-in-spite-of-opening-delays

Pick n Pay Investor Relations. 2015. Corporate Profile. Pick n Pay Investor Relations (Online). http://www.picknpay-ir.co.za/store_foot_print.php

Piper, L. "The BRICS Phenomenon: From Regional Economic Leaders to Global Political Players." Working Paper 3: BRICS Initiative for Critical Agrarian Studies (BICAS) Conference, Cape Town, April, 2015.

Reardon, T., P. Timmer, C. Barrett, and J. Berdegue´. "The Rise of Supermarkets in Africa, Asia, and Latin America." *American Journal of Agricultural Economics* 85 (2003): 1140–1146.

Reardon, T., and A. Gulati. *The Supermarket revolution in Developing Countries: Policies for 'Competitiveness with Inclusiveness'*. Washington, DC: International Food Policy Research Institute, 2008.

Reardon, T., S. Henson, and A. Gulati. "Links between Supermarkets and Food Prices, Diet Diversity and Food Safety in Developing Countries." In *Trade, Food, Diet and Health: Perspectives and Policy Options*, edited by C. Hawkes, C. Blouin, S. Henson N. Drager, and L. Dube, 111–130. Chichester: Wiley-Blackwell, 2010.

Resilient Africa. Resilient Africa Real Estate. www.resilientafrica.com.

Sherry, S. 2013. "Africa Now Tops SA Agriculture Exports." *Financial Mail*, October 10. http://www.financialmail.co.za/features/2013/10/10/africa-now-tops-sa-agriculture-exports

Shoprite Holdings Limited. 2014. Integrated Report 2014. *Shoprite Holdings*, (Online). http://shopriteholdings.co.za/InvestorCentre/Documents/2014/IntergratedReport2014/5206_Integrated_Report.pdf.

Shoprite Holdings Limited. 2015. Geographical Spread. http://www.shopriteholdings.co.za/OurGroup/Pages/Geographical-Spread.aspx.

Southern Africa Customs Union (SACU). wwwsacu.int.

USDA. 2015. "Angola: Agricultural Economic Fact Sheet." www.fas.usda.gov/data/angola-agricultural-economic-fact-sheet-0.

Van der Heijden, T., and N. Vink. "Good for whom? Supermarkets and Small Farmers in South Africa – A Critical Review of Current Approaches to Increasing Access to Modern Markets." *Agrekon: Agricultural Economics Research, Policy and Practice in Southern Africa* 52, no. 1 (2013): 68–86.

Wangalwa, E. 2015. "Nakumatt Opens Former Shoprite Store in Tanzania." *CNBC Africa*, February 12. http://www.cnbcafrica.com/news/east-africa/2014/07/28/nakumatt-shoprite-tanzania/.

Weatherspoon, D., and T. Reardon. "The Rise of Supermarkets in Africa: Implications for Agrifood Systems and the Rural Poor." *Development Policy Review* 3, no. 21 (2003): 333–355.

Wesgro. 2014. *Country Sector: Africa Food and Beverage Sector Fact Sheet 2014*.

Wegerif, M. "Exploring Sustainable Urban Food Provisioning: The Case of Eggs in Dar es Salaam." *Sustainability* 6, no. 6 (2014): 3747–3779.

Wrigley, N., and M. Lowe. 2010. "The Globalisation of Trade in Retail Services." *Report commissioned by the OECD Trade Policy Linkages and Services Division for the OECD Experts Meeting in Distribution Services, Paris 17 November 2010*.

Wrigley, N., and M. Lowe. "Introduction: 'Transnational Retail and The Global Economy'." *Journal of Economic Geography* 7, no. 4 (2007): 337–340.

Zambeef Products PLC. www.zambeefplc.com

"Shoprite in milk scandal." 2015. *Zambia Daily Nation*, December 5. Accessed April 8, 2016. http://zambiadailynation.com/2015/12/05/shoprite-in-milk-scandal

Brazil and China: the agribusiness connection in the Southern Cone context*

John Wilkinson, Valdemar João Wesz Junior and Anna Rosa Maria Lopane

ABSTRACT
This article explores the ways in which the Brazil–China axis is reshaping patterns of trade and investment in soy and related commodities. On the Brazilian side, we are particularly interested in the characteristics and dynamics of the models of investment and farming on the soy frontier. China's extensive interests in Brazilian soy provide a privileged perspective to analyse the different ways in which it is trying to reshape the dynamics of global agricultural commodity trading. We also incorporate insights from China's involvement in other Southern Cone countries, particularly Argentina. We explore the hypothesis that the scale of China's food and raw material demands even at low levels of import dependence have led it to adopt 'more-than-market' strategies of control which raise important questions for existing patterns of world agricultural trade.

Introduction

In this paper, we analyse the evolution of trade/investment and diplomatic relations between Brazil and China, focusing on agricultural resources and food, and extending the analysis to the Southern Cone countries[1] as a whole in our discussion of the soy and meat sectors. We draw attention to the contrast between the suppositions of parity in diplomatic interests and the deepening of 'neo-colonial' trade and investment patterns. China's current development strategies, as previously in the cases of Britain, Continental Europe and Japan, are geared toward ensuring supplies of a broad range of raw materials, both extractive and agricultural. Food security concerns, however, are central and become increasingly so as China's per capita income advances and urbanisation accelerates. The scale of even small levels of food and raw material dependence, especially in today's volatile conjuncture, makes China's exclusive reliance on world markets and trade increasingly problematic. While China's strategies to ensure resources are global, Brazil and the Southern Cone have become central to the supply of grains and meats for the dietary transition, along with cotton, pulp and tobacco. We explore China's initiatives in this region to move towards hands-on control over the supplies of these resources, involving investments in land, long-term contracts, joint-ventures, direct investments, the promotion of infrastructure and logistics, and more recently the transformation of COFCO[2] into a global trader. In the shift away from policies of food

---

*Article initially prepared for the BICAS Small Grants Award. This version updated and expanded.

and raw material self-sufficiency, China initially limited its perspective of dependence on outsourcing to specific non-food and feed products. As China's dietary transition deepens, its dependence on global supplies becomes more far-reaching. Brazil and the Southern Cone, given their centrality in feed grains and meats, are privileged arenas for investigating the 'more-than-market' strategies currently being developed by China to ensure its food security. Our central hypothesis, therefore, is that the scale of China's food and raw materials demands, even at low levels of import dependence, are leading this country increasingly to adopt 'more-than-market' strategies for controlling these resources which raises important questions for existing patterns of world trade.

Evolving economic, diplomatic and geopolitical relations: China and Brazil

In April 2015, the Brazil–China Business Council published a special issue to celebrate 40 years of diplomatic relations between the two countries, which was initiated in 1974.[3] In the 1970s and 80s, the terms of trade were determined by Brazil's more advanced industrial structure, exporting intermediary manufactured products from its steel and petrochemical industries in exchange for petroleum. Nevertheless, by the 1990s, current patterns of trade were already in evidence as more than half (56% in 1991) of Brazil's exports earnings came from iron ore and soy oil, with imports from China increasingly concentrated on cheap final consumer goods reflecting China's rapid industrialisation.

Economic cooperation was woven into and highly influenced by the consolidation of diplomatic ties formalised on China's initiative, as a 'Strategic Partnership' in 1993. On both sides, the convergence of diplomacy, trade and investment was stimulated by the centrality of state-owned enterprises and/or firms centrally involved in public investment programs.

Between 2004 and 2013 (Figure 1) trade flows exploded, rising from USD 9 billion to over USD 80 billion, an average annual growth of 30%. China's exports shifted from cheap final consumer goods to machines, equipment and electronic goods, whereas some 75% of Brazil's exports consisted of iron ore and soybeans, with other basic commodities (cellulose, petroleum) making up the remainder.

Trade was increasingly accompanied by direct foreign investment on the part of China, amounting to USD 56.5 billion in announced investments between 2007 and 2013, as it

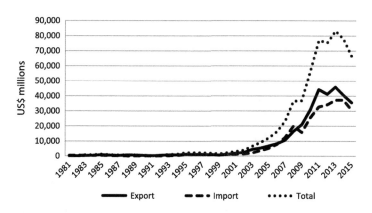

Figure 1. Trade Brazil–China 1981–2015. Source: MDIC (2016).

entered telecommunications, petroleum, transport and the automotive industry.[4] Brazilian investments in China have been largely firm-specific and sporadic.

Since 2009, China has become Brazil's leading trade partner both for imports (17, 9%) and for exports (18.6%).[5] The contrary, however, is not the case – with Brazil accounting for only 3% of China's imports and 1.5% of its exports. In the 1970s, the two countries had similar sized economies, with Brazil having a more advanced industrial base.[6] Forty years later, China's GDP grew six times that of Brazil and accounted for 11.7% of total global trade, compared to 1.3% in the case of Brazil.[7]

Brazil and much of Latin America have become strategic natural resource suppliers for China's economic growth. It is important, however, to distinguish between the different components in China's demand – minerals, petroleum and biomass. This article is primarily concerned with agricultural-based resources. While China has been heavily dependent on mineral extraction imports, agricultural resource dependence is quite selective, China has exhibited a surprising level of agricultural, and particularly food self-sufficiency during these decades of accelerated economic expansion (Figure 2).

Over the last 20 years, China's imports of agricultural products have represented just 7% of its total imports. With total agricultural imports of over USD 80 billion, China exports around USD40 billion in agricultural products and is a leading exporter of fresh and processed fruit and vegetables, particularly to the US, Japan and Europe.[8] The imports are heavily concentrated in feed and raw materials (soy and cellulose, timber, cotton and tobacco). While exhibiting global concerns for raw material and food provisions which are reminiscent of those of England and Japan, when these countries experienced their industrial take-off, what is exceptional about China is its high degree of agricultural and especially food self-sufficiency. Nevertheless, the scale of its demand means that proportionately moderate imports can have a decisive impact on world trade. For this reason, concerns for food security are leading China to trade agreements and investments strategies that aim to minimise the risks of world trade.

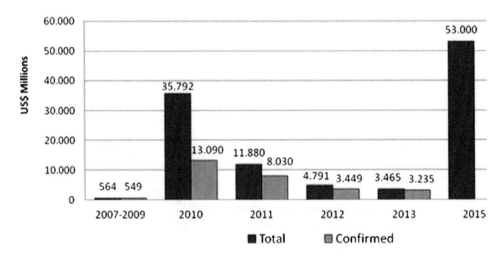

Figure 2. Announced Chinese investment in Brazil 2007–2015. Source: CEBC, MDIC Adapted by the authors for 2015.

The 'centre-periphery' characteristics of Brazil and China's economic complementarity contrast sharply with the strengthening of diplomatic cooperation, which was protocoled as a 'Global Strategic Partnership' in 2012.[9] Along with India, Russia and South Africa, China and Brazil have assumed the mantle of 'large emerging countries', in the formalisation of the BRICS, highlighting their common interests as developing countries. This collective identity was confirmed in the creation of the G20, with Brazil playing a leading role in negotiating 'developing country' interests within the WTO negotiations. While, therefore, the profile of Brazil and China's trade and investment pointed more to a new version of 'South-North' relations, diplomatically Brazil assumed a leading role as spokesperson for the developing world.[10]

China's food security and resource-seeking strategies

Food regime analysis, which has provided the dominant historical frame for interpreting the macroeconomic and political trends in the world agrifood system, has also promoted an over-exclusive focus on agriculture as the source of food. While we cannot explore this point here, a rereading of the earlier industrialisations of Britain and Japan reveals a much broader, simultaneous, concern with food, raw materials (biomass and mineral) and market access.[11] Agrifood trade and investment between Brazil and China need to be situated within this broader perspective. As noted above, China has been remarkable in its ability to maintain a high level of food self-sufficiency during three decades of unprecedented rates of economic growth and urbanisation. China is closer to post-Second World War continental Europe in its selective dependence on raw material imports. The Chinese State has traditionally assumed responsibility for food security, a concern accentuated in recent periods through isolationism and famine.

Nevertheless, self-sufficiency in food has been to a surprising extent maintained – first through an indigenous green revolution followed by market incentives from the later 1970s, and more recently through the promotion of large-scale agroindustry.[12] Of non-food biomass, timber has perhaps been the principal import priority as China's natural forests have disappeared.[13] Although China has promoted planted forests for pulp and paper, it remains highly dependent on imports, with Brazil, as its leading exporter. A range of non-food raw materials has also been opened to imports – such as cotton (although China remains the largest producer and has the largest stocks) and tobacco. Brazil is a leading supplier to China of both of these products, although traditional exporters of tobacco in Africa (such as Zimbabwe) are re-establishing their production.[14]

With urbanisation and rising incomes, the principal pressure on the agrifood system comes from the effects of the transition to an animal protein diet. In the 1960s, continental Europe opted for selective dependence on soy while maintaining their priority for self-sufficiency in grains. As from the 1990s, China adopted the same strategy, even at the expense of its traditional soy production. While the US continues to be a leading supplier of soy, the Southern Cone has now assumed dominance and is also the region which has most possibilities for expanding its production in the short term. At the beginning of 2000s, China joined the WTO, which demands minimum levels of market access of its members. At the same time, urbanisation leads not only to the adoption of an animal protein diet but also to a diversification of food consumption habits with a range of other products becoming included in trade – such as fruit juice, coffee and fish. Trade in meat products (poultry, beef) also begin to assume importance, even with the shift to large-scale industrial operations in China itself.[15]

In spite of the diversification of the urban food diet, basic commodities remain central – oils, grains (maize, wheat), milk, rice and sugar – and even with high levels of self-sufficiency, shortfalls provoke tremors in global commodity markets. The recent surge in dairy product imports in China was a notable example.[16] Maize imports increased sharply after 2008, but have declined over the last two years. Wheat imports have also oscillated, although at lower levels (Figure 7). High levels of volatility have been a key feature of agricultural commodity prices in the 2000s. Many analyses associate these sharp price fluctuations with the financialisation of agricultural commodity markets, and this whole debate was reviewed in the 2011 HLPE Report on price volatility and food security.[17] Others have identified the sudden new pressures on demand created by the biofuels targets, as the main culprit.[18] In all these analyses, surging Chinese demand has also been cited as a contributory, if not a major factor. The response to such price fluctuations has also increased the risks associated with dependence on global trade. Key agricultural commodity exporter countries (Thailand, Indonesia and Argentina) have imposed bans on exports, which in addition to aggravating prices have threatened availability.[19]

China has maintained a remarkable level of basic food self-sufficiency in a period of continuous and rapid economic growth and urbanisation. It has selectively outsourced raw materials (timber, cotton and tobacco) and feedstuffs. Its concern with food security has led China to revise its biofuels programme excluding the further use of food crops (wheat and corn). This occurred at a time when membership of the WTO and projections of future demand called into question food self-sufficiency. At different times since 2008, basic foodstuffs have been imported in significant quantities (wheat, corn, rice, dairy products and meats). China, therefore, has to confront the issue of dependence on world markets and world supplies at a time of volatility in prices and supply. It is not so much a question of the degree of dependence, which as a percentage of domestic supplies, is modest. Rather, the issue is the scale of even modest Chinese demand in relation to the size of the world market, whose predictability is equally problematic and whose control is in the hands of the global traders. We will come back to these questions when analysing China's trade and investment strategies in Brazil and the Southern Cone, situating this within a broader global context.

Brazil's agribusiness, global trade and China

Until 2008, Europe was still by far the principal regional destiny for Brazil's agroindustrial exports although China had moved into second place above Latin America, the Middle East and the United States. Between 2008 and 2015, exports to all other regions, with the exception of the Middle East, were in decline and China was edging towards first place, (Table 1), a position which was confirmed in 2015.

Even though China has now become the leading destination, Brazil's agroindustrial exports continue to be widely marketed among the world's principal regions (Table 2). Only one product – soybeans – has China as its almost exclusive customer, accounting for over two-thirds of Brazil's total exports. For other products, China accounts for between a third and a fifth of total exports (peanut oil, hides and cellulose). On the other hand, China's participation in Brazil's other leading export markets – sugar, tobacco, cotton, soy oil, alcohol, poultry and beef, is currently modest. By value, as we have seen above, China accounts for only a quarter of Brazil's total agro-industrial exports (Table 2).

Table 1. Principal markets for Brazilian agribusiness by economic bloc/country.

Years	Agribusiness exports (US$ millions)	Participation in Brazil´s agribusiness exports					
		European Union (EU-28) (%)	China (%)	Latin American and Carib. (%)	Middle East (%)	USA (%)	Others (%)
2000	20.605	41.0	2.7	12.9	4.6	18.0	20.6
2001	23.866	39.2	3.7	11.5	6.3	15.3	24.0
2002	24.846	38.0	5.5	8.4	6.2	16.7	25.2
2003	30.653	38.0	7.4	8.1	6.8	15.7	24.0
2004	39.035	36.2	7.6	8.6	7.1	14.8	25.8
2005	43.623	34.1	7.1	8.3	7.0	13.7	29.8
2006	49.471	32.4	7.6	8.5	8.4	14.2	28.9
2007	58.431	36.0	8.0	9.3	8.1	11.0	27.7
2008	71.837	33.4	11.0	10.5	7.1	8.7	29.2
2009	64.786	29.5	13.8	8.6	9.0	7.0	32.1
2010	76.442	26.9	14.4	9.3	10.1	7.1	32.2
2011	94.968	25.3	17.4	9.1	9.1	7.2	31.9
2012	95.814	23.6	18.8	9.1	8.8	7.3	32.4
2013	99.968	22.1	22.9	8.9	8.3	7.1	30.7
2014	96.748	22.2	22.8	9.0	7.5	7.2	31.3
2015	88.224	20.7	24.1	8.9	8.2	7.3	30.8

Source: MAPA (2016) – Elaborated by the authors.

Table 2. China´s participation in Brazil´s global agribusiness exports.

Products	Exports to the world				Participation of China in exports (%)			
	2000	2005	2010	2015	2000	2005	2010	2015
Soybeans	26.185	5.341	11.035	20.982	15.4	32.1	64.6	75.2
Sugar	1.199	3.919	12.762	7.641	0.0	0.0	4.0	10.0
Poultry meat	829	3.509	6.808	7.071	1.3	2.2	3.2	8.6
Coffee	1.784	2.929	5.765	6.159	0.0	0.1	0.1	0.2
Bovine meat	814	3.060	4.795	5.795	0.1	0.1	0.1	8.2
Cellulose	1.602	2.034	4.760	5.590	3.4	13.3	23.7	33.1
Bovine leather	742	1.378	1.725	2.250	3.2	18.1	20.4	27.6
Tobacco	841	1.707	2.762	2.186	6.0	14.6	12.4	12.1
Juices	1.090	1.185	1.925	2.050	0.2	3.1	3.9	2.8
Cotton and derivatives	843	1.532	1.446	1.776	0.2	7.1	10.6	10.9
Soy oil	359	1.267	1.352	1.154	5.9	13.4	58.1	12.0
Fruits	387	711	906	889	0.0	0.3	0.3	0.1
Alcohol	35	766	1.014	880	0.0	0.0	0.0	6.2
Tea	119	136	197	481	0.0	0.0	0.1	0.0
Drinks	364	202	264	424	0.0	0.0	0.1	0.1
Cocoa	163	387	419	375	0.3	0.1	0.2	0.1
Milk and derivatives	14	150	155	319	0.1	0.3	0.0	0.0
Fish	239	406	216	220	1.2	1.1	2.7	3.9
Animal feed	61	61	139	208	0.0	5.6	3.3	0.8
Bee products	9	25	60	87	0.3	6.6	0.9	1.4
Peanut oil	0	18	29	75	0.0	0.0	9.0	66.6
Total	20.605	43.623	76.442	88.224	2.7	7.1	14.4	24.1

Source: MAPA (2016) – Elaborated by the authors.

Soy is central not so much in terms of the value of its exports, which is not dissimilar to the value of exports from the sugarcane sector or the combined meats sector, but for the role this crop plays at a number of different levels. In the first place, we need to consider the spatial dimensions of the crop which in Brazil occupies some 28 million hectares, three times that of sugarcane, four times that of planted forests and nine times that of coffee.[20] Furthermore, it is combined with the planting of corn. Sixty per cent of this production is now located on lands newly incorporated for commercial production and, in combination with cattle, has been the primary basis of regional development in the Centre-West of the country – now pushing ever further to the North.[21] Fifty per cent of this soy is exported as grains and a further 25% as meal.[22] This huge regional expansion has been fuelled by China's demand, which has ensured a long period of high commodity prices. High levels of agricultural accumulation from soy production have attracted outside investments and consolidated a new model of large-scale farming in this region.[23]

The interactions between soy, cattle and logging and the pressure to create new export routes exert a relentless pressure on the Amazon ecosystem. With the traditional ports over 2000 kilometres to the South and accessible only by clogged and badly maintained roadways, further investments are being attracted to develop the logistics and infrastructure for exports. Highways have to be paved, railways laid down, waterways made navigable, and river and deep-water port terminals constructed. Exports via the Pacific are also being cogitated. A recent study has drawn attention to the indirect effects of China's soy demand for the strengthening of the political power of rural interests.[24]

Soy in no way exhausts the dynamic of agribusiness trade and investment between Brazil and China and this will be evident from our analysis below. Nevertheless, the extra demand for this product is having a societal impact precisely because of the regional, environmental and political spill-over effects.

China and Brazil: towards a new style of market relations

Brazil maintains a small trade surplus with China but the terms of trade are almost entirely an exchange of basic commodities for manufactured goods, as indicated in Figure 3. Nevertheless, the reach of China's agricultural exports can be surprising. In 2013, the Association of Garlic Producers in the State of Goiás, (the same State which received a USD 7 billion proposal from the Chinese firm CNADC[25] for investments in grains production), brought an anti-dumping suit against China, which was supported by the Brazilian Chamber of Exports (CAMEX). Conversely, in the same year, tariffs were waived on imports of black beans (Brazil's most traditional foodstuff) from China to cover a shortfall in the harvest that year.[26]

The China–Brazil Business Council has accompanied Chinese investments in Brazil since the early 2000s and although the values of these investments are often not revealed, it is possible to identify their principal objectives. Initially the primary focus was on the three types of natural resources – mining, petroleum and land. Market access opportunities quickly

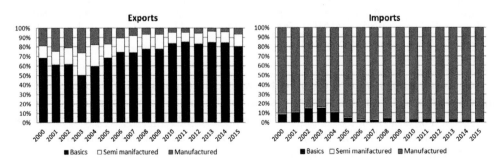

Figure 3. Brazil–China: Comparison of the profile of exports and imports. Source: MDIC (2016).

came to account for a range of investment proposals in telephones, telecommunications and the car industry. More recently, infrastructure (energy transmission, railways and ports) has become a more prominent target.[27]

In the case of agribusiness, in addition to the soy complex, cellulose, sugarcane, cotton, leather, tobacco, poultry and more recently beef, are important items of trade with Brazil. Continuing with our hypothesis, that for China simple dependence on global markets is intrinsically fraught with risk given the scale of its demand and the increasing volatility of markets – which are in the hands of global traders or subject to intervention by key producer states – we would expect these product sectors to become the object of investments or contract arrangements to influence the conditions of supplies.

Timber was just such an example in the 1990s and the perceived threat of 'Asian' investors in the Brazilian Amazon led to a mobilisation of civil society groups.[28] It was thought that Asian and Chinese firms were moving into the Brazilian Amazon as forests in Asia were depleted and access to African forests was blocked by the dominance of European logging companies. While these Asian investments did not materialize, China has accessed Amazon timber via Peru and has developed its own global value chain importing timber for the re-export of finished wood products, all under the control of Chinese firms.[29]

In 2012, China imported 65% of its demand for cellulose becoming the world's largest importer.[30] In contrast, China is the world's largest producer of paper, (99 million tons in 2011), with imports of less than 5 million tons in the same year. Brazil's pulp exports to China have increased sharply, doubling in value between 2008 and 2012, although they still fall behind the US and Canada as China imports from a broad range of countries.[31] The same source projected that Brazil would triple its exports of pulp by 2025. In 2010, the Chinese Company, Rizhao, was reported to have plans to invest in Brazil for the production of 1.5 million tons of cellulose. This investment, however, seems not to have materialised, and in 2012 restrictions on foreign land investments[32] severely affected foreign investments in this sector. Suzano Paper and Cellulose, one of Brazil's leading firms in this sector, trades directly on a contract basis with Chinese firms rather than through the market, and due to its pur-chase of the British Futurogene also has research facilities in China.[33] Three firms dominate the Brazilian tobacco market: Souza Cruz, Phillip Morris and Alliance One. China is the world's largest market for cigarettes with an annual growth rate of 3–4%.[34] Half of China's imports come from Brazil and for Brazil's China has become its leading export market. In 2012, China Tobaco Internacional do Brasil (CTIB), a subsidiary of China Tobacco International, established a joint venture with Alliance One Brazil in which CTIB would have a 51% partnership. Through this agreement, some 6000 contracts with small tobacco farmers in the southern State of Rio Grande do Sul, (the only State then authorised to export to China), representing a fifth of Alliance One Brasil's contracts, were transferred to the new company. In recent years, China has become a major importer of sugar from Brazil, a trend which is likely to continue given its current below average per capita consumption of 10 kilos as against a world average per capita consumption of 15 kilos in the context of continued urbanisation and economic growth.[35] China was largely absent from the huge wave of investments which poured into Brazil's sugar-alcohol sector in the middle-2000s.[36] Noble, the then Hong Kong-based trading company, backed by China's sovereign fund, already had 2 sugar mills and acquired 2 more in 2010, increasing its sugar producing capacity to 1.34 million metric tons. With the purchase of Noble, COFCO now assumes control of four sugar plants in the State of São Paulo. As in the case of pulp exports, a Brazilian firm took the lead in developing direct trade relations for sugar with China and the Asian market. In 2012, Copersucar, Brazil's leading sugar producer and exporter, established a subsidiary (Copersucar Asia) in Hong Kong in the same year that China became Brazil's leading export market. In 2014, Copersucar united in a 50–50 joint venture with Cargill to form Alvean, creating the world's largest sugar trading company. This joint venture parallels the creation of Raizen between Brazil's then leading sugar producer Cosan and Royal Dutch Shell. A similar pattern has emerged in the new soy frontier where the Brazilian Amaggi Group has created joint ventures with both Bunge and Dreyfus. The global traders, who pride themselves on the self-sufficiency and secrecy of their operations, are now finding it advantageous to ally themselves with increasingly powerful national players. Copersucar maintains its independence in the ethanol market and with its purchase of the US Eco-energy is now the leading global exporter of ethanol.[37]

The China, Brazil and the Southern Cone soy nexus

In each of the above sectors where China and Brazil have substantial commodity trading relations, we have seen moves on both sides to go beyond the classical trading model establishing different forms of more direct negotiation – such as long-terms contracts with clients, contract integration for the supply of raw material, direct investments in production and joint-ventures. In none of the above sectors, however, is China's strategic dependence on imports so pronounced as in the case of soybeans. Within a vision of food security dominated by the concept of self-sufficiency, China decided to outsource feed in an effort to secure basic food grain autonomy. This decision was taken even at the cost of seriously weakening China's domestic soy complex, which underwent a rapid internationalisation after 2004.[38]

Soy and grains more generally are seen to be the products most subject to the global institutions of the agricultural commodity market, with prices decided by the Chicago Board of Trade (CBOT) and supply managed and controlled by the Big Four, ABCD, traders – Archer Daniel Midlands, Bunge, Cargill and Dreyfus.[39] An influential interpretation of Brazil's and the Southern Cone's emergence as the new global pole of soy and grains production by Turzi, highlights the region's comparative advantage and its integration into an expanding global value chain orchestrated by the ABCD players, creating the regional Southern Cone 'Republic of Soy'.[40] While we cannot here address this view with the detailed analysis it deserves, our research suggests the need for serious qualification. Firstly, such a view underestimates the role of public policies, in the two major countries of the Southern Cone, Brazil and Argentina, and their different consequences for the trajectories of soy expansion in each country. It similarly underplays the differences in domestic consumption and demand patterns in these countries. It also fails to appreciate the decisive role played by Japan as from the 1970s in the opening up of Brazil's huge new frontier region in the Center-West of the country.[41]

In the 1990s, it may well have seemed that Brazil and Argentina's soy complexes would be integrated on a regional basis. The advance of Brazilian soy was still concentrated in the States of Goias and Mato Grosso and Argentinian firms, along with the ABCD traders, concentrated their new crushing investments along the Rio de la Plata. With the implementation of the Kandir's Law[42] in Brazil providing a special stimulus to the export of soy as grain and the contrary policy of taxing (called 'retenciones'), grain exports in Argentina favoring the export of oil and meal, the new crushing capacity along the Rio de la Plata seemed to provide the basis for increasing regional integration of the soy complex.[43] However, with the explosion of Chinese demand for soy grain and the unexpected rapid advance of Brazil's soy frontier up the Center-West to the North of the country, this regional integration became less realistic and the central challenge became that of new investments in crushing, storage and logistics to ship soy out via the North of the country. While the ABCD group has taken the lead this entirely new scenario is creating opportunities for the entry of a wide range of actors[44] reflecting the increasing importance of local and regional capital along with new global players.[45]

China has frequently declared its interest in establishing greater independence in relation to the ABCD traders and COFCO's recent purchases of Noble and Nidera suggest that it might soon be in a position to add its initials, creating the 'Big Five'. China's activities in the Brazilian and the Argentine soy sector can be divided into four phases, which overlap and have been influenced by changes in the regulatory climate. Initially, the primary focus was on the purchase of land, a strategy limited by the reactivation of restrictive regulations on foreign land purchases in 2010 in Brazil and 2011 in Argentina. A second approach was via negotiation with State and Provincial Governments in the soy regions of both Brazil and Argentina. Proposals here had to take into account public policies and particularly the broad concern regarding China's demand for soybean, rather than processed soy products, an issue discussed during Brazil's Presidential visit to China in 2012. Goiás and Bahia were the two States that became the object of ambitious investment plans, but the results to date have been insignificant.[46]

In Argentina, the Chongqing Grain Group (CGG) acquired 130,000 hectares in Santiago del Estero and established a partnership with Molino Cañueças, producer of vegetable oils and flour, for the purchase of a further 10,000 hectares in the province of Cordoba.[47] The most significant investment was that by Beidahuang in partnership with Cresud, Argentina's largest agricultural firm, for the acquisition of 320,000 hectares in the province of Rio Negro.[48] The Governor of Rio Negro ceded the land together with use of the port and offered fiscal advantages for the proposed investments. The Argentine Federal Government found these terms unacceptable, accusing the Provincial government of exceeding its constitutional authority and stopped the project.[49]

A third approach has been evidenced in China's commitment to large-scale infrastructure investments to improve the export logistics of Brazil's new soy frontier, on an average some 2000 kilometres from the southern ports. China's main focus here is on the creation of railway systems linking production to northern port outlets and the Pacific. In 2016, China's largest infrastructure company, China Communications Construction Company (CCCC), has established itself in Brazil and is investing in a key Port Terminal for the export of grains and minerals via the North of the country. In addition, it has become a major supplier of infrastructure equipment and services.[50] In Argentina, China shifted its focus to the financing of logistics and infrastructure in an investment agreement covering railways and port facilities with Belgrano Cargas, Argentina's largest railway company.

China's fourth approach consists in directly challenging the control of the global grains trade by the Big Four. As we have mentioned, COFCO acquired Nidera (USD 1.2 billion) and Noble (USD 1.5 billion) in 2014, which provides this state firm with an important direct entry into the procurement and marketing of soy in the whole of the Southern Cone, (see Figure 4).[51] With these acquisitions, COFCO's total revenue reaches USD 63.3 billion, in the same league therefore as the Big Four.[52] Noble operates with a wide range of commodities – grains, oils, sugar, cocoa, cotton and coffee – and is present in 40 countries on the 5

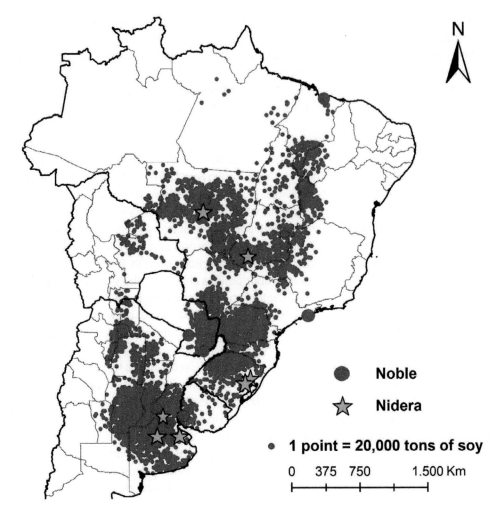

Figure 4. Soy production in the Southern Cone (2010/11) and location of Noble and Nidera´s investments in the region. Source: Adapted from Wesz Jr (2014) and updated with news disclosed by the company.

continents. It is the largest commodity trader in Asia, and has one of the largest crushing capacities in China with five plants in this country. Noble is present in the four countries of the Southern Cone, beginning its investments in Argentina in 2000, with a focus on the construction of storage and port capacity which provided a basis for direct negotiations with farmers. In 2009, Noble inaugurated its first crushing plant in Rosário, the Province of Santa Fé, with a capacity for 9,500 tons/day, some 5.5% of Argentina's total crushing capacity and is now responsible for around 10% of Argentine's soy grain exports, 6% of its feed and 9% of soy oil.[53]

In 2004, Noble began investments in Brazil employing the same strategy of constructing storage capacity in Mato Grosso and Paraná. This was followed in 2010 by the inauguration of a port terminal in Santos, São Paulo at a cost of USD100 million. A year later, Noble announced investments of some USD200 million for a soy crushing plant in Rondonópolis in Mato Grosso, with a capacity for 4,000 tons/day and 300 million tons/year of biodiesel.[54]

In Paraguay, Noble has formed a joint venture with a local logistics firm, Baela, for the development of fluvial transport capacity for grains and built a crushing plant in the port of Villeta.[55] In Uruguay, Noble maintains a terminal in partnership with Barraca Jorge Erro e Evera in the Nueva Palmira Port, with a capacity for 14,500 tons.[56]

In all these countries, Noble is also active upstream in the supply of fertilisers, technical assistance and finance, in a similar fashion to the other global traders. From 2005 to 2011, Noble's exports from the Southern Cone experienced explosive growth, increasing from USD 300 million to USD 3.7 billion, and which has now stabilised to between 2.7 and 3.2 billion in the last 4 years.[57]

Nidera is present in 20 countries and operates in all sectors of agrifood, including seeds and has investments in all 4 Southern Cone countries. It accounts for some 8% of Argentina's crushing capacity and 10% of Brazil's transgenic seed supply. Nidera has two crushing plants in Argentina, in Buenos Aires and Santa Fé provinces, with a capacity for 11,000 tons/day, some 8% of Argentine capacity. In Brazil, Nidera acquired the Brasil Óleo de Mamona (BOM) firm in the State of Bahia and, in 2005, bought up Bayer's soy and corn seed operations in Patos de Minas (MG) and Rio Verde (GO) and formed Nidera Seeds, which now controls some 10% of the transgenic soy seed market in Brazil.[58] Nidera Brazil Grain and Oil (BG&O) operates in the marketing of grains and oils and Nidera Nutrientes e Proteção de Cultivos (Nidera NPC) in plant protection. In Uruguay and Paraguay, Nidera focuses on the supply of seeds. In contrast to Noble, Nidera's share in exports has increased significantly in the last 5 years and it now exports more than Noble (Noble with USD 2.7 billion and Nidera with USD 3.5 billion in 2015).[59]

With these two purchases, COFCO has established a solid presence in a broad range of agricultural commodity markets, particularly in the soy complex in the Southern Cone, where its presence also in seeds may offer advantages in relation to the ABCD group. COFCO is now particularly strong in Argentina, with 12.8% of this country's crushing capacity,[60] and 12, 15 and 15%, respectively, of soy feed, oil and grains exports – leaving COFCO second only to Cargill, pushing Bunge and Dreyfus into third and fourth places.[61] In 2015, COFCO occupied third place in volume of grain exports in Brazil (behind Bunge and Cargill) after years of Big Five supremacy – ABCD + Amaggi.[62] In Mato Grosso, Brazil's leading agricultural State, total exports by Noble and Nidera increased 226% between 2009 and 2014, significantly more than the combined increase in the big five AABCD which was 27% for Brazil as a whole and 75% for the State of Mato Grosso. In addition, Noble controls some 10% of this State's crushing capacity and its biodiesel production.[63] Since 2011, the share of Brazil and Paraguay in the exports of these two firms has increased by 40%, whereas those from Argentina declined by 15%.[64]

Trade and investments: from feed to meats

The challenges of transitioning to an animal protein diet in China, due to growing per capita income and urbanisation, translated itself into a policy of feed imports and the promotion of the intensive industrial meat production model. Two factors introduced the need for more specific policies to address rising meat consumption. In the first place, China's meat diet has been based on pork – producing and consuming 50% of the global supply. Even with the remarkable expansion of intensive production in China,[65] demand is outstripping supply. Although imports are currently marginal, at 2% of domestic consumption, China is now the world's second largest importer of pork, and the current volume of world trade in pork would quickly prove inadequate if China's import demands continued to increase. The purchase of the U.S company Smithfields, the world's largest hog firm, by Shuanghui (with the help of CDH Investments, a Chinese private equity firm, and the Bank of China), is a further indication of the degree to which China is looking beyond trade to ensure food security.

Although pork consumption is increasing in China, urbanisation and rising incomes are also bringing changes in the profile of food consumption (Figure 5). Per capita consumption of chicken has risen from 1 kg in 1990 to 9 kg in 2014. Here again, the industrial contract integration model has been diffused with the arrival of Tyson in the 1990s followed by the C.P. Thailand Group. The largest domestic group, Guangdong Wens Group, which has also adopted this model, now produces more than 700 million broilers per year.[66] Nevertheless, imports of half a million metric tons were reached in the early 2000s and are projected to reach this figure again in 10 years, in spite of the intense modernisation this segment has undergone in this period.[67] After two years of negotiations, China and Brazil resumed trade in poultry in 2008 with the authorisation of exports from 22 Brazilian plants. In 2010, a trade dispute between China and the US, which until then was responsible for 75% of China's broiler meat imports, shifted trade in Brazil's favour, and its exports to China exploded from 24.000 tons in 2009 to 196.000 tons in 2011. Brazilian firms Marfrig, through its acquisition of Keystone Foods which supplies food service chains, and Brazil Foods, (BRF) in a joint venture with Dah Chong Hong (DCH), have initiated investments in China.[68]

Perhaps, most surprising has been the rapid growth in beef consumption (4.55 kg per capita in 2014) and beef imports (Figures 5 and 6). Given China's restrictions in terms of land and water, together with the effects of agricultural mechanisation and rural–urban migration, a modern beef industry will be very difficult to consolidate. Chinese cattle slaughter declined by 3.7 million (8%) between 2008 and 2013, and beef production also declined by a similar amount in the same period. Prices have increased by 81% between 2011 and 2014 and yet consumption per capita has continued to increase in this same period. At the same time, beef is a more attractive animal protein for the rising middle class and is more positively associated with health than pork. As a result, imports have exploded rising from 60.524

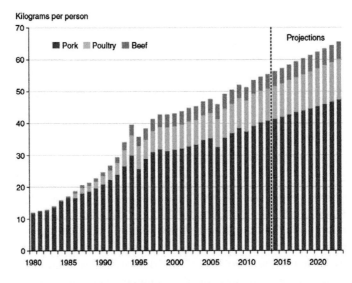

Figure 5. Continued growth projected in China's per capita meat consumption. Source: USDA Production, Supply and distribution database and projections.

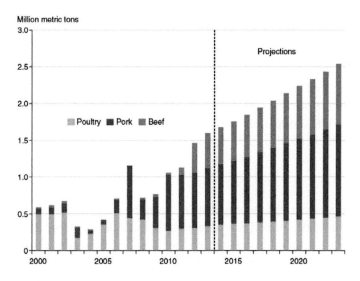

Figure 6. China's global meat imports projected to continue upward trend. Source: USDA Production, Supply and distribution database and projections.

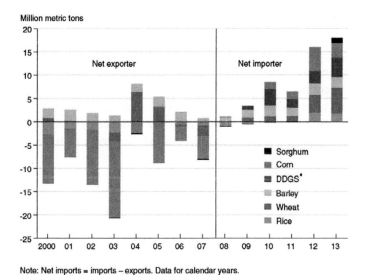

Note: Net imports = imports – exports. Data for calendar years.
*DDGS= Distillers Dried Grains With Solubles.

Figure 7. China's net imports of grains surged during 2012–2013. Source: USDA, Economic Research Service analysis of China customs statistics.

metric tons in 2012 to 295.011, metric tons in 2014.[69] If imports by Hong Kong and Vietnam are included, the total for the greater China region comes to 1.39 million metric tons, making this the world's largest importer region.[70] Most imports have come from Oceania and Canada with the US excluded since the early 2000s because of the incidence of the Bovine Spongiform Encephalopathy (BSE).

In the more recent period, however China has been looking to the Southern Cone, not only for trade but also for direct investments in this sector. China is now Argentina's third largest beef export market after an agreement was signed for the export of frozen boned meat in 2012. Uruguay for its part is authorised to export chilled meat on the bone. Brazil's beef exports have been suspended since 2012 after an atypical case of BSE was identified, but renewed authorisation of exports is currently underway. Chinese investors are now in negotiations with middle-sized Brazilian slaughterhouses through the intermediation of CDH Investments, the private equity firm, worth US$14 billion which was responsible for the Shuanghui, (now WH Group after launching an IPO on the Hong Kong stock exchange), purchase of Smithfield Foods.[71]

Conclusions

China's food and raw material security policies are in the process of revision as its dependence on global food and non-food flows deepens. The outsourcing of feed and oils (soybeans) marked a first move in this direction and was seen as a measure also to ensure basic food grain (corn) self-sufficiency. Membership of the WTO brought with it a more general commitment to open up trading relations. As the new millennium has advanced, we can see a shift to a broader recourse to basic food grain imports, including corn (Figure 7). Urbanisation and rising incomes have produced more diversified food consumption patterns and the increase in animal protein has also been accompanied by a relative decline in pork and increases in poultry and beef consumption. Both of these trends have reinforced the need to negotiate new sources of food supply.

We have traced China's evolving trade and investments relations in Brazil, with reference also to Argentina and the Southern Cone. A range of strategies has been deployed – land purchases, harvest contracts negotiation, direct client–supplier agreements, joint ventures, direct investments, promotion of infrastructure and logistics to improve and cheapen trade flows and the acquisition of global traders. All these initiatives reveal China's 'more-than-market' strategy to deal with dependence on outside sourcing which, even when proportionately modest, makes unprecedented demands on global trade. COFCO's purchase of Noble and Nidera exemplifies China's move to a 'hands-on' control of all the stages of global grains/oils production and trade flows as its dependence on food and raw material imports both widens and deepens. Its most recent advances into the Brazilian meats sector suggest that this strategy may only be in its initial stages.

In the early sections of this article, we called attention to the asymmetry between the 'partnership of equals' on the diplomatic 'development' front and the 'center-periphery' style of trade and investment relations between Brazil and China. It might be argued that it no longer makes sense to consider Brazil's soy complex within the framework of traditional commodity markets. It is certainly true that soy has become a high technology sector, increasingly dependent on advances in biotechnology and informatics. Nevertheless, it maintains the demand and price elasticity problems of a commodity which are now becoming evident as even China's demand slows down. When warning signals went out on the impending decline in demand for extractive raw materials, it was argued that demand for foodstuffs would keep the agricultural commodity markets buoyant for a considerable period to come. Since then, prices have plummeted and although in the years of boom there was significant scope for accumulation by large farming enterprises which then upgraded along the soy chain, even establishing partnerships with the Big Four, it is these latter, and now COFCO which will likely call the tune as margins tighten.[72] Beyond the trade asymmetry of commodity exports for manufacturing and technology imports, Brazil (and the Southern Cone) now faces moves to exert more direct control over their soy and eventually their meat complex, placing enormous strains on their continued diplomatic parity as leaders of the developing world.

In this article, we have provided a detailed analysis of the new strategies and policies which are redefining Brazil's and China's agrifood trading relations. In doing so, we have focused on the increasingly divergent forms of integration into global soy/grains/meat markets on the part of the Southern Cone countries, revealing their different strategies and institutional frameworks. In the Brazilian case, new actors are emerging, both Brazilian and global, as the soy/grains complex has moved up into the central and northern regions of the countries, who begin to challenge the monopoly of the ABCD traders. The principal source of change in the global soy/grains market and trading system, however, comes from China, which has moved beyond trade and land investment strategies to establish itself as a leading player in the global soy/grains complex marking the beginning of the end of the ABCD global trading hegemony.

Disclosure statement

No potential conflict of interest was reported by the authors.

Acknowledgement

The authors would like to acknowledge the valuable contributions made by our colleague Luciana Muniz.

Notes

1. Argentina, Brazil, Uruguay, and Paraguay.
2. China National Cereals, Oils and Foodstuffs Corporation, is one of China's state-owned food processing holding companies.
3. CEBC, *Carta Brasil China* [Letter Brazil China] *2015.*

4. Ibid.
5. In 2000, the US was the leading importer of Brazilian products, accounting for 23.9% by value, followed by Argentina (11.3%), Holland (5.1%), Germany (4.6%) and Japan (4.5%). China, which was in twelfth position in 2000, increased its position year-by-year and ended 2015 in first place accounting for 19% of Brazil´s exports as against 12% in the case of the US. The same tendency can be identified in the case of Brazil´s imports with China accounting for 18% and the US 15% by the end of the decade (MDIC, *Indicadores e Estatísticas de Comércio* [Trade Indicators Statistics]).
6. Wilkinson and Wesz Jr., "Underlying Issues in the Emergence of China."
7. CEBC, *Carta Brasil China* [Letter Brazil China] *2012.*
8. Ibid.
9. The significance of strategic partnerships for China is analysed by Zhongping and Jing (2014) as a response to China´s increasing involvement in a multilateral world. In the words of Wen Jiabão, China´s Prime Minister from 2003 to 2013, strategic 'means that the cooperation should be long term and stable … transcending differences in ideologies and social systems', and 'partnership' means that the cooperation should be equal-footed, mutually beneficial and win-win.' (Zhongping and Jing, *China's Strategic Partnership diplomacy,* 7).
10. Cabral and Shankland, *Narratives of Brazil–Africa Cooperation.*
11. Wilkinson and Goodman, "Food Regime Analysis."
12. Aglietta and Bai, *China's Development.*
13. Naughton, *The Chinese Economy.*
14. Valor Econômico, *Notícias* [News].
15. APEX, *Brazilian Chicken.*
16. Sharma, *Evolution and Future Trends.*
17. HLPE, *Price Volatility and Food Security;* Fairbairn, "Like Gold with Yield"; and Isakson, "Food and Finance."
18. HLPE, *Biofuels and Food Security.*
19. Von Braun, *Rising Food Prices.*
20. MAPA 2016.
21. Wesz Jr., "Hybrid Dynamics of Soy Transnational Companies."
22. ABIOVE, *Estatística* [Statistics].
23. Wilkinson and Pereira, "Brazilian Soy. New Patterns of Investment."
24. Fearnside and Figueiredo, "China's influence on deforestation in Amazonia."
25. China National Agricultural Development Group Corporation.
26. See note 21.
27. D'Atri, "Analise econômica"; and Frischtak and Soares, "As relações Brasil China."
28. See note 20.
29. Putzel, Padoch and Pinedo-Vasquez, "The Chinese Timber Trade."
30. CEBC, *Carta Brasil China* [Letter Brazil China] *2015.*
31. Ibid.
32. For a detailed analysis of these restrictions see Wilkinson, Reydon, and Di Sabbato, "Concentration and Foreign Ownership of Land."
33. Ibid.
34. See note 9.
35. OECD-FAO, *Agricultural Outlook.*
36. Wilkinson and Herrera, "Biofuels in Brazil."
37. Gomes, "Copersucar e Eco-Energy formam maior trading de etanol do mundo" (*Estadão,* October 5, 2012).
38. Oliveira, "Geopolitics of Brazilian Soybeans."
39. Murphy, Burch, and Clapp, *Cereals secrets.*
40. Turzi, "The Soybean Republic."
41. See note 20.
42. The Law Kandir, which came into force in 1996, eliminated taxes on the export of raw materials but maintained these for processed products. For the soy sector, this led to an immediate and

sharp increase in grain exports (from 5% to 30% in the years 1996–1998) and a proportionate decline in the export of soy oil and soy meal (Wesz Jr., "Strategies and Hybrid Dynamics.").

43. Gutman, *Cadenas Agroindustriales en el Mercosul ampliado* [Agroindustrial Chains in the Extended Mercosul].

44. The advance of soy in Argentina was accompanied by the development of a new model of agricultural production whereby specialised logistical firms provided all the services for a fundamentally rentier farmer class. Los Grobos and El Tejar were the most notable firms promoting this model and their entry into Brazil seemed to mark an 'Argentinization' of Brazilian agriculture on the new soy frontier. The Brazilian farming model, however is more 'hands-on', owner-producer oriented. In addition, subcontracting what are seen to be activities essential to the farming operations are illegal in Brazil (an issue currently being heatedly debated in Congress). El Tejar (O Telhar in Brazilian Portuguese) has had to cut its operations back and its ownership has now changed hands. Los Grobos has also left Brazil, with its investments in soy in Brazil being acquired by the Japanese trader, Mitsubishi. In complementary fashion, Brazil´s largest soy farming group Maggi began operations in Argentina but then withdrew with complaints about the very different conditions under which Argentine soy producers must operate.

45. See note 29.

46. Lucena and Bennett, "China in Brazil."

47. Revista Globo Rural, "Soja: China negocia parceria de US$10 milhões com empresa argentina" ["Soy: China negotiate 10 million USD partnership with Argentine firms"] (July, 2, 2012).

48. Ellis, "Las iniciativas por parte de las firmas agrícolas chinas" [Initiatives on the part of Chinese agricultural firms].

49. Ibid.

50. Pires and Ribeiro, "Gigante chinês desembarca no país e investe em porto da WTorre" [Giant Chinese firm arrives in the country and invest in the WTorre Port] (*Valor*, May 13, 2016); and valor econômico, *Notícias* [News].

51. Ibid.

52. Ibid.

53. CIARA, *Estadísticas del Sector* [Sector Statistics].

54. See note 59.

55. Chicago Tribune, *Noble proyecta construir planta* [Noble plans to build industrial plant].

56. See note 59.

57. MDIC, *Indicadores e Estatísticas de Comércio* [Trade indicators and statistics]; INDEC, *Comercio exterior* [Foreign trade]; Capeco, *Estadísticas* [Statistics]; and CIARA, *Estadísticas del Sector* [Sector statistics].

58. Ibid.

59. ibid.

60. Hinrichsen, *Annual Yearbook on Oilseeds Markets*.

61. Clarin, 'Los chinos ya se quedan con el 10% de los embarques de granos' ['Chinese firms already account for 10% of grain exports'] (2014).

62. MDIC, *Indicadores e Estatísticas de Comércio* [Trade Indicators and Statistics].

63. See note 28.

64. The purchase of Syngenta, second only to Monsanto, (now Bayer), in the Brazilian market, by ChemChina enormously strengthens China´s presence in the upstream markets of the soy/grains complex.

65. Sharma and Schneider, *Agribusiness and Development in China's Pork Industry*.

66. Poultry Production News, 2015.

67. Xie and Marchant, "Supplying China's Appetite for poultry."

68. www.marfrig.com.br.

69. "China´s Beef Imports Forecast to Increase in 2015" (*Food Alert, Irish Food Board,* February 6, 2015). http://www.bordbia.i.e./industry/manufacturers/insight/alerts/Pages/Chinasbeefimports forecasttoincreasein2015.aspx?year=2015&wk=7.

70. CEBC, *Carta Brasil China* [Letter Brazil China].

71. Ibid.

72. Prior to the rise of China, Japan was the largest grains/oils/meats importer in Asia. As we have mentioned, it was a key player in the development of the Brazilian soy frontier from the middle-70s onwards but has large relied on world trade for its supplies. Now faced with the challenge of Chinese demand, it is also adopting a more hands-on strategy investing in origination, storage and transport. Hall, "The Role of Japan's General Trading" provides an excellent analysis of Japan´s traders in the recent period.

Bibliography

ABIOVE - Associação Brasileira das Indústrias de Óleos Vegetais. *Estatística*. 2016. http://www.abiove.org.br/.

Aglietta, Michel, and Guo Bai. *China's Development: Capitalism and Empire*. Paris: Routledge, 2013.

APEX. *Brazilian Chicken*. Brasília, 2009.

Cabral, Lidia, and Alex Shankland. *Narratives of Brazil-Africa Cooperation for Agricultural Development: New Paradigms?* 2013, March, Working Paper 05. Brighton: Future Agricultures.

Capeco - Camara Paraguaia de Exportadores y Comercializadores de Cereales y oleaginosas. *Estadísticas*. 2016. http://www.tera.com.py/capeco.

CEBC. *Carta Brasil China: Especial Agronegócio Brasil-China*. 2012, November. Rio de Janeiro: Conselho Empresarial Brasil China.

CEBC. *Carta Brasil China: Visão do Futuro.*2015, March. Rio de Janeiro: Conselho Empresarial Brasil China.

Chicago Tribune. *Noble proyecta construir planta procesadora de soja en Paraguay*. 2012. http://articles.chicagotribune.com/2012-11-19/news/sns-rt-granos-paraguay-sojal1e8mj20n-20121119_1_oleaginosas-planta-cereales.

Ciara – Camara de la Industria Aceitera de la Republica Argentina. *Estadísticas del Sector*. 2016. http://www.ciaracec.com.ar/ciara/bd/index.php.

Clarin. *Los chinos ya se quedan con el 10% de los embarques de granos*. 2014. http://www.ieco.clarin.com/empresas/chinos-quedan-embarques-granos_0_1117088323.html.

D'Atri, Fabiana. "Análise Econômica." In *Carta Brasil China: Visão do Futuro*. Rio de Janeiro: CEBC, 2015.

Ellis, Evan. "Las iniciativas por parte de las firmas agrícolas chinas para establecer su presencia en América Latina y el Caribe." In *Política Exterior China: relaciones regionales y cooperación*, edited by R. I. L. Rosa and J. C. G. Maya (Coord.), 307–336. México: Puebla, 2015.

Fairbairn, Madeleine. "Like Gold with Yield: Evolving Interests between Farmland and Finance." *Journal of Peasant Studies* 41, no. 5 (2014): 777–795.

Fearnside, Philip M., and Adriano M. R. Figueiredo. "China's Influence on Deforestation in Brazilian Amazonia: A Growing Force in the State of Mato Grosso." BU Global Economic Governance Initiative Discussion Papers 2015-3, Boston University, Boston, MA, 2015, pp. 51.

Frischtak, Claudio R., and André Soares. "As Relações Econômicas Brasil-China: trajetória recente e perspectivas." *Estudos e Pesquisas*, no. 510 (2013). Rio de Janeiro: INAE.

Gutman, G. A. *Trajetorias y Demandas Tecnologicas de las Cadenas Agroindustriales en el Mercosur Ampliado: Oleaginosas, Soja y Girassol*. Montevideo: Procisur, BID, 2000.

Hall, Dereck. "The Role of Japan's General Trading Companies (Sogo Shosha) in the Global Land Grab." Conference Paper no. 3, *Land Grabbing, Conflict and Agrarian-environmental Transformations: Perspectives from East and Southeast Asia*. International Academic Conference Chiang Mai University, 2015.

Hinrichsen, J. J. *Annual Yearbook on Oilseeds Markets*. Buenos Aires, Argentina, 2015.

HLPE. *Price Volatility and Food Security*. Rome: HLPE FAO, 2011.

HLPE. *Biofuels and Food Security*. Rome: HLPE FAO, 2013.

Indec – Instituto Nacional de Estadística y Censos. 2016. *Comercio exterior*. http://www.indec.mecon.ar/.

Isakson, S. Ryan. "Food and Finance; the Financial Transformation of Agrofood Supply Chains." *Journal of Peasant Studies* 41, no. 5 (2014): 749–775.

Lucena, Andrea Freire de, and Isabella G. Bennett. "China in Brazil: The Quest for Economic Power meets Brazilian Strategizing." *Associação Brasileira de Relações Internacionais* 8, no. 2 (2013): 38–57.

Mafrig anuncia joint-venture na China. 2011. www.marfrig.com.br/pt/documentos?id=137.

MAPA – Ministério da Agricultura, Pecuária e Abastecimento. Agro Stat. 2016. http://agrostat.agricultura. gov.br/ Accessed March 2016.

MDIC - Ministério do Desenvolvimento, Indústria e Comércio Exterior. *Indicadores e Estatísticas de Comércio Exterior*. 2016. http://www2.desenvolvimento.gov.br/sitio/secex/secex.

Murphy, Sophia, David Burch, and Jennifer Clapp. *Cereal Secrets. The World's Largest Traders and Global Agriculture*. Minneapolis, MN: OXFAM Research Reports, August, 2012.

Naughton, Barry. *The Chinese Economy*. Cambridge, MA: MIT Press, 2007.

OECD-FAO. *Agricultural Outlook, 2014–2023*. Paris/Rome: FAO, 2014.

Oliveira, Gustavo de L. T. "The Geopolitics of Brazilian soybeans." *The Journal of Peasant Studies* 43 (2016): 348–372.

Poultry Production News. "WENS Group to merge with Guangdon Dahuanong," August 7, 2015.

Putzel, Louis, Christine Padoch, and Miguel Pinedo-Vasquez. "The Chinese Timber Trade and the Logging of Peruvian Amazonia." *Conservation Biology* 22, no. 6 (2008): 1659–1661.

Rama, Ruth, and John Wilkinson. "Asian Agribusiness Investment in Latin America with case studies from Brazil." In *The Changing Nature of Asian-Latin American Economic Relations*, edited by G King, J. C. Mattos N. Mulder, and O. Rosales, 33–73. Santiago: ECLAC, 2012.

Sharma, Shefali, and Mindi Schneider. *China's Pork Miracle? Agribusiness and Development in China's Pork Industry*. Institute for Agriculture and Trade Policy, 2014.

Turzi, Mariano. "The Soybean Republic." *Yale Journal of International Affairs*, Spring/Summer (2011). https://www.ucema.edu.ar/conferencias/download/2011/10.14CP.pdf.

Valor Econômico. *Notícias*. 2016. http://www.valor.com.br.

Von Braun, Joachim. *Rising Food Prices: What Should be Done?* Washington, DC: IFPRI Policy Brief, April, 2008.

Wesz Jr, V. J. "O Mercado da soja e as Relações de Troca entre Produtores Rurais e Empresas no Sudeste de Mato Grosso (Brasil)." PhD diss., CPDA/UFRRJ, Rio de Janeiro, 2014.

Wesz Jr, V. J. "Strategies and Hybrid Dynamics of Soy Transnational Companies in the Southern Cone." *The Journal of Peasant Studies* 43, no. 2 (2016): 286–312. doi:10.1080/03066150.2015.1129496.

Wilkinson, John. *Brazilian Cooperation and Investment in African Agriculture*. Rio de Janeiro: Actionaid, 2013.

Wilkinson, John, and Selena Herrera. "Biofuels in Brazil: Debates and Impacts." *The Journal of Peasant Studies* 37, no. 4 (2010): 749–768.

Wilkinson, John, and Paulo Pereira. *Brazilian Soy. New Patterns of Investment, Finance and Regulation*. Rio de Janeiro: Mimeo, 2015 (mimeo).

Wilkinson, John, and V. J. Wesz Jr. "Underlying Issues in the Emergence of China and Brazil as Major Global Players in the South-South Trade and Investment Axis." *International Journal of Technology Management & Sustainable Development* 12, no. 3 (2013): 245–260.

Wilkinson, John, Baastian Reydon, and Alberto Di Sabbato. "Concentration and Foreign Ownership of Land in Brazil in the Context of Global Land Grabbing." *Canadian Journal of Development Studies*, 33, no. 4 (2012): 417–438. doi:10.1080/02255189.2012.746651.

Wilkinson, John, and David Goodman. "Food Regime Analysis: A Reassessment." In *La Grande Transformation de l `Agriculture Vint Ans Après (provisional title)*, edited by G. Allaire and D. Benoit, Paris (in press), 2015.

Xie, Chaoping, and Mary A. Marchant. "Supplying China's growing appetite for poultry." *IFAMA* 18 (2015).

Zhongping, Feng, and Huang Jing. *China's Strategic Partnership Diplomacy: Engaging in a Changing World*, Working Paper, June. Virginia, VA: ESPO, 2014.

Index

For Product Safety Concerns and Information please contact our EU
representative GPSR@taylorandfrancis.com Taylor & Francis Verlag GmbH,
Kaufingerstraße 24, 80331 München, Germany

Printed and bound by CPI Group (UK) Ltd, Croydon, CR0 4YY
01/05/2025
01858358-0001